QUALITATIVE SECONDARY ANALYSIS

Sara Miller McCune founded SAGE Publishing in 1965 to support the dissemination of usable knowledge and educate a global community. SAGE publishes more than 1000 journals and over 800 new books each year, spanning a wide range of subject areas. Our growing selection of library products includes archives, data, case studies and video. SAGE remains majority owned by our founder and after her lifetime will become owned by a charitable trust that secures the company's continued independence.

Los Angeles | London | New Delhi | Singapore | Washington DC | Melbourne

QUALITATIVE SECONDARY ANALYSIS

KAHRYN HUGHES **ANNA TARRANT**

Los Angeles | London | New Delhi
Singapore | Washington DC | Melbourne

Los Angeles | London | New Delhi
Singapore | Washington DC | Melbourne

SAGE Publications Ltd
1 Oliver's Yard
55 City Road
London EC1Y 1SP

SAGE Publications Inc.
2455 Teller Road
Thousand Oaks, California 91320

SAGE Publications India Pvt Ltd
B 1/I 1 Mohan Cooperative Industrial Area
Mathura Road
New Delhi 110 044

SAGE Publications Asia-Pacific Pte Ltd
3 Church Street
#10-04 Samsung Hub
Singapore 049483

Editor: John Nightingale
Assistant editor: Eve Williams
Production editor: Martin Fox
Marketing manager: George Kimble
Cover design: Stephanie Guyaz
Typeset by: C&M Digitals (P) Ltd, Chennai, India
Printed in the UK

Library of Congress Control Number: 2019940991

British Library Cataloguing in Publication data

A catalogue record for this book is available
from the British Library

ISBN 978-1-5264-4524-7
ISBN 978-1-5264-4525-4 (pbk)

At SAGE we take sustainability seriously. Most of our products are printed in the UK using responsibly sourced
papers and boards. When we print overseas we ensure sustainable papers are used as measured by the PREPS
grading system. We undertake an annual audit to monitor our sustainability.

Anna: I dedicate this, my first edited collection, to my husband Jamie and my children, Lorelei and Wilfryd.

Kahryn: To Simon, Robert and Harry. With love.

CONTENTS

ABOUT THE EDITORS

Kahryn Hughes is an Associate Professor in Sociology at the University of Leeds, and Director of the Timescapes Archive. She has received ESRC funding for several of their flagship methodological programmes, including under the Research Methods Programme and Timescapes. Her research over the past 15 years has primarily aimed at methods innovation and development. Her current research interests relate to three overlapping areas: the sociology of health, sociological theory and research methodology. More specifically, she is interested in addiction, poverty, time and process.

Anna Tarrant is Associate Professor in Sociology at the University of Lincoln and a UKRI Future Leaders Fellow. Since 2014, she has been researching men's care responsibilities in low income families. Her work has been supported by funded studies including 'Men, Poverty and Lifetimes of Care' (funded by the Leverhulme Trust Early Career fellowship scheme) and 'Responding to Young Fathers' (funded by the Leeds Institute of Social Sciences Impact Acceleration Account). From January 2020, she will commence a UKRI Future Leaders Fellowship to conduct a qualitative longitudinal and participatory study about the lives and support needs of young fathers.

ABOUT THE CONTRIBUTORS

Joanna Bornat is Professor Emerita of Oral History at the Open University. While her undergraduate and postgraduate degrees were in sociology she has had a career-long interest in oral history and continues in retirement to be a trustee of the Oral History Society and an editor of the UK journal *Oral History*. She has researched and written on the re-use of archived interviews, publishing the results in a number of articles and collections where she maintains an interdisciplinary perspective.

Graham Crow is Professor of Sociology and Methodology in the School of Social and Political Science at the University of Edinburgh, where he has worked since 2013. He previously worked at the University of Southampton. He has taught and published in the fields of community sociology, family sociology, comparative sociology, sociological theory and research methods. He has a particular interest in unusual combinations of methods, and is using contrasting methods to research end-of-career transitions. His latest books are *Revisiting Divisions of Labour* (co-edited with Jaimie Ellis, Manchester University Press, 2017) and *What are Community Studies?* (Bloomsbury Academic, 2018).

Emma Davidson is a Leverhulme Early Career Research Fellow in Sociology at the University of Edinburgh, and co-director of interdisciplinary consortium, the Centre for Research on Families and Relationships. She has expertise in qualitative research, specifically participatory research, collaborative ethnography and computerised qualitative data analysis. Emma's work has largely focused on understanding the lived experiences of inequality in the UK, with research interests spanning diverse topics including literacy in the early years; youth justice; young people's experiences of care; complex multiple needs homelessness; public libraries and other 'third spaces'; and the enactment of civil society. Her ongoing Leverhulme research (https://anewpage.org/) is an exploration of the everyday social world of the public library and the challenges of austerity.

Rosalind Edwards is Professor of Sociology and a co-director of the ESRC National Centre for Research Methods at the University of Southampton, and a co-editor of the *International Journal of Social Research Methodology*. Rosalind's areas of interest encompass family lives and policies, and qualitative and mixed research methods. Currently she is collaborating with colleagues on methodological projects investigating indigenous and non-indigenous research partnerships (www.indigenous.ncrm.ac.uk), and the secondary analysis of large volumes of qualitative longitudinal data.

Ruth Geraghty is a Project Specialist in the Centre for Effective Services, with expertise in research data management, evidence curation and open data. Ruth previously worked as Data Curator for the Children's Research Network Prevention and Early Intervention (CRNINI-PEI) Research Initiative, supporting community organisations to archive and re-use their evaluation data. Prior to joining CES in 2016, Ruth worked as a social researcher in the university sector and is co-author of the sociological textbook *Family Rhythms: The Changing Textures of Family Life in Ireland* (MUP, 2016).

John Goodwin is a Professor of Sociology and Sociological Practice at the University of Leicester. As a sociologist his principal research interests include the broad areas of youth, community and research methods as well as the history of sociology. John is a recognised expert on the life and sociology of Pearl Jephcott; and also has a significant interest in the works of Norbert Elias and C. Wright Mills. He has expertise in qualitative secondary analysis, re-studies, biographical methods and the use of unconventional data sources in sociological research.

Jane Gray is Professor of Sociology and a research associate in the Social Sciences Institute at Maynooth University. Her scholarship centres on questions relating to families, households and social change. She led the development of the Irish Qualitative Data Archive and is a member of the management team for the Digital Repository of Ireland. Her co-authored textbook (with Ruth Geraghty and David Ralph), *Family Rhythms: The Changing Textures of Family Life in Ireland*, was published by Manchester University Press.

Maureen Haaker is a Lecturer in Early Childhood Studies and the course leader for the MA Childhood Studies. In 2010, Maureen graduated from Marian University in Indianapolis, Indiana with a BA in Sociology and Political Science. In 2012, she received her MA Sociology at University of Essex. Following the completion of her postgraduate degree, Maureen collaborated on an ESRC-funded project hosted by the UK Data Service called Digital Futures, which looked at methodological issues surrounding data management and re-use of qualitative datasets. Maureen is a member of the Social Research Association, British Sociological Association, and American Sociological Association.

Sarah Irwin is Professor of Sociology at the University of Leeds. She is Director of the Centre for Research into Families, the Life Course and Generations. She has published extensively in the areas of family, youth, parenting and social inequalities and has a long-standing interest in research methods, including qualitative longitudinal research and qualitative secondary analysis.

Lynn Jamieson is Professor of Sociology at the University of Edinburgh. She is a co-director of the Centre for Research on Families and Relationships, and a co-editor of the journal *Families, Relationships and Societies* and of the Palgrave Macmillan monograph series Studies in Family and Intimate Life.

Dawn Lyon is Reader in Sociology in the School of Social Policy, Sociology and Social Research at the University of Kent, UK. She has published in the fields of the sociology of work, time, gender, migration, youth studies, and visual and sensory sociology. In her work on young people's imagined futures, she is interested in the importance of the future in everyday life and she is currently working with a film-maker on a documentary entitled *Remembering the Future*. She is also interested in the rhythms of working life. Her book, *What is Rhythmanalysis?* was published by Bloomsbury Academic in 2018.

Bren Neale is Emeritus Professor of Life Course and Family Research at the University of Leeds, UK, and a fellow of the Academy of Social Sciences. She was director of the ESRC-funded Timescapes Qualitative Longitudinal Study during 2007–12. She has contributed to advances in qualitative longitudinal research across academia, government and the voluntary sector, and continues to provide training and support in this methodology for new and established researchers.

Henrietta O'Connor is Professor of Sociology at the University of Leicester. Her research interests focus on the sociology of work, youth employment and gender. She also has an active interest in research methods ranging in scope from her early work on online research methods to more recent research based around the secondary analysis of qualitative data, qualitative longitudinal research and community re-studies.

Susie Weller is a Senior Research Fellow in the ESRC National Centre for Research Methods and the MRC Lifecourse Epidemiology Unit, University of Southampton, UK. She has expertise in conducting creative, participatory and qualitative longitudinal research with young people and families. She has published over 50 articles, chapters and papers exploring: lived experiences of health care interventions; caring relations, identities and practices; young people's trajectories to adulthood during economic change; participation, citizenship and democracy in schools; friendship and social networks; social capital and choice; sibling relationships over time; and qualitative methods. She is co-founder of the Big Qual Analysis Resource Hub (http://bigqlr.ncrm.ac.uk/) – the first online multimedia collection designed to assist researchers in analysing complex qualitative data.

ACKNOWLEDGEMENTS

There are many people we would like to thank for their valuable support and contribution to this book, which is undoubtedly a collective endeavour. This collection would not have been possible without the pioneering contributions of our colleagues. Together, their chapters capture and map out a new terrain of methodological innovation and advance in approaches to Qualitative Secondary Analysis. The intellectual contributions and the professionalism the contributors have shown, in responding to comments and meeting the deadlines we have suggested, continue to inspire us in the work we do.

The comments from the seven reviewers of our book proposal were also invaluable, helping us to identify areas of strength but also where our collective work considerably advances debate. We would like to thank our Editor at SAGE, Natalie Aguilera, for early advice and support. This not only strengthened our proposal but also brought our methodological focus into sharper perspective. This was a master class in editing and we thank her for it. We would also like to thank Eve Williams for taking the book forwards in its later stages of production, and everyone at SAGE who has been involved in bringing the book to print stage. This is work that we are incredibly proud of.

I

CHANGING DATA LANDSCAPES AND QUALITATIVE SECONDARY ANALYSIS

ONE

AN INTRODUCTION TO QUALITATIVE SECONDARY ANALYSIS

Kahryn Hughes and Anna Tarrant

--- CHAPTER CONTENTS ---

1.1 Introduction

This book brings together chapters from leading scholars and researchers who have developed innovative theories and methods of Qualitative Secondary Analysis (QSA). Combined, the chapters provide a comprehensive introduction to the range of epistemological, ethical and pragmatic aspects of QSA. This book especially addresses researchers new to debates on qualitative data re-use. It aims to present both depth understanding of the key methodological challenges of QSA, and also offer practical tools and strategies you can apply in your own research practice.

To provide a broad overview, our Introduction charts the rise of debates on Qualitative Secondary Analysis. We show how QSA has emerged as a distinct methodological approach in tandem with changes in the research data landscape. We briefly introduce the main critiques and challenges of QSA and signpost to the relevant chapters where such questions are addressed in depth. As with all other chapters in this volume, we include pedagogical resources at the conclusion of this chapter along with references.

1.1.1 Re-using qualitative data

Interest in the possibilities of re-using qualitative research data blossomed as resources through which to do so began to flourish. In 2007 Niamh Moore identified two particular events characterising this development. The first was the establishment of the Qualitative Data Archival Resource, originally known as QUALIDATA, now part of the UK Data Service. The second was a move by the Economic and Social Research Council (ESRC), the major funder of social research in the UK, to require funded researchers to deposit copies of their data into QUALIDATA (Moore, 2007).

These developments had followed an ESRC scoping review by Jennifer Mason (2002) of existing data resources for the purposes of data sharing and re-use in the social sciences community and the potential for capacity building in this area (see also Holland et al., 2006; Mason, 2007). Mason's focus was on re-using qualitative research data in an attempt to redress an imbalance in existing investments in quantitative rather than qualitative resources. The review identified two key benefits to building capacity in qualitative data re-use. First, the immersive, depth and time-consuming nature of qualitative research means qualitative datasets are expensive to produce, and the tendency for these to be used solely for one study was potentially wasteful (Holland et al., 2006). Re-use would therefore facilitate the realisation of the original financial investment. Second, the same intensive and time-consuming nature of qualitative research often constrains sample size. By amalgamating qualitative datasets relating to similar topics, however, it might be possible to 'scale up' qualitative findings (Neale et al., 2012; Thomson and McLeod, 2015). We will come back to discuss the implications of these two benefits below. For now, though, we confine ourselves to pointing out that changing attitudes towards data re-use characterise priorities set by European Funding Councils, who increasingly require the re-use and QSA of extant data (e.g., ERC Horizon 2020, European Commission) whilst minimising collection of new data. Elsewhere, the USA, Canada and Australia have also seen a growth in research data archives and scholastic debate supporting the re-use of data. While this has mainly been in relation to quantitative data, there have nevertheless been significant developments in qualitative resources and engagement.

1.2 What Data Are Out There?

In order for QSA to be feasible, the data need to be 'out there' (Mauthner et al., 1998). In their landmark paper raising early methodological and ethical cautions about QSA, Mauthner et al. (ibid.) identified a wealth of digital and non-digital data available for re-use. Since then, the data landscape has changed entirely. In response to global digitisation and accessibility of data, an international data landscape of vast research potential and activity has emerged, characterised by an explosion in the numbers and sizes of research data archives and repositories. These repositories have become more complex in both intention and functionality in response to the increasingly diverse range and formats of academic data generated.

The data, therefore, are certainly out there, and it is worth mentioning some key *qualitative* data resources to give a flavour of the diversity and wealth of data now available to researchers. Principal data collections in the UK are held at the Mass Observation Archive, a key historical resource of accounts of everyday life; the National Social Policy and Social Change Archive, University of Essex, a paper archive of special collections; the Irish Qualitative Data Archive, which holds a range of studies on growing up and living in Ireland; and NIQA (the Northern Ireland Qualitative Archive), which has two archives on ageism and conflict. Chapter 11 by Jane Gray and Ruth Geraghty demonstrates what can be done with the data held there. The UK Data Service (UKDS) houses the largest collection of digital data in the social sciences and humanities in the UK and has an impact agenda of advancing research, building skills and informing social policy. The resources provided by UKDS are not only research data, but include a broad range of services supporting best practice, data preservation and sharing standards.

Other university-based archives include that at the London School of Economics Archive, with a range of thematic collections, and the Timescapes Archive at the University of Leeds, which is a specialist repository for qualitative longitudinal data.

International qualitative data archives include repositories such as the Australian Data Archive (ADA), the Qualitative Data Repository at Syracuse University (NY), the Henry A. Murray Research Archive at Harvard, and the Inter-University Consortium for Political and Social Research (ICPSR) in the USA. In Europe there has also been a flourishing of qualitative data archives, many of which are members of the Council of European Social Science Data Archives (CESSDA), the long list of which is included on the UK Data Service website.

This catalogue is in no way exhaustive, and in this volume Chapter 5 by Rosalind Edwards and colleagues, and Chapter 7 by Maureen Haaker, review the broad range of archives and data repositories available for qualitative secondary analysis. Many large-scale panel studies which ostensibly lend themselves more to quantitative analyses may well also contain qualitative components. For example, the *Born in Bradford* study has collected numerous observations and open-ended responses as part of their various research strands. While these are not listed on their study website, these qualitative data are nevertheless *there*. Our point is that while working with data that have been collected, organised and deposited in ways that make them available for re-use, it would be mistaken to concentrate solely on such data. There are rich possibilities for research using 'found' qualitative data, which may include muted components of quantitative datasets (Savage, 2010).

The infrastructures listed above are composed in the main of purposefully collected research data, but if we include repositories with thematic data holdings, collections such as those in the Feminist Archive may form valuable resources for research. This archive holds an assortment of objects, indicating the great diversity and wealth of 'human documents' (Plummer, 2001; see also Chapter 4 by Bren Neale) that researchers might want to investigate as part of our research:

> periodicals, books, pamphlets, diaries, calendars, conference papers, personal letters, photographs, stickers, postcards, drawings, posters, banners, badges, vinyl records, mini-disks, audio cassettes, video cassettes, 16mm film, clothing, digitised audio and film and various other ephemera. (http://feministarchivesouth.org.uk/about/)

The Feminist Archive is not necessarily large, or even situated in the same place. The Feminist Archive has its North collection in the University of Leeds and its South in the University of Bristol. If we cast our net a little wider, we can include collections such as those held by the British Library. Their Sound Archive, which is among the largest collections of recorded sound in the world, includes music, spoken word and ambient recordings and holds more than six million recordings.

Its counterpart in the USA, the World Listening Project, is one of many different data repositories, including a vast array of materials, that can be repurposed for what Duncan (2012: 313) describes 'as a sort of comparative research, but using comparisons over time instead of over space'.

The drive to archiving has not only been confined to institutional collections. Community archives have a considerable lineage, shaped by the premise that personal histories of specialised, marginalised or politicised groups need protecting and promoting simply to preserve their stories in the historical frame. Further, these archives can be seen as part of broader trends in digital social participation whereby people collect data on themselves as part of a complex project of self-knowing. In the UK, examples of this include a host of living archives in communities organised around vanished industries such as coal mining, or steel working. The Aylesham Community Heritage Archive (UK) is one example, built via inter-generational contributions of memories, photographs and other ephemera to support the protection and continuity of both family and community histories of coal miners. The collections tell not only of industrial change, but also of longer historical diasporas, and shifting histories of community identity. Archives may sustain community identities that are not geographical, but formed through politicised identities. For example, the Lesbian Herstory Archives in Brooklyn (USA) not only archives materials contributed by women, but also promotes itself as a research resource. Chapter 4 by Bren Neale and Chapter 8 by Joanna Bornat explore how these types of materials may be reconceived as both objects and subjects of research using QSA, connecting to wider debates in sociology and oral history respectively.

Finally, there are paper datasets kept in offices, bedrooms and attics where researchers have retired, or which have simply been boxed up and left somewhere a long time ago. The chapter by John Goodwin and Henrietta O'Connor (Chapter 10) exemplifies the possibilities and challenges of working with 'found datasets' of this nature. Even less accessible are the datasets in electronic folders either on people's private computers, degrading as their technology degrades, or in their accounts on university servers, kept there until the account is deleted when the researcher either moves institution, or in recent cases where overzealous data managers driven by misguided compliance to GDPR regulations delete whole drives. Such data are *there*, but they are disappearing as rapidly as new data are generated. Our growing orientation to *visible*, and by that we mean online, data sources may mean these other data are increasingly discarded and lost in a digital data landscape that in its very formation marginalises and threatens data such as these.

And there is no hiatus in this rapidly changing data landscape. As new forms and larger volumes of data continue to be generated, new infrastructures are being developed to collect and store them. In the UK, this drive to create new data infrastructures, especially in university contexts, is in large part due to a move by UK funding councils to devolve responsibility to universities for archiving, curating and making available for re-use all council-funded research. However, this does not account for the broader, more comprehensive international change in orientation towards, and investment in, resources for storing data. Such changes must be ascribed to the wider historical terrain in which the explosion of 'big data', and imperatives towards their analysis and re-use, are part of what has been described as 'knowing capitalism' (Savage and Burrows, 2007). Interestingly, and in subversion of this, the processes and activities around archiving or collecting data, as in the community archives listed above, can be seen as both resource and conduit for social and political resistance (see also Geiger et al., 2010).

In the social sciences, these comprehensive changes have ushered in a 'data turn', namely a turn towards understanding the research process as more than that involved in the primary or preliminary study, but one which attends to longitudinal questions of data legacy and preservation, recognising the longer-term processes of data re/production through their re-use (Moore, 2007; Bishop, 2009; Hammersley, 2015). In other words, this tsunami of data and data infrastructures compounds a series of challenges for social scientists, including how to work with them, and how to understand or make use of the new research possibilities they offer. One such methodological approach is QSA, but how and what is QSA? In response to this question, we return to the 'two benefits' of re-using data identified earlier to help us work through the challenges and questions it raises.

1.3 Challenges and Questions Raised by QSA

To recap: the benefits were first, that data re-use may realise more fully the original financial investments from funding councils, and second, that re-using extant data may enable researchers to 'scale up' their findings. These two claims have been heavily criticised from the outset across the social sciences, and the rest of this section outlines why this has been the case.

In brief response to the first benefit, the task of undertaking QSA is as time consuming, intensive and potentially as costly as any other qualitative research (Tarrant and Hughes, 2019; see also Chapter 5 by Edwards and colleagues). In order to understand why this is the case, and why for example it is just not possible to lift a dataset out of a repository and drop it into one's own dataset, or receive it from another research team to bulk up one's own sample, it is necessary to consider the epistemological *work* required to address the key challenges of QSA. To do this, we have organised the remainder of our discussion on the challenges of QSA and how various scholars have addressed them via a series of questions.

We have ordered these questions so that they map onto the overarching structure of the book, and we signpost to relevant chapters which contain worked examples of how particular questions or topics have been addressed.

1.3.1 Data re-use or Qualitative Secondary Analysis?

First, we need to settle on an appropriate language for Qualitative Secondary Analysis. Early debate on whether it was possible to re-use qualitative data maintained somewhat rigid distinctions between primary and secondary analysts based on their connections or otherwise to their contexts of production (Moore, 2007; Geiger et al., 2010). It was argued that direct researcher experience informs on data analysis in ways which secondary, unconnected, analysis cannot (Mauthner et al., 1998). In her seminal paper, Niamh Moore (2007) questioned the distinction between primary and secondary analysis, pointing out that for analysis to become 'secondary', data must become 'secondary' too. She argued that to talk about 'pre-existing data' blinds us to how data are co-produced in new contexts (ibid.). Instead, she proposes that (re)using data involves primary analysis of a different order of data (Moore, ibid; see also Henderson et al., 2006).

While we agree with Moore that the boundaries between primary and secondary researchers are often blurred (see our reflections on collective QSA in Chapter 6), we nevertheless prefer the language of qualitative *secondary* analysis. If data are co-produced, QSA researchers must develop strategies for the comprehensive capture of how this occurs. They must be able to reflect on the 'embedded contexts' of both their own and the previous study (Irwin et al., 2012) in order to 'make sense' of what those data are and how their 'usefulness' may be understood.

We suggest that the language of QSA allows us to interrogate the precise means used by researchers to recontextualise, rework or repurpose data for new research. This also includes reflexive engagement on how we may bring differently constituted datasets into analytic conversation and alignment (Irwin, 2013). Thus recontextualising data/sets involves recasting them as theoretical objects, identifying not only how they were produced, but how they may be re-used (see also Hughes et al., 2016). Making distinctions between different phases of data re-use through the language of QSA also enables us to 'write in' temporality and modes of analytical engagement in QSA. In effect, the language of QSA is one infused with particular temporal modes of epistemological reflexivity. The substance of such theoretical reflection is elaborated upon in Sarah Irwin's chapter (Chapter 2), which examines some of the practicalities, challenges and methodological implications of undertaking QSA across several datasets. It does so with a particular focus on analytic strategies and conceptual development.

However, you will find throughout the volume a diversity of opinions on this. For example, Bren Neale in Chapter 4 makes a case for the language of 'revisiting' data. Rosalind Edwards and colleagues use the language of 'big qual analysis' which reflects both a conceptual and material recasting of qualitative data. Sarah Irwin in Chapter 2 uses the language of secondary analysis but cautions against considering this as therefore second-class analysis, whereas Maureen Haaker in Chapter 7, from the UK Data Service, employs the language of data re-use.

Consequently, while we (the editors) use the language of Qualitative Secondary Analysis both in the title of this book, and throughout our jointly authored chapters, this is not necessarily a shared nor 'settled' definition. The book therefore offers a journey both through the history of this methodological approach, and a range of different approaches to conceiving of it.

1.3.2 Can we do QSA ethically?

As part of deciding on a language of Qualitative Secondary Analysis, we need to understand how and whether it is possible to conduct QSA ethically. Much early caution focused on how QSA rewrites relationships of researcher/researched, and researcher/researcher. QSA changes the possibilities for original participants to be aware of the re-use of their data (Neale, 2013). How, then, might researchers solicit consent for archiving and re-use where future research in which the data will be used is inevitably unclear?

Ethical questions also include those around the politics of anonymity and confidentiality in an increasingly digitised data landscape in which the opportunities for data linkage and individual profiling are continually enhanced (see Irwin, 2013). These questions connect to those concerning data legacy and preservation. For example, what balance should be struck between protecting participants and preserving their data in processes of anonymisation (Moore, 2012)? Where data are identified as especially sensitive, how long do data remain sensitive and how long is 'long'? If archives and research teams are considering timed embargo on sensitive data, when might that embargo reasonably expire? How and who is involved in negotiating these decisions? What happens to data that aren't archived, or which do not contain consent for re-use because they simply date from a time when such consent was not sought?

In addressing these ethical questions, new stakeholder models of ethical data sharing have been developed, drawing especially on work on qualitative longitudinal methodology, which builds 'time' into a broad range of ethical strategies, dispositions and practices that run throughout the lifetime of data (see Bishop, 2009; Neale and Bishop, 2012; Neale, 2013). Historical distance thus enhances innovation in ongoing ethical reflection and engagement in QSA, facilitating attention to and recognition of the unique and varied ways in which researchers (and others) are connected to the data that have been generated. These and other debates are mapped out in our chapter on Ethics (Chapter 3), which concludes with a 'legacy ethics' of QSA.

1.3.3 How can we build time into QSA?

The idea of 'scaling up' as a benefit of QSA requires a temporal reorientation to the 'lifetime' of data. Along with other writers (e.g., Edwards, 2008; Thomson and McLeod, 2015), we suggest that an increased methodological engagement with data re-use can be linked with a 'temporal turn' in the social sciences more generally (see Thomson et al., 2012; Thomson and McLeod, 2015). Such a 'turn' has been fuelled by an increasing interest in, and commitment to, more processual theoretical engagement (Thomson et al., 2012; Hughes et al., 2016) where time and temporality have become both the medium for, and the subject of, research (Neale, 2019). The question of temporality is an unsurprising element of QSA, not only because of the protracted time frames of data re-use, but also because the antecedents of much debate in QSA began in discussions around qualitative longitudinal research, a methodology fundamentally attuned to questions of time (Neale, 2019).

In considering time as a *medium* for QSA, research design must take into account how data may become 'heritage data', e.g., either the data on which new research may be developed by originating teams or secondary analysts, or 'travelling data' (Thomson et al., 2012), where data may also come to characterise certain social moments and places, through given historical periods (Tarrant and Hughes, 2019). Re-imagining data as 'travelling data' provides the opportunity for the '[re]contextualising of material in new times and places and with different audiences' (Thomson et al., 2012: 311). Building a temporally-informed analytic orientation towards data enhances opportunities for epistemological engagement with the process of recasting datasets as theoretical objects, as discussed earlier.

There are pragmatic benefits too. When time is recognised as an irreducible aspect of data, and of the research process as a whole (Bornat, 2005; Henderson et al., 2007), analysis can be flexible in new ways (Åkerström et al., 2004). Temporal distancing facilitates longitudinal analysis and extended reflection. Nick Emmel (2016, 2017), for example, has described how revisiting his data at several points over time has enabled him to rethink and refine a relational model of social vulnerability that has already been through several iterations. Further, linking datasets that have been collected at different historical moments may extend researchers' temporal reach beyond the contemporary contexts within which they are work-ing, and new questions can be brought to bear on data in the context of new theoretical sensibilities.

QSA builds out of a long history of practice such as in oral history research where a wide range of data are re-used in order to both engage with questions of the past, and comparisons with the present (Bornat, 2013). In this work, time becomes a *sub-ject* of investigation. Building time into QSA allows us to theoretically rework 'pasts' and bring them into comparison with the present, and may facilitate analytical engagement with questions of the future. Identifying and working with *memory* in people's accounts may bring them into new fields of analytic visibility. Joanna Bornat's chapter demonstrates how there may be a multiplicity of times within people's accounts. In considering the question of temporality, she argues that it is important to acknowledge that time is not a thing; nor are data solely of *one time*, or one moment. The histories they speak of are those of the momentary context of data production but these accounts are histories in and of themselves. They speak of longer processes of temporal production, engagement and meaningfulness. Bornat develops three temporal categories to indicate *what's happening* within an interview, giving us new intellectual and analytical tools to approach our own QSA.

Dealing with how we might build time into our research design, Bren Neale's chapter develops three strategies for QSA based on three different temporal cases. These include looking at extant, 'old' data through a contemporary lens; compar-ing 'past' and 'present' by bringing historical and contemporary data into ana-lytical conversation; and revising collections of data which are characterised by *seriality*, such as diaries or letters. Neale, too, offers strategies and new analytic tools to approach our own QSA. Taken together, these two chapters contribute to key epistemological debates around how data may be reworked and repurposed for new research, and related questions of how archives shape possibilities for QSA.

1.3.4 How can we sample from archives?

QSA opens up the ambition of research, changing how we think of research design in terms of how we might use what is already there. However, the somewhat sweeping suggestion that qualitative data may be used to 'scale up' new research ushers in a host of pragmatic challenges. The process of 'getting to grips' with the contextual embeddedness of data, an integral part of QSA, requires the researcher to identify, access and familiarise themselves with large datasets, as well as the study sample characteristics.

However, there is *so much* data out there, stored in an international constel-lation of data repositories. Which data should we use and why? How might we go about identifying it? How is the work of 'familiarisation' to be achieved across so much diverse data? How can we avoid cherry picking from datasets, and falling into the analytical trap of the 'juicy quote' syndrome and false 'completeness' claims (Savage, 2008)? Being required to collate and manage vast quantities of data may not suit all timescales or research budgets. This raises the question of how QSA researchers balance the competing demands of finance, time and opportunity in producing high-quality, valuable research findings.

These challenges have provoked a wave of novel research design and innovation, including new and more collegial research relationships. QSA is therefore emerging as both a mainstream methodological strategy, and yet one which is characterised by innovation where such innovation has yet to become established. Our (the editors') chapter (Chapter 6) on collective secondary data analysis, outlines one approach, and details how research teams may be assembled specifically for the purposes of QSA using a method of collective analysis workshops that draws on a longer history (Bornat et al., 2008). This chapter sets out a potential framework for collective QSA, exploring the possibilities of theoretically generated small samples in purposefully gathered research teams, and discusses the methodological implications of bringing data together for collective analysis.

While collective QSA workshops may facilitate depth analysis of small samples, of two or three datasets, Rosalind Edwards and colleagues in Chapter 5 develop a 'big qual' approach to analysing large collections of archived qualitative data. Their chapter engages with questions of computer-aided analytical software that might be used to sample from across datasets in ways which facilitate the simultaneous process of *familiarisation* with a vast array of data, alongside the development of meaningful *questions* and *analytic directions* the data may support. Using a 'breadth and depth' approach, they explore the potentials and pitfalls of bringing together data and searching across them, using a number of strategies including the use of key words, thematic analysis and depth case analysis. They demonstrate how new empirical insights can be generated through this 'big qual' approach, and offer structured tools for your own research.

So far in our discussion of QSA, we have focused entirely on research projects. However, QSA has an array of possibilities, including in teaching contexts. The rise of QSA may reconfigure or, at the very least, reframe our understanding of the long chains of stakeholders involved in research funding and participation, and the value of data. The drive by funding councils for their investments to work harder has led to demands whereby research partners provide 'in kind' resources in the form of time, staff and data (Hughes et al., 2014). Significantly, data are becoming a resource, which can be redeployed as a form of capital in new and emerging research designs. In this context, there has been a fresh demand for training in QSA, and some more forward-thinking universities are beginning to make their repositories available to students, introducing a new set of practical (resource, management, legal) and ethical challenges. Chapter 7 by Maureen Haaker, from the UK Data Service, provides a detailed overview of data services in the education sector. She signposts to existing teaching resources and the key skills they may foster in students through experiential learning. These skills have practical value for all QSA researchers and need not only apply in teaching contexts. Her chapter provides a discussion of how the need for training in QSA may in part be addressed through educational contexts.

1.3.5 What data are included in QSA?

Even where questions of how we may access data or bring datasets together are addressed, the data infrastructure landscape is characterised by considerable variation. In a world of increasing data complexity and variety, new methods are required for understanding and reconciling data in different formats, other than those of, say, the more traditional transcripts from interviews, or focus groups. Furthermore, archives capture not only what are seen as core research data, but also metadata. Some of these may be deliberately produced, for example to a template designed by the data management team of an infrastructure (Neale et al., 2016). However, a rich source of data are the unintentional data, marginalia and so forth that occur within the data. These may be seen as data happenstance, but nevertheless require methodological framing and understanding in QSA. What, then, count as research data and how might we use such for research? Chapter 10 by John Goodwin and Henrietta O'Connor details how 'found data' produce the opportunity for both an interrogation of the original study and a re-study.

The happenstance of 'finding' data is also described in the chapter by Dawn Lyon and Graham Crow (Chapter 9). They tell how, on a visit to QUALIDATA in 2008 to explore the archive of the Sheppey Studies, they discovered a collection of 'future essays' written by schoolchildren from the Isle of Sheppey in 1978. On reading them they were able to compare how they had been used in the original study by Ray Pahl. This prompted QSA of the essays from their own standpoint, which they then brought into conversation with newly gathered essays from young people of similar ages in the same geographical contexts. The chapter goes on to chart a third stage in their research, where the authors used tools from arts practice, moving away from essay format to disrupt the 'illusions' somewhat inherent in biographical approaches. Thus, their chapter looks at how working across a diverse range of materials offers new opportunities for comparison in QSA.

Finally, the possibilities of bringing qualitative data into new contexts for the purposes of comparison and theoretical refinement are not necessarily confined to *qualitative* contexts. Jane Gray and Ruth Geraghty in Chapter 11 discuss the opportunities presented by bringing *quantitative* data into dialogue with qualitative data in qualitative secondary analysis. They draw on examples from linked studies to show how dialogue between qualitative and quantitative data can take place in the original study design; to situate the qualitative data for the purposes of QSA; and finally, to support empirically-driven theoretical development.

1.4 Conclusion: Organisation of the Book

As this Introduction demonstrates, QSA cannot be understood as a discrete set of methodological techniques. Instead, we have presented a diverse array of questions and approaches, with high epistemological and ethical stakes. Even so, there are several overarching themes that comprise the three sections of this book, and they are as follows:

- **Part I** covers the epistemological underpinnings of QSA, discussing the ethical challenges and potential ways forward for re-using data, and engaging with questions of how we may build time into QSA.
- **Part II** addresses the central questions and challenges of building QSA into a study design. This section informs on new and innovative research design and orientation, addressing such questions as how researchers might approach breadth and depth, and teaching-focused QSA.
- **Part III** of this book questions what we mean by 'data', and how we might think creatively about using different sorts of data in QSA.

Each chapter presents a structured overview of the key features raised by the author's topic. Chapters dealing with new methodologies map out how their own particular innovations have been applied, what the outcomes have been and the limitations of their approach. Pedagogical resources, where appropriate/available (e.g., time lines, grid analysis, search terms, metadata) take the form of weblinks. Taken together, the chapters provide a rounded account of contemporary advances and innovations in QSA, responding to the host of questions raised in this Introduction.

Finally, many of the questions addressed across the chapters in this book link to broader questions around 'big data', and the challenge for social scientists of remaining distinctive in a changing data world (Savage and Burrows, 2007). The debates explored here may also offer meaningful engagement with questions of data re-use more generally, principally because the chapter authors engage with epistemological challenges of making sense of 'evidence' in the contexts of qualitative data re-use.

1.5 Pedagogical Resources: Links to Qualitative Archives

Australian Data Archive – https://ada.edu.au

Aylesham Community Archives and Heritage Group – www.communityarchives.org.uk/content/organisation/aylesham

The Council of European Social Science Data Archives (CESSDA) – www.cessda.eu

The Feminist Archive North – https://feministarchivenorth.org.uk

The Feminist Archive South – http://feministarchivesouth.org.uk/

Henry A. Murray Archive, Harvard University – https://murray.harvard.edu

Inter-University Consortium of Political and Social Research – www.icpsr.umich.edu/icpsrweb/

Irish Qualitative Data Archive – www.maynoothuniversity.ie/iqda

Lesbian Herstory Archives – www.lesbianherstoryarchives.org

The London School of Economics Archive – www.lse.ac.uk/library/collections/collection-highlights/collections-highlights

Mass Observation Archive – www.massobs.org.uk

The Northern Ireland Data Archive on Conflict and Ageism – www.ark.ac.uk/qual/

Qualitative Data Repository, Syracuse University – www.google.com/search?client=safari&rls=en&q=qualitative+data+archive+america&ie=UTF-8&oe=UTF-8

The Timescapes Archive – https://timescapes-archive.leeds.ac.uk

UK Data Service – www.ukdataservice.ac.uk

UK Data Service, International Qualitative Archives – https://ukdataservice.ac.uk/get-data/other-providers/qualitative/european-archives.aspx

The World Listening Project – www.worldlisteningproject.org

1.6 References

Åkerström, M., Jacobsson, K. and Wasterfors, D. (2004) 'Re-analysis of previously collected material', in C. Seale, S. Silverman, J.F. Gubrium and G. Gobo (eds), *Qualitative Research Practice*. London: Sage.

Bishop, L. (2009) 'Ethical sharing and reuse of qualitative data', *Australian Journal of Social Issues*, 44(3): 255–72. Available at: www.data-archive.ac.uk/media/249157/ajsi44bishop.pdf (accessed 24 February 2011).

Bornat, J. (2005) 'Recycling the evidence: Different approaches to the reanalysis of gerontological data', *Forum: Qualitative Social Research*, 6(1).

Bornat, J. (2013) 'Secondary analysis in reflection: Some experiences of re-use from an oral history perspective', *Families, Relationships and Societies*, 2(2): 309–17.

Bornat, J., Bytheway, B. and Henwood, K. (2008) *Report of Meeting between Timescapes' 'Men as Fathers' and 'The Oldest Generation' Projects*, University of Cardiff, 21

July. Available at: www.timescapes.leeds.ac.uk/assets/files/report-fathers-oldest-generation-projects-july08.pdf (accessed 20 May 2019).

Duncan, S. (2012) 'Using elderly data theoretically: Personal life in 1949/1950 and individualisation theory', *International Journal of Social Research Methodology*, 15(4): 311–29.

Edwards, R. (ed.) (2008) *Researching Families and Communities: Social and Generational Change*. Abingdon, GB: Routledge.

Emmel, N. (2016) *Revisiting Yesterday's Data Today*. Available at: http://bigqlr.ncrm.ac.uk/2016/12/14/guest-post-6-nick-emmel-revisiting-yesterdays-data-today/ (accessed 20 May 2019).

Emmel, N. (2017) 'Empowerment in the relational longitudinal space of vulnerability', *Social Policy and Society*, 16(3): 457–67.

Geiger, T., Moore, N. and Savage, M. (2010) *The Archive in Question*, National Centre for Research Methods NCRM/016. Available at: http://eprints.ncrm.ac.uk/921/1/Moore_review_paper_march_10.pdf (accessed 4 April 2019).

Hammersley, M. (2015) 'On ethical principles for social research', *International Journal of Social Research Methodology*, 18(4): 433–49.

Henderson, S., Holland, J. and Thomson, R. (2006) 'Making the long view: Perspectives on context from a qualitative longitudinal (QL) study', *Methodological Innovations Online*, 1(2): 47–63.

Henderson, S., Holland, J., McGrellis, S., Thomson, R. and Sharpe, S. (2007) *Inventing Adulthoods: A Biographical Approach to Youth Transitions*. London: SAGE.

Holland, J., Thomson, R. and Henderson, S. (2006) *Qualitative Longitudinal Research: A Discussion Paper*, London Southbank University. Available at: www.researchgate.net/publication/242763174_Qualitative_Longitudinal_Research_A_Discussion_Paper (accessed 20 May 2019).

Hughes, K., Neale, B. and MacMillan, R. (2014) *Changing Landscapes for the Third Sector: Enhancing Knowledge and Informing Practice*, under ESRC Knowledge Exchange and Transfer Scheme. Available at: http://changinglandscapes.leeds.ac.uk (accessed 20 May 2019).

Hughes, K., Goodwin, J. and Hughes, J. (2016) 'Documenti e reperti umani come figurazioni', *CAMBIO: Rivista sulle trasformazioni sociali [Journal of Social Transformations]*, 6(11): 123–38.

Irwin, S. (2013) 'Qualitative secondary data analysis: Ethics, epistemology and context', *Progress in Development Studies*, 13(4): 295–306.

Irwin, S., Bornat J. and Winterton, M. (2012) 'Timescapes secondary analysis: Comparison, context and working across data sets', *Qualitative Research*, 12(1): 66–80.

Mason, J. (2007) '"Re-using" qualitative data: On the merits of an investigative epistemology', *Sociological Research Online*, 12(3). Available at: www.socresonline.org.uk/12/3/3.html (accessed 22 May 2019).

Mauthner, N.S., Parry, O. and Backett-Milburn, K. (1998) 'The data are out there, or are they? Implications for archiving and revisiting qualitative data', *Sociology*, 32(4): 733–45.

Moore, N. (2007) '(Re)using qualitative data?', *Sociological Research Online*. Available at: http://socresonline.org.uk/12/3/1.html (accessed 20 May 2019).

Moore, N. (2012) 'The politics and ethics of naming: Questioning anonymisation in (archival) research', *International Journal of Social Research Methodology*, 15(4): 331–40.

Neale, B. (2013) 'Adding time into the mix: Stakeholder ethics in qualitative longitudinal research', *Methodological Innovation*, 8(2): 6–20.

Neale, B. (2019) *What is Qualitative Longitudinal Research?* London: Bloomsbury.

Neale, B. and Bishop, L. (2012) 'The Timescapes archive: A stakeholder approach to archiving qualitative longitudinal data', *Qualitative Research*, 12(1): 53–65.

Neale, B., Henwood, K. and Holland, J. (2012) 'Researching lives through time: An introduction to the Timescapes approach', *Qualitative Research*, 12(1): 4–15.

Neale, B., Hughes, K., Blyth, G., Proudfoot, R. and Phillips, P. (2016) *Managing Qualitative Longitudinal Data for Longer-Term Use and Re-use: A Practical Guide for Researchers*. Leeds: University of Leeds Institutional Repository.

Plummer, K. (2001) *Documents of Life 2: An Invitation to a Critical Humanism*. London: Sage.

Savage, M. (2008) *Sampling, Validity and the Longitudinal Archive*, NCRM Seminar Series on Archiving and Reusing Qualitative Data. Available at: www.restore.ac.uk/archiving_qualitative_data/projects/archive_series/papers.shtml (accessed 20 May 2019).

Savage, M. (2010) *Identities and Social Change in Britain since 1940: The Politics of Method*. Oxford: Oxford University Press.

Savage, M. and Burrows, R. (2007) 'The coming crisis of empirical sociology', *Sociology*, 41(5): 885–99.

Tarrant, A. and Hughes, K. (2019) 'Qualitative Secondary Analysis: Building longitudinal samples to understand men's generational identities in low-income contexts', *Sociology*, 53(3): 599–611.

Thomson, R. and McLeod, J. (2015) 'New frontiers in qualitative longitudinal research: An agenda for research', *International Journal of Social Research Methodology*, 18(3): 243–50.

Thomson, R., Moe, A., Thorne, B. and Bjerrum Nielson, H. (2012) 'Situated affect in travelling data: Tracing processes of meaning making in qualitative research', *Qualitative Inquiry*, 18(4): 310–22.

TWO

QUALITATIVE SECONDARY ANALYSIS: WORKING ACROSS DATASETS

Sarah Irwin

CHAPTER CONTENTS

2.1 Introduction: Why Work Across Multiple Datasets?

Secondary analysis holds challenges for researchers looking only at one dataset so why would they compound their difficulties by working across multiple datasets? Tantalisingly, such work offers the prospect for extending the explanatory reach of qualitative research projects and perhaps enhancing possibilities for building cumulative knowledge. There are different reasons why analysts pursue secondary analysis across qualitative datasets (for reviews see Heaton 2008; Watters et al., 2018). They might wish to evolve their own primary research through grounding it with reference to analyses of extant data (e.g., Tarrant and Hughes, 2019; Watters et al., 2018). They might seek to extend their sample or the analytic reach of data in addressing their questions by working with data across contiguous datasets (Funk et al., 2015). Or they might see scope for new analyses and insight in working across more disparate datasets (Irwin and Winterton, 2011b; Gray et al., 2016; Davidson et al., 2018). Accordingly, existing datasets may provide a rich resource for social science researchers pursuing secondary analysis.

This chapter examines some of the challenges and methodological implications of undertaking secondary analysis across more than one dataset and some strategies which have been employed to this end. There has been much debate about the epistemological implications of pursuing secondary analysis of qualitative data (e.g., see Bishop, 2007; Mason, 2007; Moore, 2007; Heaton, 2008; Irwin and Winterton, 2012; Sherif, 2018). I will not explore such debates here. The aim of this chapter is primarily that of offering a picture of some exemplar studies and a set of considerations for the secondary analyst. I reiterate a case for the importance of creativity, rigour and resourcefulness in undertaking QSA (cf. Mason, 2007; Irwin and Winterton, 2012). This includes strategies for building an interrogative account of social processes, prospects for refining understanding, and clarity over the limits and possibilities of QSA.

Data are embedded within the conditions in which they are made, so theoretical understanding and analytic rigour are important when working across datasets. Extensive preparatory and analytic work is required in grasping the contextual shaping of data and the possibilities for alignment of data and/or evidence. This is then a baseline for developing substantive analysis. Undertaking secondary analysis across more than one dataset is a tall order and relatively unusual, most especially when this embraces datasets in which the researchers have not been involved as primary investigators. This chapter considers some diverse examples of QSA practice and will be of interest to those contemplating working across datasets. It also invites broader reflection on the relationship between data, evidence and sociological understanding.

2.2 Considerations in Working with Data from Different Sources

In this section I address some preliminary issues that secondary analysts will need to consider in working across datasets. The salience of the dataset(s) in facilitating analysis of new research questions is an obvious requirement but their capacity to do so may not be self-evident at the outset; in-depth knowledge of data is needed for good judgements about this. A second key question about fit relates to how different datasets articulate with one another. The secondary analyst must reflect on the contextually embedded nature of data and, in cross-project working, if and how diverse project data can be brought into meaningful alignment. They must have a grounded and theoretical take on this and, as Mason suggests, be 'analytically critical about what the data they use can tell them about, and how they can do so' (Mason, 2007: 4.1).

In developing analyses, qualitative researchers immerse themselves in data, establishing an understanding and ordering of the data along thematic and conceptual lines of inquiry. In so doing they evolve and test out, and sometimes transform, their understanding. Compared to primary investigators, secondary analysts will hold a different perspective on the dataset, being distant from its original generation and its immediate contextual shaping. Assuming that the data can yield new insights through re-use it is crucial to understand the contexts in which data are embedded. Sometimes secondary analysts are themselves primary investigators returning to data well known to them as part of the originating team (e.g., Funk et al., 2015; Tarrant and Hughes, 2019; and see Tarrant and Hughes, Chapter 6). Here re-use is effectively an extension of the original research, albeit that analysts may be revisiting the data with a new focus. However, where secondary analysts are approaching data as first-time users they need to do extensive groundwork. To understand often quite complex data, secondary analysts must ensure a thoroughgoing understanding of its nature, content and originating contexts. They need to understand the project design, objectives and methods. Formally archived data will offer metadata and documentation which provides an orientation to the research project context and data: this could include a record of publications and other outputs from the project and an account of the research design, including the methodology, sampling decisions, achieved sample and a routemap of the project data. The latter would usefully include the data collection tools, most obviously interview schedules and protocols relating to all data collection.

Data reflect not only the wider social contexts in which they are generated but also proximate project contexts (by virtue of the sample, the method, the nature of interview schedules and so on). Data embeddedness is not an obstacle to successful primary analysis and nor need it be for secondary analysis, although the challenges can be greater in the latter. Working across datasets quickly crystallises the question of if, and how, the data can be brought into alignment, or into a common analytic frame of reference. If they cannot we may as well stick with meta-analysis, at the level of project findings. In the following I sketch some different approaches to secondary analysis across more than one dataset.

2.3 Working Across Datasets: Examples of Practice

2.3.1 Introduction

Using data from different datasets can extend the reach of the data (Heaton, 2008; Davidson et al., 2018). It can aid in the design of new research to build on an existing dataset (cf. Watters et al., 2018), or it might enable new analysis and insight through the breadth of diverse datasets. In this section I will describe in some detail examples of secondary analysis drawing on data from multiple datasets. Several of these have drawn on data from ESRC Timescapes. The Timescapes projects were designed to bring a nuanced set of approaches to exploring complexity, crucially doing so through qualitative longitudinal methods for accessing the temporal and dynamic aspects of participants' lived experiences (Neale, 2007; see also Neale, 2018). The seven substantive primary empirical projects had common foci, including life course and familial transitions, and relations across generations, but they also had diverse designs, disciplinary foci and substantive research questions meaning that there were extensive differences in the nature of the data collected. In such a situation, how do we bring diverse data together in analytically meaningful ways? As an integral part of the overall programme of research, the Timescapes Secondary Analysis Project sought to explore the potential and prospects for developing qualitative secondary analysis in single (and across two or more) datasets. Through the rest of the chapter I will consider some strategies there, and elsewhere, for working across datasets: from working with data which can be treated as contiguous across datasets to working with complexly different data.

2.3.2 Working with data which can be treated as contiguous

I elaborate an example here based on one of the Timescapes Secondary Analysis Projects in which we treated data from two different datasets as more or less continuous. I will sometimes use the term contiguous here to imply correspondence rather than imply that the data simply 'runs on' across datasets. The approach here is akin to Heaton's description of an amplified approach to secondary analysis, within her typology (2008). It is cumulative in its approach to bringing together data from different projects. Three of the Timescapes projects included interviews with young people. Early agreement had been made to include some common questions relating to young people's expectations for the future. In one analysis we explored data collected in young people's short 'essays' on their imagined futures, a task asked of the young people in the studies: *Young Lives and Times: The Crafting of Young People's Relationships and Identities Over Time* (YLT) (Neale, 2012) and *Siblings as Friends: The Changing Nature of Children's Lateral Relationships* (SAF) (Edwards and Weller, 2012).[1] (Also see Lyon and Crow, Chapter 9.) It echoed the National Child Development Study question asked of 11-year-olds in the early phase of that study (Elliott and Morrow, 2007). The young people were asked: 'Imagine you are now 25. Write about the life you are leading, your interests, your home life and your work at the age of 25.' YLT held 18 responses and SAF held 24 responses. The projects had differing objectives, samples, research designs and lines of questioning. However, our review of the projects and their data gave confidence that we could treat the answers to this question as contiguous across the datasets for our analysis purposes. We remained transparent about participants' study origin in presenting the data with illustrative examples of the (usually paragraph-long) accounts of young people from both projects (Winterton and Irwin, 2011).

Particularly interested in classed diversity in young people's expectations, Mandy Winterton[2] undertook preliminary readings and re-readings to 'map' all the data in respect of salient themes without any initial reference to data on their socio-economic attributes or circumstances. The essays revealed a pattern of diverse expectations amongst the young people. Some were strongly suggestive of a confident and 'normalised' expectation of higher education and a graduate job, travel and no mention of parenthood by the age of 25, and other young people pointed to non-graduate employment and/or being parents by the age of 25. A third set of accounts seemed anomalous, describing both university or having a graduate job, but also having started a family by the age of 25, dimensions which would not typically go together for young women or men. Examined then with reference to data on the young people's circumstances, it was clear that the first two kinds of accounts sat consistently with diverse social class backgrounds while the third (on the face of it more anomalous) kind of account came from young people with no family background of higher education and yet who also

[1] I am grateful to Professor Rosalind Edwards and Dr. Susie Weller for providing the Secondary Analysis team with access to the SAF data.

[2] Dr Mandy Winterton worked as the Research Fellow on the Secondary Analysis Project throughout its duration from 2010 to 2012.

held – usually very provisional – expectations of going to university. This diversity, and the particular interest of investigating this 'middle' group (and diversity within it), became an important stepping stone for our subsequent qualitative longitudinal analysis of class diversity and the shaping of young people's evolving educational expectations (Winterton and Irwin, 2011, 2012), including a subset of youth on quite contingent pathways presaged in this early analysis. In sum we worked across two projects to broaden the analytic sample and extend the reach of our work, bringing into comparison more cases than there would have been from either one of the studies.

Following a more recent project (see e.g., Irwin and Elley, 2011; Irwin, 2017), I have been asked by researchers working in parallel areas to share my semi-structured interview schedules and questions. Seeking to use other researchers' interview questions, the primary investigator would need permission and must acknowledge their source. Such a practice might be an interesting avenue to pursue in building 'bridging points' across empirical studies and could enrich opportunities for re-analysis, as well as offering opportunities for theoretical refinement across new and diverse study contexts. Some agreed questions were integrated into all the Timescapes project interview schedules, and as secondary analysts we explored resultant data across the datasets (see e.g., Irwin et al., 2012). We learned a good deal about the project-specific shaping of responses which also informed how we progressed our own subsequent cross-project analyses. As we will see, such embeddedness is not necessarily an obstacle to cross-project analysis, and it may create new opportunities for exploring phenomena across diverse settings.

2.3.3 Working with complexity across projects

Within any single project, its sample, methods and focus will create a unified (if complex) dataset which coheres in relation to the originating research design and questions. As these important dimensions may differ across project datasets, the secondary analyst may need to engage with data created in different ways and for different purposes. The issue is different to triangulation where different methods may be brought to bear on the same research question. In this section I will illustrate some of the issues which arise where data are not contiguous across projects. I do not want to imply that diverse data needs present an obstacle to analysis nor, indeed, that analysts should get hung up on this as an impediment to advancing research. Indeed, as Halford and Savage (2017) argue in their reflections on sociology and big data, social scientists could be both more ambitious and more creative in bringing together disparate data. However, in working across datasets we do need to ask: How do we move beyond project specificity and construct data as conjoint? Can this aid analysis? Can it then add to knowledge or understanding?

I will describe some different approaches pursued by secondary analysts. They all bring together data produced in different contexts and sometimes with rather different characteristics. They follow a common objective of ensuring sufficiency in understanding how data stands as evidence in pursuit of their particular lines of enquiry, and in the movement between data, evidence and theoretical refinement (cf. Hammersley, 2010). In working across datasets, analysts do not expect to develop straightforward 'cumulative' insights but rather seek insight from working across broad sources of data, utilising diversity and developing and refining conceptual understanding. These aims parallel those of primary and single dataset analysts except that researchers are making creative virtue of working across datasets.

2.3.4 Bringing diverse data into analytic conversation

Firstly, I consider an example of cross-project working as part of the Timescapes Secondary Analysis project. This was undertaken within the lifetime of Timescapes when the projects were still generating primary data, across successive waves of data collection. With Mandy Winterton I had pursued a range of diverse approaches to secondary analysis of Timescapes project data (a) working within projects or across contiguous data as described above, (b) working across projects to explore the contextual embeddedness of data as this related to those interview questions asked in common across projects and (c) through working across disparate projects in pursuit of a new research question of our own. It is this latter example which I consider here. The work was exploratory. We sought to evolve a line of analysis which could be developed across different projects which had not been designed with our question in mind and which had distinct foci and approaches. We had familiarised ourselves with the Timescapes projects' aims, research designs and fieldwork instruments, and read extensively across project transcripts and data as well as undertaking our more targeted analysis of the small set of common questions discussed above. We identified a list of themes and potential questions for further exploration (Irwin and Winterton, 2011b) and shared these with the project teams, with whom we then met for dedicated project meetings to discuss secondary analysis. We decided on a set of questions relating to gender and time stress in the family lives of parents with young (primary school age) children in two of the Timescapes projects, specifically: *Work and Family Lives: The Changing Experiences of 'Young' Families* (abbreviated to *Work and Family Lives*, or WFL) and

Masculinities, Identities and Risk: Transitions in the Lives of Men as Fathers (abbreviated to *Men as Fathers*, or MaF).[3] For overviews of the research designs and methods see Backett-Milburn et al., 2012 and Harden et al., 2014 on *Work and Family Lives*, and Henwood et al., 2012 on *Men as Fathers*). We found it difficult to adequately research our own questions through longitudinal data analysis so we focused on cross-sectional data.

The *Work and Family Lives* (WFL) project explored the experiences of working parents and their primary-school-aged children in negotiating and managing work and family commitments. In our earlier readings of the WFL project data, we had observed sharply gendered divisions of labour across working mothers and fathers, but also their very different accounts of their experiences. Although 'inductive', our understanding of gendered experiences of time pressure connected to a broader conceptual knowledge rooted in wider evidence and research on gender, time pressure and work–life stress. For example, mothers of pre-school children are more routinely in paid employment than in previous generations (e.g., Walby, 1997) and they are more exposed to resulting structural stresses of managing work–life balance (e.g., Crompton, 2002). Additionally, evidence suggests that women increasingly take on the work of *managing* work–life balance for their families (e.g., Vincent et al., 2004). We read and re-read all transcripts of adult participants who were co-residing with their partner or spouse (and later read outwards to include lone-parent interviews). We sought to 'map' all individual participant cases within the dataset in respect of the specific dimensions of experience in which we were interested. We did this both as textual description but also through visual representation of how individuals compared in respect of how straightforwardly, or otherwise, they

[3]*Work and Family Lives: The Changing Experiences of Young Families* was directed by Professor Kathryn Backett-Milburn at the University of Edinburgh. I am grateful to Kathryn and her team, including Jeni Harden, for providing the Secondary Analysis team with access to the *Work and Family Lives* data and for having a dedicated project meeting with us in winter 2010-11. *Masculinities, Identities and Risk: Transition in the Lives of Men as Fathers* was directed by Professor Karen Henwood at the University of Cardiff. I am grateful to Karen and her team, including Fiona Shirani, for providing the Secondary Analysis team with access to the *Men as Fathers* heritage data, from interviews conducted in Norfolk during 2000-2008 and for having a dedicated project meeting with us in winter 2010-11. Additionally, I am grateful to the *Work and Family Lives* and *Men as Fathers* project teams and, in particular, Jeni Harden and Karen Henwood, for their comments on an earlier draft of our analyses relating to their project data. The fuller analysis is written up elsewhere: see Irwin and Winterton, 2014. The data analysis was done by myself and Mandy Winterton and does not necessarily correspond with the primary analysts' views.

found managing the day-to-day scheduling of care and work commitments, at least as described in their accounts.

As the focus of this chapter is on methods I will not develop the substantive analysis in detail (for which see Irwin and Winterton, 2014) but a brief account is helpful in elaborating our secondary analysis strategies. On our readings, the data interestingly echoed wider evidence on experiences of gender and time pressure. The women's accounts suggested a particular social positioning (who did what) but also a cultural positioning in the meanings mothers and fathers accorded to their experiences. For example the mothers commonly described a feeling of guilt both in compromising their role as parents *and* in their achievements at work. Women across diverse circumstances appeared more likely to *manage* the work of work–life balance than did men, and where they had extensive paid work (full-time or approaching full-time hours), they were likely to experience pressure, and they expressed a substantial degree of guilt and anxiety about sufficiently meeting their commitments. In line with extant evidence our analysis suggested that those who were mothers *and* had extensive paid work commitments described their work and family commitments in terms of compromise, conflict and spreading themselves thinly. Such anxieties were present in (some) men's accounts but it was a more common and significantly more marked motif amongst working women.

We explored the extent to which participants' accounts reflected simple material divisions of labour. For example, did stress follow the doubling up of paid work and extensive practical care commitments, regardless of gender? We drew on the empirical data to test out such questions by looking at atypical circumstances. We asked if fathers in atypical positions (working men with extensive *practical* caring commitments) provided accounts more similar to the working mothers. We also examined the very few cases where working mothers might have fewer practical childcare commitments than typical since their husbands took on extensive childcare duties. Such women still described extensive time stress. It could be that such accounts stemmed from specificities in their circumstances. The data nevertheless fitted with wider evidence that an adequate understanding of work–life stress needs to move beyond a descriptive account of divisions of labour to an understanding of their linkages with cultural expectations and with power (e.g., Vincent et al., 2004; Doucet, 2009). We posited that three possible explanations of the gendered manifestation of time stress were as follows. Women generally are much more likely to *manage* the work of work–life balance than are men, making practical arrangements and also anticipating and reacting to contingencies, and are therefore more prone than fathers to recount experience of pressure and compromise. Secondly, women's positions in paid work give them less authority to exert control over managing family time where this potentially clashes with paid work time. Thirdly, mothers' cultural positioning as primary nurturing carer may sharpen their emotional experiences of tension between paid work and childrearing. Unsurprisingly, because we evolved our own questions distinct from the original project aims, the scope for testing them out was limited although the evidence was suggestive that all of these factors were salient.

Whilst pursuing this analysis with data from the WFL dataset we started to analyse data from the project *Masculinities, Identities and Risk* (MaF – see Henwood et al., 2012, 2014 for details of the project). Men were interviewed about their own masculine identities and experiences as these evolved from before the birth of their first child to when this child was eight years old. The study rationale, disciplinary grounding, sample, interview contexts and lines of questioning all contributed to rather different kinds of account than in the contexts of the WFL interviews. We began with a more deductive way of entering into the MaF project dataset, starting with cases which looked potentially 'productive' with respect to our questions about household divisions of labour, for example, where there was a high density of paid work within households. We sampled initially based on project metadata (supplied to us by the team), but having followed this more deductive strategy we then read 'outwards' to give confidence we were interpreting the evidence in a way which was consistent with cases and evidence across the study sample. We read full transcripts and then focused on areas of the interview where men discussed issues relating to the intersection of work and care commitments, for themselves and their partners. Again, we sought to understand the spread of perspectives and their link to circumstances in ways which were not always visible through summary metadata.

In WFL we had explored parents' gendered experiences of time stress and compared mothers and fathers in typical and, where possible, rather less typical divisions of labour. In our analysis of MaF data we sought a complementary strategy, examining the experiences of men across both more conventional and less conventional divisions of labour. In the former were those who seemed at ease within a conventional division of labour. In the latter were some men who both worked extensively *and* desired extensive practical hands-on care of their young children. The latter contexts suggested an interesting counterpoint to the WFL analysis where this pattern was the predominant one for working mothers. Would men in such circumstances feel stretched and experience time stress? We developed a more in-depth case-based approach, strategically sampling for diversity within our analytic themes. We explored links between these men's experiences, their circumstances and values around childcare and their experiences of time pressure. In so doing we could draw comparisons with the WFL dataset. It was not possible to draw hard and fast conclusions from the analysis. However, it lined up with wider evidence about work–life stress and gender. (For a more extended discussion of the substantive questions see Irwin and Winterton, 2014.) We conjectured on some of the manifold social, economic and cultural processes which position mothers and fathers differently and shape their experiences, by exploring and comparing diverse cases within and across the datasets. We examined what we took to be markers of the same processes (gendered accounts of divisions of labour and mothers and fathers' accounts of their experiences and linked perceptions) and explored how these manifested across diverse circumstances. This was enabled by *translating* our research questions across the project data, so these questions had integrity within the project contexts but were also commensurate, allowing us to bring project data into a kind of analytic conversation.

2.3.5 'Casing' across project data and analytic correspondences

In their recent secondary analysis work, Tarrant and Hughes (2019) undertook analyses across two datasets: *Intergenerational Exchange* (Hughes and Emmel, 2012, part of the original Timescapes data) and *Following Fathers* (Neale, 2012). The projects both hold evidence on the social positioning and experience of fathers in vulnerable and marginalised circumstances, and how they are positioned by policy assumptions and linked service practices. The datasets hold extensive parallels in the geographical locale of the samples; in their common thematic focus on low-income livelihoods and the articulation of family lives, generational exchange and relationships and service provision; and in the researchers' interest in temporal processes. There are also some key differences across the studies in the different samples and profile of participants, notably their ages, and in the immediate project foci and research questions. Tarrant and Hughes pursued detailed participant case-based analyses across samples, seeking to bring the evidence into alignment, and comparing data through a very close reading of how the cases were situated in respect of key processes under investigation (Tarrant and Hughes, 2019). Bringing the cases together added to understanding, for example through shedding light on how young fathers are positioned by social services and by extended kin, often in ways which render young fatherhood especially problematic. The analysis does not treat data as continuous, and the cases cannot be treated as 'cumulative' but are configured as evidence in the service of specific research questions. Tarrant and Hughes develop their case-based analyses to build conceptual understanding of young fatherhood, generational and age identities, vulnerabilities and policy across different contexts. This is then developed (and tested out) within and through the project datasets. In so doing they seek to generate insights into disadvantaged fathers' vulnerability through time in ways which are both sensitive to, and gain insight from, distinct datasets (Tarrant and Hughes, 2019).

Importantly too, Tarrant and Hughes highlight the absolute importance of clarity over the potential limitations of qualitative secondary analysis. As with the previous examples the researchers evolved hypotheses and lines of theoretical interest which they sought to test out and refine, but at times such questions over-reached the capacity of the data, and 'theoretical refinement highlight(ed) how the boundaries of these studies limit the extent to which we can explore new and emerging questions' (Tarrant and Hughes, 2018: 12). In addition, as noted by the authors, the extensive parallels across the studies suggested significant potential for alignment. Such potential is relatively unusual. Where researchers seek to pursue new lines of enquiry as secondary analysts, whether within or across datasets, it is possible that such research will be exploratory or be limited to informing the design of new questions. Testing out and refining avenues of enquiry requires data which very precisely fit the research questions. Data will quickly reveal their inability to evidence questions which do not fit within their boundaries. It is still an open and empirical question as to the capacity of combined but disparate qualitative datasets to enable new or transformative understandings. I move now to consider approaches which pool data and seek expansive analyses which benefit from drawing across multiple datasets.

2.3.6 Pooling data across projects

After the completion of Timescapes, Davidson and colleagues (2018) developed a project to undertake secondary analysis drawing on archived data from across six of the original empirical projects. They pursued strategies to bring together data from diverse project data sources into an 'assemblage of data', that is, a new dataset or datasets in which cross-project data are pooled in new ways. They might be sorted with reference to particular demographic criteria which are common across datasets, or descriptive themes based on project metadata. Assembling data in this way provides for analyses which embrace different project data and allows for researchers to progress 'big data' analysis. Again, this proceeds not through simple accumulations or merging of data but by retaining knowledge and understanding of project and contextual specificities, and ensuring this is integral to analysis. The approach holds promise for the secondary analyst as it 'enable(s) analysis of issues beyond the foci of the constituent parts' (2018: 2), and the researchers' ambition is that the diversity and reach of data, when appropriately aligned, allow for theoretical refinement and enhanced understanding of social processes. Davidson and colleagues' use of computational algorithms is an interesting way to refine the iterative process, and to manage very large amounts of qualitative data. For them the aim then is to bring together data in strategic ways in the service of expansive understanding which can also be tested out against the available data and wider evidence (Davidson et al., 2018; see also Edwards and colleagues, Chapter 5). It is how the data are brought together that allows them to ask questions which make a virtue of the extensive and diverse datasets. They seek to bring data into meaningful comparison, aided by an extensive cross-project mapping of the content, contours and research-question-driven relevancies of subsets of data, in conjunction with intensive, in-depth interpretive analysis in which they progress their understanding of project data and build cases which enable comparison along the dimensions of interest. Their focus is on vocabularies and practices of care, how these are gendered and if and how they change across biographical and historical time. Thus they seek to address questions in a more holistic way than enabled by any of the single datasets, gaining insights which benefit from the reach across datasets.

Another variation on bringing together datasets is one more centred around cross-project team working in a context of a cohesive set of theoretical concerns. In their study of energy poverty and social relations Middlemiss and colleagues (forthcoming) are exploring experiences of vulnerability through a secondary qualitative analytic perspective. Across a network are several primary investigators of diverse studies holding datasets with potential overlaps and connections. The researchers are interested in secondary analysis and, as primary investigators, in bringing their own data into a common pool for evolving conjoint analyses. The researchers have worked in a collaborative way in sharing data, identifying questions of analytic interest and identifying exemplar cases within and across datasets. They have then come together to collaborate over their analyses, particularly focusing on cases in order to test out and refine evolving theoretical understandings of energy poverty, vulnerability, service provision and social relationships (Middlemiss et al., forthcoming).

In this section of the chapter I have considered examples of secondary analysis across datasets where the data are not contiguous but complex in how they align. In my own work on the Timescapes Secondary Analysis project, with Mandy Winterton, we undertook cross-project analyses, retaining an emphasis on the salience of project contexts in which the data were embedded, whilst also seeking both to enable analytic 'conversations' across datasets and to build evidence in addressing our research questions. The work of Davidson and colleagues brings together data (from several datasets) into a unified corpus or assemblage, along given criteria, and with extensive analytic work to ensure data align in meaningful ways. Tarrant and Hughes (2019) and Middlemiss and colleagues (forthcoming) pursue approaches which are more centred on a case-based approach. The projects follow differing strategies in organising data in order to proceed with testing out and refining their analyses. All of them seek to align data from across projects to enable analysis across disparate datasets. In turn this requires:

a   a thorough understanding of the data: both its contours (sample, content, etc.) but also the study context and embeddedness of data;

b   judgements about 'fit', in essence a theoretical understanding of how the data might be brought together to yield fresh insight and enable forms of conjoint analysis;

c   meaningful bases for constructing data as evidence in support of explanation and theoretical refinement. This might include pertinent comparisons within and across datasets, or analyses of strategically chosen cases, in testing out and refining theories.

2.4 Conclusion: Reflections on Working Across Datasets as a Qualitative Secondary Analyst

It has been clear throughout that caution is important in pursuing analysis across multiple qualitative datasets. It is relatively straightforward in particular circumstances where secondary analysis and new research are designed hand in hand, perhaps with overlap across a sample and clear comparability across data around defined themes. Another (overlapping) possibility is that the projects are more independent but data are deemed to be more or less contiguous across projects, and lend themselves to exploration within the same frame of analysis. However, in examples where project data do not align so readily there is some significant complexity in working across datasets. I have focused on some different approaches here. In reflecting on whether to work across disparate datasets, researchers need to consider how well the data fit the new research questions. They need to assess how much time is required for secondary analysis and for developing sufficient understanding of the contours and contents of unfamiliar datasets. They need to ask if they can develop sufficient familiarity to map the data and understand the implications of subsampling where this is appropriate. They need a grounded understanding of ways in which data are shaped by the contexts and conditions in which they are created. They then need to make an informed assessment of scope for bringing data within the same analytic framing. I have described ways in which analysts have sought to ensure commensurability across datasets. Researchers need to make judgements about fit: whether the data are a fit for their research questions, and how diverse datasets can be brought together whilst retaining nuanced understanding of *both* their specificities and common scope. Although challenging, there is interest and some promise in building secondary analyses drawing on extant datasets. Through the examples described in this chapter I have considered some analytic strategies for working across disparate datasets and the linked ways in which researchers seek to progress their analyses, construct evidence and refine theoretical understanding.

2.5 **References**

Backett-Milburn, K., Harden, J., Maclean, A., Cunningham-Burley, S. and Jamieson, L. (2012) *Work and Family Lives: The Changing Experiences of 'Young' Families*, Timescapes Final Report Project 5. Available at: www.timescapes.leeds.ac.uk/research/work-family-lives.html (accessed 22 May 2019).

Bishop, L. (2007) 'A reflexive account of reusing qualitative data: Beyond primary/secondary dualism', *Sociological Research Online*, 12(3). Available at: www.socresonline.org.uk/12/3/2.html (accessed 22 May 2019).

Crompton, R. (2002) 'Employment, flexible working and the family', *British Journal of Sociology*, 53(4): 537–58.

Davidson, E., Edwards, R., Jamieson, J. and Weller, S. (2018) 'Big data, qualitative style: A breadth-and-depth method for working with large amounts of secondary qualitative data', *Quality and Quantity*, 53(1): 363–76.

Doucet, A. (2009) 'Gender equality and gender differences: Parenting, habitus and embodiment' (the 2008 Porter Lecture), *Canadian Review of Sociology*, 46(2): 1103–21.

Edwards, R. and Weller, S. (2012) *Your Space! Siblings and Friends: The Changing Nature of Children's Lateral Relationships*, Timescapes Final Report Project 1. Available at: www.timescapes.leeds.ac.uk/assets/files/Final-Reports/Final-report-project-1.pdf (accessed 22 May 2019).

Elliott, J. and Morrow, V. (2007) *Imagining the Future: Preliminary Analysis of NCDS Essays Written by Children at Age 11*, Centre for Longitudinal Studies WP 2007/1, UCL. Available at: https://core.ac.uk/download/pdf/83638.pdf (accessed 22 May 2019).

Funk, L.M., Stajduhar, K.I. and Outcalt, L. (2015) 'What family caregivers learn when providing care at the end of life: A qualitative secondary analysis of multiple datasets', *Palliative and Supportive Care*, 13: 425–33.

Gray, J., Geraghty, R. and Ralph, D. (2016) *Family Rhythms: The Changing Textures of Family Life in Ireland.* Manchester: Manchester University Press.

Halford, S. and Savage, M. (2017) 'Speaking sociologically with big data: Symphonic social science and the future for big data research', *Sociology*, 51(6): 1132–48.

Hammersley, M. (2010) 'Can we re-use qualitative data via secondary analysis? Notes on some terminological and substantive issues', *Sociological Research Online*, 15(1): 47–53. Available at: www.socresonline.org.uk/15/1/5.html (accessed 22 May 2019).

Harden, J., Maclean, A., Backett-Milburn, K., Cunningham-Burley, S. and Jamieson, L. (2014) 'Responsibility, Work and Family Life: Children's and Parents' Experiences of Working Parenthood', in J. Holland and R. Edwards (eds), *Understanding Families Over Time: Research and Policy*. Basingstoke: Palgrave Macmillan. pp. 124–41.

Heaton, J. (2008) 'Secondary analysis of qualitative data: An overview', *Historical Social Research*, 33(3): 33–45.

Henwood, K., Shirani, F. and Coltart, C. (2012) *Masculinities, Identities and Risk: Transitions in the Lives of Men and Fathers*, Timescapes Project Guide 4.

Available at: www.timescapes.leeds.ac.uk/assets/files/P4-Men-as-Fathers-guide-28Feb12.pdf (accessed 22 May 2019).

Henwood, K., Shirani, F. and Coltart, C. (2014) 'Investing in involvement: Men moving through fatherhood', in J. Holland and R. Edwards (eds), *Understanding Families Over Time*. London: Palgrave.

Hughes, K. and Emmel, N. (2012) *Intergenerational Exchange: Grandparenting and the Texture of Poverty*, Timescapes Final Project Report 6. Available at: www.timescapes.leeds.ac.uk/assets/files/Final-Reports/final-report-project-6.pdf (accessed 22 May 2019).

Irwin, S. (2017) 'Parenting teenagers as they grow up: Values, practices and young people's pathways beyond school in England', *The Sociological Review*, 66(1): 241–56.

Irwin, S. and Elley, S. (2011) 'Concerted cultivation? Parenting values, education and class diversity', *Sociology*, 45(3): 480–95.

Irwin, S. and Winterton, M. (2011a) *Debates in Qualitative Secondary Analysis: Critical Reflections*, Timescapes Working Paper 4. Available at: www.timescapes.leeds.ac.uk/assets/files/WP4-March-2011.pdf (accessed 22 May 2019).

Irwin, S. and Winterton, M. (2011b) *Timescapes Data and Secondary Analyses: Working Across the Projects*, Timescapes Working Paper 5. Available at: www.timescapes.leeds.ac.uk/assets/files/WP5-March-2011.pdf (accessed 22 May 2019).

Irwin, S. and Winterton, M. (2011c) *Qualitative Secondary Analysis in Practice: An Extended Guide (with Reference to Concepts, Contexts and Knowledge Claims)*, Timescapes Working Paper 7. Available at: www.timescapes.leeds.ac.uk/assets/files/methods-guides/timescapes-irwin-secondary-analysis.pdf (accessed 22 May 2019).

Irwin, S. and Winterton, M. (2012) 'Qualitative secondary analysis and social explanation', *Sociological Research Online*, 17(2). Available at: www.socresonline.org.uk/17/2/4.html (accessed 22 May 2019).

Irwin, S. and Winterton, M. (2014) 'Gender and work–family conflict: A secondary analysis of Timescapes data', in J. Holland and R. Edwards (eds), *Understanding Families Over Time*. London: Palgrave.

Irwin, S., Bornat, J. and Winterton, M. (2012) 'Timescapes secondary analysis: Comparison, context and working across data sets', *Qualitative Research*, 12(1): 66–80.

Mason, J. (2007) '"Re-using" qualitative data: On the merits of an investigative epistemology', *Sociological Research Online*, 12(3). Available at: www.socresonline.org.uk/12/3/3.html (accessed 22 May 2019).

Middlemiss, L., Albala, P.A., Emmel, N., Gillard, R., Gilbertson, J., Hargreaves, T., Mullen, C., Ryan, T., Snell, C. and Tod, A. (forthcoming) 'Energy poverty and social relations: Characterising vulnerabilities using a capabilities approach', *Energy Research & Social Science*.

Moore, N. (2007) '(Re)Using qualitative data?', *Sociological Research Online*, 12(3). Available at: www.socresonline.org.uk/12/3/1.html (accessed 22 May 2019).

Neale, B. (2007) *Timescapes: Changing Relationships and Identities Through the Life Course*, ESRC Qualitative Longitudinal Study. Available at: www.timescapes.leeds.ac.uk/assets/files/TIMESCAPES_Blueprint.pdf (accessed 24 May 2019).

Neale, B. (2012) *Young Lives and Times Project Report*, Timescapes Final Project Report 2. Available at: www.timescapes.leeds.ac.uk/assets/files/Final-Reports/final-report-project-2.pdf (accessed 2 May 2019).

Neale, B. (2018) *What is Qualitative Longitudinal Research?* London: Bloomsbury Academic.

Sherif, V. (2018) 'Evaluating preexisting qualitative research data for secondary analysis', *Forum Qualitative Sozialforschung/Forum: Qualitative Social Research*, 19(2): Art. 7. Available at: www.qualitative-research.net/index.php/fqs/article/view/2821/4211 (accessed 22 May 2019).

Tarrant, A. and Hughes, K. (2018) 'Qualitative Secondary Analysis: Building longitudinal samples to understand men's generational identities in low-income contexts', *Sociology*, doi: 10.1177/0038038518772743.

Tarrant, A. and Hughes, K. (2019) 'Qualitative Secondary Analysis: Building longitudinal samples to understand men's generational identities in low-income contexts', *Sociology*, 53(3): 599–611.

Vincent, C., Ball, S.J. and Pietikainen, S. (2004) 'Metropolitan mothers: Mothers, mothering and paid work', *Women's Studies International Forum*, 27: 571–87.

Walby, S. (1997) *Gender Transformations*. London: Routledge.

Watters, E.C., Cumming, S.J. and Caragata, L. (2018) 'The lone mother resilience project: A qualitative secondary analysis', *Forum Qualitative Sozialforschung/Forum: Qualitative Social Research*, 19(2): Art. 23. Available at: http://dx.doi.org/10.17169/fqs-19.2.2863 (accessed 22 May 2019).

Winterton, M. and Irwin, S. (2011) 'Youngster's expectations and context: Secondary analysis and interpretation of imagined futures', in M. Winterton, G. Crow and B. Morgan-Brett (eds), *Young Lives and Imagined Futures: Insights from Archived Data*, Timescapes Working Paper 6. Available at: www.timescapes.leeds.ac.uk/assets/files/secondary_analysis/working-papers/WP6-final10Oct.pdf (accessed 24 May 2019).

Winterton, M. and Irwin, S. (2012) 'Teenage expectations of going to university: The ebb and flow of influences from 14 to 18', *Journal of Youth Studies*, 15(7): 858–74.

THREE

THE ETHICS OF QUALITATIVE SECONDARY ANALYSIS

Kahryn Hughes and Anna Tarrant

--- **CHAPTER CONTENTS** ---

3.1 Introduction: Ethics and Qualitative Secondary Analysis

This chapter explores key debates on the ethical questions raised by the use of Qualitative Secondary Analysis (QSA) over the past two decades, covering familiar ethical concerns such as *consent, representation* and *confidentiality*. Our discussion also demonstrates how the ethics of QSA involves more than reworking familiar issues (Neale, 2013; Wiles and Boddy, 2013) and necessitates a conceptual reframing of research contexts themselves.

Organised along chronological lines, the chapter charts how the debate on the ethics of QSA has developed. First, we introduce early concerns and prohibitions against the re-use of data. Second, we examine the impact of a changing data landscape including a growth in data archives and infrastructures and new methodologies of QSA. We consider how these ushered in ethical attention to the 'duties' of the 'stakeholders' in the longer chains of relationships and networks involved in the production and curation of research data (Neale and Bishop, 2012; Neale and Hanna, 2012). Third, we discuss the usefulness of a temporal, relational framing of the ethical challenges raised by these realationships. We consider the broader social context of 'datafication', including how this has prompted a new focus on data protection and a resurgence of 'rights-driven ethics' stressing *data privacy*. Finally, we advance an ethics of *legacy* and explore the multi-directional and layered character of ethical reflexivity involved in QSA methodology.

3.2 Ethics of Risk

Debates on the ethics of QSA have been informed by growing public unease around risks, especially to personal privacy, associated with developments in the digital data landscape. Such changes have been accompanied by parallel developments in data re-use, or QSA, in the social sciences (see Introduction for a discussion of these terms). These developments have been underscored by increasing emphasis on data re-use by UK and European research funding councils, who increasingly require researchers to consider re-using data resources that have been expensive to produce. Funding councils have also devolved responsibility to universities for the archiving and curation of new research data, with the requirement that these data be made available for re-use, pursuing an open access agenda. This effectively passes on the ethical risks associated with data re-use to universities and the academics they employ. In new funding applications, researchers are increasingly required to describe how they will protect and manage their data, what they will do with their data once their study has concluded, and how they will resource this.

Such requirement has also been integrated into institutional ethical review processes. Applicants are now expected to set out their data-management plans, including a rationale on how they will store their data once their study has completed, and for a justification if applicants plan to destroy their data. The ethical stakes around QSA are therefore high. At the least, they involve reputational risks to both institutions and individuals; they require researchers to manage a host of new and uncertain risks to participants that relate to the re-use of data in unknown future research contexts; and they involve new and emerging relationships between technology and research methodology.

Early ethical questions about QSA were raised as part of an accelerating debate about ethics in social sciences research more generally. This debate had changed the research landscape such that what might once have been considered to be an added dimension of research (and not always necessarily attended to) was now embedded throughout the entire research process (Mauthner et al., 1998; Hammersley, 2009). Edwards and Mauthner (2002) describe how in the 1980s–90s a number of professional associations such as the British Psychological Society and British Sociological Association drew on definitions, principles and codes from across the social sciences in producing guidelines for their members (2002: 15). This was in response to several high-profile studies that caused public and professional outcry (Becker 2005) which demonstrated the political impacts of research (Zago and Holmes, 2015), as they stimulated public debate on researchers' integrity. They articulated what we might describe as a growing 'public trust deficit' in social science research more generally. In response, social scientists have developed more sophisticated ethical frameworks supported by extensive epistemic reflection from across the academy.

The emerging debate on the ethics of QSA demonstrated the inseparability of epistemological and ethical reflexivity. Driven by a concern that different methods produce different realities, researchers felt they had a moral responsibility to understand what they were doing before they did it (see Mauthner, 2012). In considering risks to the participants whose data were being re-used, questions were raised about *representation*. For example, how might secondary analysts so removed from the relationships and contexts of the participants in the original study be able to represent their meanings? Also, given the long time frames and distanciation of data from their original contexts of production, the question of participant *consent* becomes ever thornier. How can people give consent to the re-use of their data when future research and researchers are unknowable? How many researchers might use those data, and for how long: a decade? two decades? a hundred years?

Destroying data at the close of a study, as had been traditional in qualitative social sciences research as an ethical means of protecting participants, was now actively discouraged. Yet at the same time increasingly sophisticated techniques for storing data for the purposes of re-use intensified questions around data perpetuity and further complicated questions of consent. The growth of archives and institutional repositories raised important questions about *confidentiality*. As research data are digitised and archived, they are increasingly discoverable. They can also be brought into analytical interplay with digitised data from other sources. This increases the risk of exposing informants' identities both through the details in data, even where they have been anonymised, and also through data linkage across a host of different sources.

New questions around *anonymisation* were also raised in the context of QSA, particularly how far data can and should be anonymised. Research data include contextual information about participants such as their age, marital status and where, when, why and by whom the research was carried out. These *metadata* (data that describe research data) are an essential component of research datasets, supporting their 'meaningfulness' in subsequent research (see Irwin, Chapter 2, and Tarrant and Hughes, Chapter 6). However, they also expose both participant and researcher to an additional level of scrutiny not previously encountered in research where re-use would have been confined to the original research team.

These early ethical concerns also pertain to researchers as well as participants. Research data are produced through a researcher's individual and distinctive engagement such that collected data are, so to speak, stamped with a researcher's 'intellectual fingerprint' (Mauthner, 2012). To re-use those data means re-using the intellectual labour of the original researchers (see Irwin, Chapter 2). Questions of endeavour, interpretation and labour including emotional investments were raised in this context. The potential for unknown researchers getting too personal and invading other researchers' privacy via the re-use of their data was also identified. Further, the *data* that are used might also relate to fieldnotes, marginalia (see Goodwin and O'Connor, Chapter 10), and other ephemera collected through the original research and therefore include items that were never meant to be included as *research data*. This raises additional questions about what the ethical boundaries of the *dataset* might be, especially items such as notebooks and diaries that had been produced as private resources. Ethical and political sensibilities change over time, resulting in changing perceptions of historical ethical practice, where researchers may use terms or frame their participants in ways shaped by their contemporary historical context but which may differ significantly from those of future researchers (Gillies and Edwards, 2012; Hughes et al., 2016). How then should those researchers be portrayed, understood or acknowledged in future work drawing on their materials? Finally, QSA requires us to consider the character of relationships between researchers and participants, and any emotional or ethical undertakings that occurred in the research encounter. These questions point to the high emotional and intellectual stakes of sharing which are often erased in accounts of research through the very enterprise of reporting research *findings* rather than research *experiences*.

QSA thus raises important ethical challenges for how we understand both the *research context* and the *research process*. Instead of occurring within a research team, or confined to one study or a series of linked studies, QSA research contexts span wide networks of data sources, and the research process consequently involves new sorts of relationships that may play out in unexpected ways over time. Unsurprisingly, in earlier scholarship the question was, although we *can* do QSA, *should* we?

3.2.1 Ethics of sharing

In her introduction to a special issue for *Sociological Research Online*, Jennifer Mason celebrated the emergence of an 'investigative epistemology' in new approaches to qualitative research data re-use championed through the papers in the collection (Mason, 2007). The special issue comprised landmark papers which shifted the debate on data re-use, or what we call QSA, out of its moralistic *impasse*. While the early questions were and continue to be important, they also risked the infantilisation of participants, and obscuring the reasons why they participate in research (Jacobsson and Åkerström, 2013; Hughes and Tarrant, 2019). New ESRC funding under the Qualitative Data programme had been granted for collections of studies to explore and demonstrate the possibilities of sharing data reflecting appreciation for the value of qualitative data, including its potential value for future generations of researchers (see http://quads.esds.ac.uk). Such work was driven by the 'investigative methodology' Mason (2007) champions. Epistemological debate shifted ground; traditional distinctions between primary and secondary analysts were challenged (Moore, 2007). Methodological debates became more nuanced, acknowledging long traditions of research practice which blurred the boundaries between primary and secondary analysis (Moore, 2007). Following these epistemic shifts, there emerged a growing climate of acceptability for QSA, albeit one characterised by caution and continuous reflexivity (Irwin et al., 2012). Such work, alongside the growth of data infrastructures, encouraged attention to the elongated relational chains of data 'prosumers' (see Ritzer and Jurgenson, 2010) – those who simultaneously consume and produce data – in research as well as in broader society. Relatedly, there emerged a new terrain of 'data stewardship' (Neale, 2017), namely all those involved in the production, archiving and reproduction of research data. As the term suggests, *duties* were seen to inhere to the responsibilities of various data stewards (Bishop, 2009; Neale and Bishop, 2012; Neale and Hanna, 2012; Irwin, 2013), opening up new areas for ethical reflection and development.

3.2.2 A temporal ethical sensibility

In Chapter 4, Bren Neale discusses potential strategies for building temporal under-standings into the process of revisiting data or, more broadly, the 'lifetime' of data and data re-use. This includes building a 'temporal sensibility' into the range of ethical concerns, considerations and challenges throughout the process of revisit-ing or re-using data. Such temporal *ethical* sensibility allows us to retain within our analytic frame the long chains and complex networks of human relationships involved in research processes, including those at play in the original contexts of data production, or those in subsequent contexts through which data are revis-ited, reworked and repurposed. A temporal ethical sensibility therefore lends itself directly to understanding not only the 'duties' which concern *participant*-facing ethics but also those which involve *researcher*–researcher relationships.

QSA necessarily involves the storing and sharing of data using various online and offline means. In this process of storing and sharing, increasing numbers of 'data stewards' comprise elongating chains of research relationships, rather than research teams of known members working alongside each other.

Such elongating chains of research relations between people who may never meet raises complex questions of whose 'rights' or ethical sensitivities should be stressed. For example, when should the interests of originating researchers be par-amount? What sorts of ethical stresses should be placed on participants' interests when sharing and re-using their data? In addressing the question of which inter-ests should be paramount, however, Bishop (2009) points towards what we might consider to be a *democratisation* of research relationships, arguing that:

> the rights and interests of research subjects are just the rights and interests of persons and must be balanced against rights and interests of other persons.

In other words, it is essential not to either over- or understate the ethical interests of any particular individual in isolation and instead attend to the complex inter-play of ethical concerns throughout.

This is arguably crucial to ethical reflexivity more generally. An over-focus on particular individuals or groups may serve to obscure or mute the interests of others, and also neglect how different interests emerge at various stages of the research process. For example, early debate questioned how far informed consent was possible from participants (see below), and also how ethical rela-tions between 'originating' researchers/teams and subsequent QSA researchers might be achieved. These questions identify a need for ethical attention to the original research contexts and also fresh ethical consideration of new ques-tions in any later research, challenging the idea of 'once and for all' ethical solutions.

Building time into understanding ethical engagement in QSA opens up temporal spaces for ongoing reflection through which researchers become able to navigate emerging ethical challenges and develop situational ethical strategies. This is important given how, in QSA, researchers may, particularly in the early stages of their study, be working with original or previous research individuals and teams (see Tarrant and Hughes, 2019; and Lyon and Crow, Chapter 9) in navigating understandings of datasets, or perhaps gaining access to the original participants. A temporal orientation towards ethics also builds in the possibility for future generations of researchers to keep pace with changing understandings of how data are managed and conserved and, importantly, how participants' interests are attended to over the lifetime of their data, even when they are no longer alive to consult.

Ethical engagement in QSA therefore involves both retrospective and prospective reflection, in which we are required to address the question of *where* ethics should be stressed in the research process. By building a temporal sensibility into our ethical orientation towards QSA, we are able to capture the multi-directional and layered character of the research process. Neale (2013) encapsulates much of this thinking by suggesting that ethics should be both proactive and reactive, where proactive ethics are those built into study design from the outset reflecting anticipated ethical concerns, and reactive ethics are those developed in response to emerging ethical challenges in the field. Where the possibility of data re-use extends into the unknowable future, the time frames of such ethics are protracted, and can be taken up repeatedly over time and reworked in new contexts by new researchers.

We now discuss this in the context of those questions raised above of consent, anonymisation, representation and confidentiality. Our discussion then introduces the ethical concerns raised by the broader context of 'datafication' and what ethical balance can be struck between *protection* and *preservation*. We conclude the chapter by advancing an ethics of *legacy*.

3.2.3 Informed consent and enduring consent

Giving people the opportunity to make an informed choice about whether or not they want to participate in research sits at the heart of research ethics. However, QSA profoundly challenges the idea of informed consent. Nowadays, researchers increasingly solicit consent for the preservation, archiving and re-use of participants' data. They must acknowledge that those data may be repurposed in ways and contexts that cannot be fully anticipated. Consent cannot therefore be granted in any fully informed way.

This problem is not only confined to QSA. There is a long history of work challenging the idea of consent ever being fully informed, even within the study for which it has been generated (Corrigan, 2003; Holloway and Jefferson, 2013). Simply put, the research process is an endeavour to generate new knowledge. If we do not know what our research will produce from the outset, how far are we able to inform our participants? As findings cannot be clear from the outset, researchers struggle to anticipate the tenor of their analyses, especially where the research team consists of more than one researcher. For example, readings of the same transcripts by different researchers may yield different interpretations (Frost et al., 2010).

Not only do different researchers bring different interpretations, but also researching over time changes researchers' sensibilities, so that period effects change both the reading and uses of data (Heaton, 2004). Instead, in qualitative social sciences research we secure consent for certain forms of *participation*, identifying the methodological strategies researchers will use to engage with participants and sharing with them any indicative questions. Even here there are challenges. Informed consent relies on *transparency* by researchers. However, the ongoing, iterative character of much qualitative research may mitigate against identifying questions to participants. This may not only be due to a lack of certainty on the part of researchers but also reflect an ethics of empowerment in the researcher–researched relationship, where the intention is that depth data should be mutually produced and formulated.

Moreover, the language used in the academy shaping particular fields of enquiry (e.g., poverty, marginalisation) may be offensive in the research encounter (Emmel et al., 2007). Therefore, language or terms used in consent seeking may not map directly onto those used by the researchers, but instead are proxies for concepts and theories underpinning the research. In such situations, the somewhat absolutist demands for 'transparency' and 'fully informed consent', while integral to ethically conducted research, may nevertheless clash with other ethical sensibilities at play.

Rather than becoming hijacked by this apparent *impasse*, Neale (2013) sensibly suggests that in seeking consent for archiving and data re-use, researchers ought to shift from the language of informed consent and instead secure *enduring* consent. Here, consent is given on the basis of uncertainty about the research purposes to which the data will be put, but on the understanding that the data will be ethically safeguarded. This could be by the research team but also, as research data repositories become more ubiquitous, in the repository or archive in which it is stored, and treated ethically in any future research.

However, with increasing legislation around data management, data ownership and data protection, there have been several well-documented cases where legal and institutional codes of ethics and data protection have collided. In 2011 Boston College was subpoenaed to hand over the tapes of interviews conducted with members of the IRA and loyalist paramilitary groups, now known as the 'Boston Tapes'. The interviews were part of 'the Belfast Project', a recorded oral archive of IRA and loyalist paramilitary testimonies housed at the Boston College Burns-Archive Library. The interviews had been gathered at great risk to all those concerned not least because the researchers were 'insiders', namely members of such paramilitary groups under threat of violent repercussions if they disclosed their membership. Assurances had been given, and agreements signed, that the taped interviews would only be released after the interviewee's death. However, the subpoena was served under the terms of a UK–US legal assistance treaty and the Crime (International Co-Operation) Act, and Boston College complied (see Inckle, 2015).

At its simplest, the case of the Belfast Project established that, despite assurances to the contrary, the safeguarding and confidentiality of archived data is not necessarily always possible, or it might only be possible for certain sorts of data at given historical moments, regardless of the contractual agreements in place at the time consent is given or sought for archiving. Legal–political changes have the power to destabilise such agreements or contracts; and thus assurances given by organisations such as universities, or individuals such as researchers, cannot be understood as enduring for all time. The Boston Tapes case is an extreme example that reflects the highly charged character of those particular data. Most interview data would not provoke international political interest and risk of this sort. Nevertheless, it is a useful example to underscore the changing and potentially fragile contexts through which data may pass, and the limits of researcher control and protection of them.

Although advances have been made in considering how we might gain consent for QSA in ongoing research, the bulk of research data both digitised and in paper or other format lacks consents for re-use. This raises the question of whether or not these data can be re-used and, if so, how.

3.2.4 Missing consents?

While the concept of enduring consent offers an ethical way forward for current research, the question of consent remains problematic for research data where re-use has not been anticipated and no consents were secured.

A key strategy for gaining consent where the research is relatively contemporary is 'revisiting' or re-contacting participants. However, what ostensibly seems a reasonable endeavour often faces several potential difficulties, many of them ethical. Pragmatically, personal data such as contact details are often missing from datasets, especially where there was no intention to continue a study, and where there was an emphasis on confidentiality and anonymity. Again pragmatically, following up on a study after some years have elapsed builds in the potential for change in the localities of participants. Methods of retracing participants may involve use of administrative data, and inevitably depends on lengthy and resource intensive investigation by the researcher. It may also involve gatekeeper access which in turn could raise ethical questions around confidentiality for participants. Less traditional methods might be used to re-contact participants, such as via online social media, but such methods may rely on happenstance or encounter generational differences in online access and participation (Goodwin and O'Connor, 2015). Unsurprisingly, re-contact raises a host of ethical issues (see Miller, 2015) where tracking participants down might be experienced rather like 'being hunted' (Neale, 2019), colliding with their rights to privacy and their right not to be researched.

The feasibility of re-contact also changes over time. Participants' circumstances may change and researcher intrusion into people's lives to satisfy a concern of the researchers can have devastating consequences, especially where family members have died. In research on grandparents in low-income contexts, Kahryn and colleagues encountered the deaths of several people during the course of the study (Hughes and Emmel, 2007–2012). This was not entirely unusual, as the high rates of mid-life morbidity and early life mortality of the study population mapped directly onto broader health statistics for the area (Hughes and Emmel, 2011; Emmel and Hughes, 2010, 2014). In one case, the interviewee's estranged husband died. His ex-wife, Sheila, the study participant, had represented him as abusive, as had his adult children in interviews from a previous study (Emmel et al., 2002–2005). But after his death, his eldest daughter embargoed Sheila from speaking about him again in the research. Her ostensible reason was that one did not speak ill of the dead. However, over the course of subsequent interviews, the estranged husband re-entered Sheila's life in photographs over her fireplace, and in gestures towards him during interviews, a muted figure who was slowly reintegrated into a family from which he had been estranged. In another case from the same study, an interviewee experienced the death of her adult daughter and subsequently removed herself from the study. Over the course of several interviews she had been highly critical of her daughter, and although she did not want to redact her data, she could not continue that particular research 'conversation'. Such cases provide insight into how people navigate the emotional pitfalls of research participation as it interweaves with events in their lives, and points to the possible consequences for individuals if researchers return to consult them about data involving a lost family member (see Edwards and Weller, 2013, 2015). Research may also have explored painful times in participants' lives (Grinyer, 2009), which is not unlikely given the sensitivity of much qualitative social sciences research. As Neale (2019: 87) argues,

> being newly confronted with an earlier version of oneself may mean re-living old hurts or traumas, or it may reveal unfavourable comparisons between how a participant envisaged their future and what has actually transpired.

In effect, transcripts from previous research may force people to confront a 'fixed' narrative from which they may wish to distance themselves (Neale, 2019). Thus, the very process of re-contact, for the best of ethical reasons, is not necessarily ethically unproblematic (Andrews, 2008). How then might we re-use data for which there are no consents?

Archiving research data might well provide a way forward in relation to this question. An established debate in research ethics more generally distinguishes between what have been called *regulatory* and *interpretive* ethics. Regulatory ethics are procedural and inhere to institutional processes of ethical scrutiny and regulation (see Hammersley, 2015). Regulatory ethics may stress institutional interests over those of individuals, containing within them particular assumptions about the relationships between institution and research. In university contexts, for example, the emphasis may be on a researcher's responsibility to their employer, rather than the other way around. While regulatory ethics may be based on a set of ethical principles, following these via standardised ethical strategies can be problematic because they often fail to accommodate the specific, contextually driven needs of the groups and individuals in research. Instead, ethical strategies need to be developed throughout research through 'careful judgement based on practical knowledge and attention to detail in context of time and place' (Edwards and Mauthner, 2002: 27). Drawing on a feminist ethics of care, such work identifies how *interpretive* ethics should be mutually negotiated within the research context with those being researched. From within this tradition, ethical principles are reconceived as strategies that are situational, negotiated and responsive to processes of ethical reflexivity throughout the research process by both researchers and participants (see especially Mauthner et al., 2012; also Guillemin and Gillam, 2004; Warin, 2011; Neale and Bishop, 2012; Neale, 2013, 2019).

Research data archives may provide contexts within which it is possible to resolve these apparently antagonistic ethical approaches. This is because archives, such as the UK Data Service[1] or the Timescapes Archive at the University of Leeds[2] (see Introduction, also Haaker, Chapter 7 for a discussion of archival resources),

---

[1]https://ukdataservice.ac.uk

[2]https://timescapes-archive.leeds.ac.uk

are required both legislatively and institutionally (say within university contexts) to have in place procedural protections which manage the depositing, access to and re-use of archived data (Neale et al., 2016). Following recent legislation such as the General Data Protection Regulation 2018 (GDPR), archives are able to develop protocols that mitigate against a wholesale drive towards open access. These ethical protocols contextualising archive use thus provide a temporal space in which researchers can engage reflexively with ethical concerns. In effect, they allow researchers to develop responsive and requisite ethical strategies on a case-by-case basis rather than more generalised principles. Archives therefore have the capacity to combine the relative strengths of both regulatory and interpretive ethics, allowing for longitudinal ethical engagement and reflexivity on the protections of, and for, the various data stakeholders in the lifetime of those data.

QSA of archived data thus offers researchers the possibility of *enhanced* ethical engagement with data, rather than the obverse, where researchers can decide on where ethics should be stressed, for example through *anonymisation, representation* and *confidentiality*. We now move on to discuss these particular ethical concerns in relation to QSA in more detail but it is worth noting that where data are not archived, more general GDPR legislation provides guidelines of data governance. While GDPR does not require that research data have consent for re-use, it does require a degree of anonymisation, and prohibits many forms of data sharing. In this emerging legislative context, it may be that the possibility of QSA with data that are not housed within archives becomes increasingly rare. Datasets will continue to be destroyed simply because they are too onerous to keep in ways which comply with legislative requirements in a context driven by principles of open access.

3.2.5 Anonymisation, representation and confidentiality

Anonymisation is the process of removing details from data such as participants' names, their addresses and so on that may enable them to be identified. A common anonymisation strategy is to assign the key participant a pseudonym, and produce anonymised versions of transcripts and other files relating to that participant (Neale et al., 2016). However, anonymising is more than a mechanistic process of simply changing names. For example, when anonymising, researchers will strive to convey a flavour of the participants' contexts and their times and situations through the names that are chosen. Drawing on Moore (2012), Neale et al. (2016) argue:

> Increasingly, the imperative to anonymize data and obscure identities sits uneasily with the view that the process may strip a dataset of its integrity, diminish its intellectual meaning and scientific value and do a disservice to participants who are airbrushed out of the historical record.

We discuss these ideas more critically below, but here we suggest that archiving for the purposes of QSA enables research data to be stored as intact as possible. For example, data may be stored in a 'dark archive', conferring responsibility for anonymisation to future researchers in any publications or outputs they may produce while at the same time preserving both the integrity of the complete dataset and protecting the participants from any abuses of anonymity or confidentiality.

The interpretive character of anonymisation (Neale et al., 2016) raises questions of *representation* and authenticity. Early debate identified questions of representation as problematic for QSA researchers (see Mauthner et al., 1998; Mauthner, 2012), especially because they were unlikely to have met or become familiar with the participants. In such cases how could researchers hope fully to represent participants' experiences? However, for the last ten years Kahryn has rarely been the interviewer in the research studies she has either led or been part of, and has often relied on the fieldworker's notes or descriptions to get a sense of the participants. Her position thus blurs the distinction between 'primary' and 'secondary' analyst and we concur with Moore (2007) that even where a researcher has been the interviewer, such distinction becomes difficult to sustain over longer time frames. As years pass and the research dates, memories become more fragmented and partial, connections weaken and the idea of 'closeness' to the participant (especially as they too have moved on in their lives) becomes less viable as a 'truth' position, already a troubled claim (Geiger et al., 2010). Susie Weller has pointed out that as time distances originating researchers from their data, their emotional ties to those data slacken, while the emotional ties to the data for the QSA researchers increase the longer they work with those data (Weller, 2019). This has certainly been the case for Kahryn and Anna. We have found QSA to be resource intensive and time-consuming (see also Irwin Chapter 2; Edwards et al., Chapter 5; Tarrant and Hughes, 2019). The process of familiarisation in our experience inevitably requires understanding and insight into the unique characteristics of the participants. In our QSA work, we found that the emotional intelligence we deployed in making sociological sense of people's stories contributed to forging emotional ties and emotional investments. While we cannot claim this facilitates a greater or lesser capacity for *authentic representation* of those participants, we draw on experiences such as these to support our claims that QSA involves prolonged and often depth engagement with participants' data, which in turn may support ethical reflexivity around how to represent the stories they have told (Tarrant and Hughes, forthcoming).

Finally, QSA raises questions of *confidentiality*. Confidentiality commonly refers to confidentiality around people's research participation and what they said, and preventing identification through how their contributions are reported.

QSA seems to offer the potential for increased breaches of confidentiality by offering new researchers unprecedented access to data they did not collect and the details of people who are not aware that they are being scrutinised by new generations of researchers. These may also include people known to the participants.[3]

However, QSA may also offer the potential for enhanced confidentiality. For example, re-situating data in new theoretical contexts may disrupt associations between respondents and original studies. More pragmatically, there is no participant contact by researchers, no access through human gatekeepers, and an increased potential for various forms of double anonymisation, all common areas of concern for confidentiality.

We would, though, urge caution here. It has also been argued that the more of a case that is used and the more details provided across outputs, the greater the possibility of identifying that participant (Hollomotz, 2018). Where participants' circumstances are so unique, say because of specific medical conditions, they may be immediately identifiable to people 'in the know' (Rachel Hewett, personal communication, 2018). It is feasible that repeated QSA of the same datasets may generate multiple opportunities for 'data linkage' where those 'data' are descriptions or analyses in publicly available outputs.

Importantly, confidentiality does not only apply to participants. Often, research ethics presume particular relational dynamics between researchers and researched in which researchers are more powerful. This rather narrow focus often leaves relationships between researchers underexplored in ethical reflection. One possible reason is that the principle of confidentiality in research moves against broader professional and legislative requirements for *transparency* and *accountability*. Academics are required to defend their theses, and have robust strategies for doing so. QSA however offers an unprecedented opportunity for wider communities of data stakeholders to observe and scrutinise the practices of the researchers who produced the original dataset. It is important not to underestimate the impacts this might have. Research methods, practices and indeed research *terms* change over time, becoming in fact out-dated, obsolete or socially unacceptable as new politics of language and indeed a politics of method (Savage, 2010; Moore, 2012) develop. Over time subsequent researchers may return to older datasets and, through methodological critique, discredit earlier researchers to the ruination of their careers, as in fact has happened (Gillies and Edwards, 2012).

---

[3] The potential for breaches of internal confidentiality is an acknowledged concern where there is prolonged engagement with participants, such as in qualitative longitudinal research (Neale and Hanna, 2012).

In developing ethical approaches to QSA it is therefore important to understand changing methodological styles and approaches as inevitable, both characterising and 'dating' datasets. Methods can become subjects of future enquiry (Savage, 2010; Hughes et al., 2016), part of the ongoing analytical engagement intrinsic to the broader questions about how datasets were produced in QSA. Indeed, the elongated time frames of QSA offer an opportunity to reconceive of researcher–researcher relationships within longer chains of data 'stewards' and, in so doing, formulate new ethics of 'co-working'. These may include relationships between the researchers in the original study and those in subsequent studies drawing on, and recontextualising, data (Irwin, Chapter 2; Tarrant and Hughes, Chapter 6; Tarrant and Hughes, 2019; Lyon and Crow, Chapter 9). Where data are drawn from studies conducted by teams that no longer exist, new and creative methodologies are emerging in the production of *theoretically interrogative* relationships with those previous teams (see Goodwin and O'Connor, Chapter 10). In effect, a temporal ethical orientation to QSA may build in additional opportunities for new and creative ethical development.

So far, we have presented ethical concerns that are local to research contexts and map onto more traditional dimensions in debate on research ethics. However, we now raise some cautions. The changing digital landscape and enhanced possibilities of data linkage make participants increasingly discoverable, in ways which may disadvantage particular individuals and groups (Boyd, 2007; Edwards et al., 2015). In the context of a drive towards open access to research data, challenges to confidentiality and anonymity intensify, and in these new data terrains, important questions of 'representation' are emerging. In this next section we move to consider broader social contexts of data re-use and present a case for a legacy ethics of QSA.

3.3 Legacy Ethics and 'Datafication'

We situate our ideas on legacy ethics and QSA in the broader context of changing social attitudes towards personal digital data. Human digital data production occurs to the extent that data are no longer what we generate, but are what we are '*immersed* and *bedded* in' (emphasis in the original, Purdham and Elliot, 2015: 26) so that we now live in (and through) *data environments* (Elliot et al., 2008, 2010). The drive to translate this captured busyness of human life into digital data points has been termed 'datafication' (Dencik et al., 2018). Public distrust has become heightened by an increasing awareness of how personal data are both economically valuable yet invisibly exploited (Welsh et al., 2003; Royal Statistical Society, 2014; Power, 2016; Lyon, 2017). A particular concern in public perception is the *futurity* of personal data as they pass through, and are repurposed in, new contexts over which their generators will have little or no control.[4] Critical reflection on these broader social contexts engenders new ethical concerns. Work on 'datafication' points to how it introduces and entrenches inequalities, discrimination and exclusion (Dencik et al., 2018; Criado Perez, 2019). This includes individuals and groups muted or marginalised through lack of access to digital participation, but may also reflect how data are being treated and analysed. In contrast, those whose social participation is more digitally visible because they are more resourced are increasingly likely to be ubiquitous in digital data. Through digital participation, people generate multiples of themselves, and where data are constantly copied, exchanged, bought and sold, these are in turn copied endlessly.

This raises new questions of representation, namely how particular individuals and groups are invisible in data, and whose voices are not heard. Qualitative research excels in forging and maintaining connections (Mason, 2018), and the broad tenets of the social justice agenda driving Dencik et al.'s programme of research often underscore much social science research. QSA, as one of many strategies in the arsenal of qualitative research, is excellently placed to address specifically what might be termed the politics of silencing and loss in a digital world. In what comes next, we employ a temporal ethical sensibility to advance *legacy ethics*, and return to the concerns raised in early writing on the ethics of QSA to discuss our thinking.

3.3.1 Ethics of legacy: The ethics of silencing and loss

The digital data divide (or more properly, unequal access to data systems through asymmetrical access to digital capture (Citron and Pasquale, 2014)) produces a context within which it is possible to argue for greater and purposeful inclusion of datasets from marginalised and silenced/muted groups in research data archives, as they are often 'hard to reach' for research purposes (Emmel et al., 2007). Such groups might include those who are less likely to value research participation. Burrows and Savage (2014) in their reflections on the Great British Class Survey, for example, described the working class as ghostly figures in the research data. These groups may also include those less able to access research contexts, such as young children with learning disabilities (Beckett, 2013), or those in highly regulated contexts such as sex offenders with learning disabilities in secure units

---

[4]For example: Electronic Frontier Foundation (www.eff.org); Tactical Technology Collective (https://tacticaltech.org); Front Line Defenders (www.frontlinedefenders.org); Security in a Box (https://securityinabox.org/en/).

(Hollomotz, 2018). Returning to the earlier question of what we should do with data for which there are no consents, we suggest that a legacy ethics moves away from over-protectionism that might emerge from a 'rights-based' ethical agenda, towards a more justice-based approach to data (Dencik et al., 2018). In the context of QSA, this would involve a process of actively ensuring the re-use of those datasets often considered especially sensitive because they come from vulnerable individuals and groups. Such datasets are more usually subjects of extra-protective ethical strategies, including their destruction. In such cases, participants' voices can only be considered as lost to research, constituting a 'double-silencing' or muting of already silenced groups.

A legacy ethics approach would instead seek to ensure that such data are stored safely, for example in the plethora of research data archives where requisite ethical data protections can be exercised. Legacy ethics thus confers ethical responsibility to QSA researchers, visible and accountable in long chains of data stewards, rather than protecting participants from them. In this way, careful archiving and re-using data even where there were no consents may allow a more balanced representation of muted or silenced voices alongside the voices of those usually more accessible to research. In this way, an ethics of legacy may facilitate attention to questions of representation that move beyond an over-focus on individual researchers, and instead produce future contexts where researchers in the round continue to value the contribution of the original participants.

3.4 Conclusion

This chapter has identified how Qualitative Secondary Analysis introduces new ethical challenges for research, particularly because it relies on the sharing and re-use of data by unknown researchers in unknowable contexts. Our discussion charted the early debate on the ethics of QSA, identifying the main risks and key stakeholders, and identified the need to reconceive of the 'research context' as one which pertains to a discrete and often contemporary group of people. Instead, we drew on Neale and Bishop's work (2012) in pointing towards the longer chains of data stakeholders, or stewards, involved in the sharing and re-use of qualitative research data.

Using the specific examples of consent, anonymisation, representation and confidentiality we explored the ways in which understanding the longer time frames available for ethical reflection and engagement in QSA may help to mitigate against some of the additional risks and dangers that data sharing and data re-use might entail. We also identified how archiving data might help to protect the interests of the broad constituency of data stakeholders as they shifted and required different emphases over time. In this context, we developed our ideas on a temporal ethical sensibility, pointing to how time builds in the possibility for additional ethical reflexivity.

Finally, we outlined the broader social context of 'datafication' within which new public concerns around the use of data are arising. We drew on Dencik et al. (2018) to elaborate a legacy ethics of QSA, underpinned by a critical social justice agenda acknowledging the need to preserve the voices of those whose contributions to research are often challenged. From this position, we suggest that a focus on an ethics underpinned by social justice rather than by a rights-driven ethical agenda may serve to act as a balance for marginalised and muted groups. We conclude by suggesting that legacy ethics, focusing on the preservation of data rather than its destruction, may utilise the very technologies which give rise to a host of new ethical concerns such as data archives, using them as contexts for *enhanced* rather than *weakened* ethical engagement.

3.5 Pedagogical Resources

Bishop, L. (2016) 'Secondary analysis of qualitative data', in D. Silverman (ed.), *Qualitative Research* (4th ed.). London: Sage. pp. 395–411.

Corti, L., Van den Eynden, V., Bishop, L. and Wollard, M. (2019, forthcoming) *Managing and Sharing Research Data: A Guide to Good Practice* (2nd ed.). London: Sage.   This book is replete with 'how to' guidance from seeking consent to anonymising and other data management strategies. This walks the researcher through the process of preparing data for archiving and re-use, attending to all the *proactive* ethical strategies (Neale and Hanna, 2012) required by legal and research ethics frameworks.

The Timescapes Archive Website: https://timescapes-archive.leeds.ac.uk   Neale, B. and Bishop, L. (2012) *The Ethics of Archiving and Re-using Qualitative Longitudinal Data: A Stakeholder Approach*, Timescapes Methods Guide Series, Guide 18. Available at: www.timescapes.leeds.ac.uk/assets/files/methods-guides/timescapes-neale-ethics-archiving.pdf.

3.6 References

Andrews, M. (2008) 'Never the last word: Revisiting data', in M. Andrews, C. Squire and M. Tamboukou (eds), *Doing Narrative Research*. London: Sage.

Becker, J.G. (2005) 'Human subjects investigation: Timeless lessons of Nuremberg and Tuskegee', *Journal of the American College of Radiology*, 2: 215–17.

Beckett, A.E. (2013) 'Non-disabled children's ideas about disability and disabled people', *British Journal of Sociology of Education*, 35(6): 856–75.

Bishop, L. (2009) 'Ethical sharing and reuse of qualitative data', *Australian Journal of Social Issues*, 44(3): 255–72.

Boyd, K.M. (2007) 'Ethnicity and the ethics of data linkage', *BMC Public Health*, 8(7): 318.

Burrows, R. and Savage, M. (2014) 'After the crisis? Big Data and the methodological challenges of empirical sociology', *Big Data & Society*, 1(1). Available at: https://journals. sagepub.com/doi/10.1177/2053951714540280 (accessed 23 October 2019).

Citron, D.K. and Pasquale, F. (2014) 'The scored society: Due process for automated predictions', *Washington Law Review*, 89(1): 1–33.

Corrigan, O. (2003) 'Empty ethics: The problem with informed consent', *Sociology of Health and Illness*, 25(7): 768–92.

Criado Perez, C. (2019) *Invisible Women: Exposing Data Bias in a World Designed for Men*. New York: Abrams Press.

Dencik, L., Jansen, F. and Metcalfe, P. (2018) *A Conceptual Framework for Approaching Social Justice in an Age of Datafication*, Working Paper, DATAJUSTICE Project. Available at: https://datajusticeproject.net/2018/08/30/a-conceptual-framework-for-approaching-social-justice-in-an-age-of-datafication/ (accessed 23 May 2019).

Edwards, R. and Mauthner, M. (2002) 'Ethics and feminist research: Theory and practice', in M. Mauthner, M. Birch, J. Jessop and T. Miller (eds), *Ethics in Qualitative Research*. London: Sage Publications.

Edwards, R. and Weller, S. (2013) 'The death of a participant: Moral obligation, consent and care in qualitative longitudinal research', in K. te Riele and R. Brooks (eds), *Negotiating Ethical Challenges in Youth Research*. Abingdon: Routledge.

Edwards, R. and Weller, S. (2015) 'Ethical dilemmas around anonymity and confidentiality in longitudinal research data sharing: The case of Dan', in M. Tolich (ed.), *Qualitative Ethics in Practice*. Walnut Creek, US: Left Coast Press.

Edwards, R., Hughes, C. and Williams, M. (2015) *Data Linkage: Ethical and Social Concerns*. Available at: www.ncrm.ac.uk/news/show.php?article=5444 (accessed 23 May 2019).

Elliot, M.J., Purdam, K., and Smith, D. (2008) 'Statistical disclosure control architectures for patient records in biomedical information systems', *Journal of Biomedical Informatics*, 41: 58–64.

Elliot, M.J., Mackey, E. and Purdam, K. (2010) *Data Environment Analysis – Annual Report*. London: Office for National Statistics.

Emmel, N. and Hughes, K. (2010) '"Recession, it's all the same to us son": The longitudinal experience (1999–2010) of deprivation', *Twenty-First Century Society*, 5(2): 171–81.

Emmel, N.D. and Hughes, K. (2014) 'Vulnerability, intergenerational exchange and the conscience of generations', in J. Holland and R. Edwards (eds), *Understanding Families over Time: Research and Policy* (Studies in Family and Intimate Life Series). London: Palgrave Macmillan.

Emmel, N., Hughes, K. and Greenhalgh, J. (2002–2005) *Developing Methodological Strategies to Recruit and Research Socially Excluded Groups*, ESRC Research Methods Programme H333250001.

Emmel, N.D., Hughes, K., Greenhalgh, J. and Sales, A. (2007) 'Accessing socially excluded people – Trust and the gatekeeper in the researcher–participant relationship', *Sociological Research Online*, 12(2). Available at: www.socresonline. org.uk/12/2/emmel.html (accessed 23 May 2019).

Frost, N., Nolas, S.M., Brooks-Gordon, B., Esin, C., Holt, A., Mehdizadeh, L. and Shinebourne, P. (2010) 'Pluralism in qualitative research: The impact of different researchers and qualitative approaches on the analysis of qualitative data', *Qualitative Research*, 10(4): 1–20.

Geiger, T., Moore, N. and Savage, M. (2010) *The Archive in Question*, National Centre for Research Methods NCRM/016. Available at: http://eprints.ncrm.ac.uk/921/1/Moore_review_paper_march_10.pdf (accessed 4 April 2019).

Gillies, V. and Edwards, R. (2012) 'Working with archived classic family and community studies: Illuminating past and present conventions around acceptable research practice', *International Journal of Social Research Methodology*, 15(4): 321–30.

Goodwin, J. and O'Connor, H. (2015) 'A restudy of young workers from the 1960s: Researching intersections of work and life course in one locality over 50 years', in N. Worth and I. Hardill (eds), *Researching the Life Course: Critical Perspectives from the Social Sciences*. Bristol: Policy Press. pp. 63–80.

Grinyer, A. (2009) 'The ethics of the secondary analysis and further use of qualitative data', *Social Research Update*, 56. Available at: http://sru.soc.surrey.ac.uk/SRU56.pdf (accessed 23 May 2019).

Guillemin, M. and Gillam, L. (2004) 'Ethics, reflexivity, and "ethically important moments" in research', *Qualitative Inquiry*, 10(2): 261–80.

Hammersley, M. (2009) 'Against the ethicists: On the evils of ethical regulation', *International Journal of Social Research Methodology*, 12(3): 211–25.

Hammersley, M. (2015) 'On ethical principles for social research', *International Journal of Social Research Methodology*, 18(4): 433–49.

Heaton, J. (2004) *Reworking Qualitative Data*. London: Sage.

Hollomotz, A. (2018) 'Successful interviews with people with intellectual disability', *Qualitative Research*, 18(2): 153–70.

Holloway, W. and Jefferson T. (2013) *Doing Qualitative Research Differently: A Psychosocial Approach*, 2nd edn. London: Sage.

Hughes, K. and Emmel, N.D. (2007–2012) *Grandparenting: Charting Trajectories of Intergenerational Social Exclusion and Health*, Project 6, ESRC Changing Lives and Times Qualitative Longitudinal Initiative Relationships and Identities through the Life Course, the Timescapes Programme.

Hughes, K. and Emmel, N. (2011) *Intergenerational Exchange: Grandparents, Their Grandchildren and the Texture of Poverty*, Timescapes Policy Briefing Paper Series 6. Available at: www.timescapes.leeds.ac.uk/assets/files/Policy-Conference-2011/paper-6.pdf (accessed 23 May 2019).

Hughes, K. and Tarrant, A. (2019) *Contextualising Qualitative Interviews: Understanding Why and When People Take Part in Research*, Freedom of Speech and Qualitative Interviews, University of Tours, 15 March.

Hughes, K., Goodwin, J. and Hughes, J. (2016) 'Documenti e reperti umani come figurazioni', *CAMBIO: Rivista sulle trasformazioni sociali [Journal of Social Transformations]*, 6(11): 123–38.

Inckle, K. (2015) 'Promises, promises: Lessons in research ethics from the Belfast Project and "The Rape Tape" case', *Sociological Research Online*, 20(1). Available at: www.socresonline.org.uk/20/1/6.html (accessed 23 May 2019).

Irwin, S. (2013) 'Qualitative secondary data analysis: Ethics, epistemology and context', *Progress in Development Studies*, 13(4): 295–306.

Irwin, S., Bornat J. and Winterton, M. (2012) 'Timescapes secondary analysis: Comparison, context and working across data sets', *Qualitative Research*, 12(1): 66–80.

Jacobsson, K. and Äkerström, M. (2013) 'Interviewees with an agenda: Learning from a "failed" interview', *Qualitative Research*, 13(6): 717–34.

Lyon, D. (2017) 'Surveillance culture: Engagement, exposure, and ethics in digital modernity', *International Journal of Communication*, 11: 824–42.

Mason, J. (2007) '"Re-Using" qualitative data: On the merits of investigative epistemology', *Sociological Research Online*, 12(3). Available at: www.socresonline. org.uk/12/3/3.html (accessed 23 May 2019).

Mason, J. (2018) *Qualitative Researching*, 3rd edn. London: Sage.

Mauthner, M., Birch, M., Jessop, J. and Miller, T. (eds) (2012) *Ethics in Qualitative Research*, 2nd edn. London: Sage.

Mauthner, N.S. (2012) 'Accounting for the tangled webs we weave: Ethical and moral issues in digital data sharing', in M. Mauthner, M. Birch, J. Jessop and T. Miller (eds), *Ethics in Qualitative Research*. London: Sage Publications. pp. 157–75.

Mauthner, N.S., Backett-Milburn, K. and Parry, O. (1998) 'The data are out there, or are they? Implications for archiving and revisiting qualitative data', *Sociology*, 32(4): 733–45.

Miller, T. (2015) 'Going back: Stalking, talking and research responsibilities in qualitative longitudinal research', *International Journal of Social Research Methodology*, 18(3): 293–305.

Moore, N. (2007) '(Re)-using qualitative data?', *Sociological Research Online*, 12(3). Available at: www.socresonline.org.uk/12/3/1.html (accessed 23 May 2019).

Moore, N. (2012) 'The politics and ethics of naming: Questioning anonymisation in (archival) research', *International Journal of Social Research Methodology*, 15(4): 331–40.

Neale, B. (2013) 'Adding time into the mix: Stakeholder ethics in qualitative longitudinal research', *Methodological Innovations*, 8(2): 6–20.

Neale, B. (2017) *Generating Data in Qualitative Longitudinal Research: A Methodological Review*, Timescapes Working Paper 8. Available at: www.timescapes.leeds.ac.uk/ assets/files/secondary_analysis/working-papers/Generating-Data-in-QL-research-Timescapes-Working-Paper-8.pdf (accessed 23 May 2019).

Neale, B. (2019) *What is Qualitative Longitudinal Research?* London: Bloomsbury.

Neale, B. and Bishop, L. (2012) 'The Timescapes Archive: A stakeholder approach to archiving qualitative longitudinal data', *Qualitative Research*, 12: 53–65.

Neale, B. and Hanna, E. (2012) *The Ethics of Researching Lives Qualitatively Through Time*, Timescapes Methods Briefing Guide 11. Available at: www.timescapes.leeds. ac.uk/assets/files/methods-guides/timescapes-series-2.pdf (accessed 23 May 2019).

Neale, B., Proudfoot, R., Blyth, G., Hughes, K. and Philips, B. (2016) *Managing Qualitative Longitudinal Data: A Practical Guide*. Available at: https://timescapes-archive.leeds.ac.uk/wp-content/uploads/sites/47/2018/10/Managing-QL-data-a-practical-guide-2016.pdf (accessed 23 May 2019).

Power, D.J. (2016) '"Big Brother" can watch us', *Journal of Decision Systems*, 25(1): 578–88.

Purdam, K. and Elliot, M. (2015) 'Exploiting New Sources of Data', in P. Halfpenny and R. Procter (eds), *Innovations in Digital Research Methods*, London: Sage.

Ritzer, G. and Jurgenson, N. (2010) 'Production, consumption, prosumption: The nature of capitalism in the age of the digital "prosumer"', *Journal of Consumer Culture*, 10: 113–36.

Royal Statistical Society (2014) *Research on Trust in Data and Attitudes Toward Data Use/Data Sharing*. Available at: www.statslife.org.uk/images/pdf/rss-data-trust-data-sharing-attitudes-research-note.pdf (accessed 23 May 2019).

Savage, M. (2010) *Identities and Social Change in Britain since 1940: The Politics of Method*. Oxford: Oxford University Press.

Tarrant, A. and Hughes, K. (2019) 'Qualitative secondary analysis: Building longitudinal samples to understand men's generational identities in low-income contexts', *Sociology*, 53(3): 599–611.

Tarrant, A. and Hughes, K. (forthcoming) 'Ethics, class and institutions: Technology choice in a photovoice methodology with men living in low-income localities', *Sociological Research Online*.

Warin, J. (2011) 'Ethical mindfulness and reflexivity: Managing a research relationship with children and young people in a 14-year qualitative longitudinal research (qlr) study', *Qualitative Inquiry*, 17(9): 805–14.

Weller, S. (2019) *Post#26: Collaborating With Original Research Teams: Some Reflections on Good Secondary Analytic Practice*. Available at: http://bigqlr.ncrm.ac.uk/2019/03/06/post26-dr-susie-weller-collaborating-with-original-research-teams-some-reflections-on-good-secondary-analytic-practice/ (accessed 23 May 2019).

Welsh, S., Hassiotis, A., O'Mahoney, G. and Deahl, M. (2003) 'Big brother is watching you – The ethical implications of electronic surveillance measures in the elderly with dementia and in adults with learning difficulties', *Aging & Mental Health*, 7: 372–5.

Wiles, R. and Boddy, J. (2013) 'Introduction to the Special Issue: Research ethics in challenging contexts', *Methodological Innovations*, 8(2): 1–5.

Zago, L.F. and Holmes, D. (2015) 'The ethical tightrope: Politics of intimacy and consensual method in sexuality research', *Nursing Inquiry*, 22: 147–56.

II

BUILDING QUALITATIVE
SECONDARY ANALYSIS INTO
RESEARCH AND TEACHING

FOUR

DOCUMENTS OF LIVES AND TIMES: REVISITING QUALITATIVE DATA THROUGH TIME

Bren Neale

--- CHAPTER CONTENTS ---

4.1 Introduction

> Sociology without history resembles a Hollywood set: great scenes, sometimes bril-
> liantly painted, with nothing and nobody behind them. (Tilley, cited in Miller, 2000: 21)

> 'The whole of anything is never told,' observed Henry James ... And the richness and
> value of qualitative studies is not exhausted or fully captured in one reading or telling,
> or in one time. (McLeod and Thomson, 2009: 125)

This chapter takes a temporal approach to the topic of revisiting research data. It does so on the grounds that all research data have an inherent temporality: they are generated, analysed and revisited in particular contexts of time and space that shape how they are interpreted and understood. Drawing on the work of Plummer (2001) the chapter begins by introducing legacy data (pre-existing, extant or 'old' data) as documents of lives and times. The discussion goes on to explore three approaches to revisiting legacy data through different horizons of time. The first involves *revisiting 'old' data*, which enables interpretations of past times through the lens of the present day. The second is *comparing 'old' and 'new' data*, past times and present times, through community-based re-studies. The third is *revisiting processual data* such as collections of letters or diaries with their inherent seriality, or data elicited prospectively, in 'real' time, from participants in qualitative longitudinal (QL) research. This kind of revisiting is not only carried out by 'secondary' researchers but is integral to the work of QL researchers as they 'grow' their datasets through time. It enables a processual understanding of biographies, individual and collective, as they evolve, and for continuities and changes, turning points and transitions to be understood over the long sweep of the life course, across the generations and through historical time. The chapter concludes with some brief reflections on the epistemological foundations for revisiting qualitative data, seen through a temporal lens.

4.2 Research Data as Documents of Lives and Times

Among the varied sources of data that underpin qualitative research enquiry, documentary and archival sources have been relatively neglected. This is despite their potential to shed valuable light on temporal processes. These data sources form part of a larger corpus of materials that Plummer (2001) engagingly describes as 'documents of life':

> The world is crammed full of human personal documents. People keep diaries, send let-
> ters, make quilts, take photos, dash off memos, compose auto/biographies, construct
> websites, scrawl graffiti, publish their memoirs, write letters, compose CVs, leave sui-
> cide notes, film video diaries, inscribe memorials on tombstones, shoot films, paint

pictures, make tapes and try to record their personal dreams. All of these expressions of personal life are hurled out into the world by the millions, and can be of interest to anyone who cares to seek them out. (Plummer 2001: 17)

Documents of life also include articles and reports in books, magazines and newsprint; digital data held in emails, text messages and on social networking sites; wills and the rich holdings of public record offices; and confidential and often revealing documents held in organisations and institutions. Seeking out such data has been described as a 'jackdaw' or 'bricolage' approach to research that is particularly characteristic of social historians and historically oriented sociologists (Thompson, 1981; Yardley, 2008; Neale, 2019). For example, letters have long provided a rich source of insight into unfolding lives. In their classic study of Polish migration, Thomas and Znaniecki (1958 [1918–20]) analysed the letters of Polish migrants to the US (an opportunistic source, for a collection of such letters was thrown out of a Chicago window and landed at Znaniecki's feet (Plummer, 2001)). Similarly Stanley's (2013) study of the history of race and apartheid was based on an analysis of three collections of letters written by white South Africans spanning a 200-year period (1770s to 1970s).

4.3 Social Science and Humanities Datasets

Documents of lives and times are commonly generated through social research, where participants create rich life course narratives, pictorial records, diaries or other forms of multimedia data in collaboration with researchers (Neale, 2019). The resulting datasets are likely to include 'field notes, transcripts, video and audio recordings, photographs, mementoes, rough drafts, working papers, case summaries, documentary sources, contemporary readings, and final published papers, books and reports' (McLeod and Thomson, 2009: 125). These offer a treasure trove of insights that can be re-examined over time to shed fresh light on the lives of the participants and the times in which they lived.

Over the past 20 years, the practice of revisiting legacy data from earlier studies has grown and is fast becoming established within the repertoire of research methods used by historically orientated researchers (Bornat, 2013). This development has been fuelled by the growing commitment and enthusiasm of researchers who wish to preserve and share their datasets for historical and biographical purposes. Of equal importance is the growth in data infrastructure (archives and institutional repositories) and funding initiatives to support this process, and a growing literature that is documenting how legacy datasets are being used, as well as appraising their strengths and weaknesses as sources of knowledge (see, in particular, Corti et al., 2005; Crow and Edwards, 2012; Irwin and Bornat, 2013).

Many qualitative datasets remain in the stewardship of the original researchers, where they run the risk of being lost to posterity (or fortuitously rediscovered; see John Goodwin and Henrietta O'Connor, Chapter 10). However, great strides have been made in recent years to build a culture of archiving, preserving and revisiting legacy data through institutional, specialist or national repositories (Valles et al., 2011; Bishop and Kuula-Luumi, 2017). Such data facilities are scattered across UK and Europe, for example, the Kirklees Sound Archive in West Yorkshire, which houses oral history interviews on the wool textile industry (Bornat, 2013; for an overview of these resources see Edwards et al., Chapter 5).

4.4 Revisiting Qualitative Datasets through Time

Before reviewing different approaches to the use and re-use of legacy datasets, it is worth teasing out the different ways in which this enterprise is understood. The process is commonly described as the analysis of legacy data by 'secondary' researchers, as opposed to the 'primary' researchers who generated a dataset. It is this definition, based on a distinction between primary and secondary research, which has tended to shape, and indeed polarise, debates about the ethics and epistemology of data re-use (see Introduction, also Sarah Irwin, Chapter 2). However, data re-use or qualitative secondary analysis (QSA) can also be defined as the process of revisiting data for purposes beyond that for which they were originally generated (Bornat, 2003; Bishop, 2009; see also Joanna Bornat, Chapter 8). For example, when Bornat (2003) revisited a series of interviews about the development of geriatric medicine, she brought a fresh vision to the dataset and discovered that issues relating to race and ethnicity were implicitly embedded in the narratives. These themes became the focus for her re-analysis. Linked to this, and of particular significance here, temporal data can be revisited over time to discern changes and continuities in individual lives and in the social fabric of society. The language of revisiting reminds us that data 'age' with time. Whether undertaken by 'primary' or 'secondary' researchers, revisiting places data in a new temporal context, with the potential to reveal fresh insights into biographical, generational and historical processes (Neale, 2019). This alternative way of conceptualising the use of legacy data provides the foundation for the discussion below.

Whatever its specific purpose, and whatever time scales are involved, revisiting data has the potential to illuminate the relationship between past, present and future (Irwin, 2013: 286; cf. Bond, 1990; Bishop, 2007). Duncan (2012: 313) describes revisiting 'as a sort of comparative research, but using comparisons over time instead of over space'. All data are temporal in an historical sense: whether they are created synchronically (at one moment in time) or diachronically (through time), they implicitly reflect the times in which they are generated (McLeod and Thomson, 2009). As data 'age' or mature, their historical value becomes more evident. Narrative (qualitative) forms of data are also likely to be temporal in a biographical sense, reflecting continuities and changes in the lives of the narrators. In addition, some forms of data are constructed in dynamic and processual ways, through time. Examples include the seriality of letters, written or visual diaries, or longitudinal data that are gathered cumulatively from a panel of research participants. Understanding documents of life as temporal data gives scope for researchers to historicise their insights and explanations, and to work towards an exciting fusion of sociology and history (Mills, 1959; Duncan, 2012; O'Connor and Goodwin, 2012; Bornat and Bytheway, 2012).

4.5 Approaches to Data Revisiting

Qualitative or qualitative longitudinal studies and data may be revisited for different purposes, in a variety of ways, by the same or by a different researcher. Three broad approaches to revisiting are described here, each of which involves a different way of engaging with time. The first is *revisiting 'old' data* (more usually described as secondary analysis), in which researchers revisit legacy data generated for an earlier study. The second, *comparing 'old' and 'new' data* through re-studies, builds on this approach, not only analysing past source materials but following up with a fresh study that explores similar themes in the same or a similar setting. This increases the scope for comparative analysis across extensive horizons of time. A third approach, *revisiting processual data*, involves the re-analysis of serial data such as diaries, photographs or letter collections, or the cumulative narratives, multimedia data and researcher observations that are gathered in 'real time' through qualitative longitudinal enquiry. These three approaches are described further below.

4.5.1 Revisiting 'old' data

This involves a 'one-off' retrospective analysis (or secondary analysis) of a legacy dataset that enables social processes to be reconstructed and reinterpreted from a different historical, theoretical and/or methodological standpoint. Here, the focus is on 're-working the past' through the lens of the present day (Neale 2020). As a prime example of this approach, Savage (2005a, 2005b) re-analysed a rich dataset (a series of detailed notebooks deposited in the UK Data Archive) that had been generated in the early 1960s by Goldthorpe and Lockwood for their *Affluent Worker Study*. Adopting a positivist approach to social research, the original researchers focused on their quantifiable survey data, leaving their rich case study evidence on the cutting room floor. Some 40 years later, Savage accessed and read these neglected data in a different way, 'against the grain', making sense of the complexities and nuances of the workers' past accounts through the lens of present day scholarship. This produced new insights into perceptions and practices of social class in post-war Britain that challenged and refined the interpretations of the earlier researchers (Savage, 2005a, 2005b). Savage was also able to shed light on the original research process and its theoretical and methodological underpinnings.

Savage's research illustrates how a retrospective, comparative lens can generate fresh theoretical and historical insights from an original dataset. In the process, he also rectified the under-utilisation of a valuable data resource. As each generation of researchers observes, qualitative research generates substantial volumes of data that are rarely fully analysed as part of an original study (Foster et al., 1979; McLeod and Thomson, 2009). Data from the Affluent Worker Study, for example, was repurposed not only by Savage but also by the social historian David Kynaston (2005), in this case for his social history of post-war Britain. In a series of publications, Kynaston created a rich tapestry of political, socio-economic and cultural insights drawn from a wide range of sources, including social science datasets held in the UK Data Archive, and participant accounts in the Mass Observation Archive.

4.5.1.1 Revisiting multiple data sources

Kynaston's research demonstrates the huge potential to use two or more datasets in parallel, bringing segments of data together to build new insights across varied social and historical contexts. This can enrich temporal understandings and open new windows onto social processes. Drawing on multiple datasets enables researchers to expand the empirical baseline for their research, and to read across complementary forms of data: historical/contemporary/processual; local/global; textual/visual; qualitative/quantitative; researcher/participant-generated; scholarly/popular, and so on. This creates 'big' rich data with the potential to combine explanatory depth with comparative breadth (Neale, 2015; see Rosalind Edwards and colleagues, Chapter 5).

4.5.2 Comparing 'old' and 'new' data: Re-studies

The second broad approach to revisiting data represents an elaboration of the first. Here, legacy data are not only revisited, but used as the baseline for a re-study that compares past and present day accounts. This brings old and new data into a common analytical framework. The process of constructing a re-study may involve modifying themes and identifying new topics of enquiry, refining methodology (for example, modifying samples and settings), and generating new data to fill substantive gaps in the original research. In these ways, the original study becomes a vital baseline for a newly constituted study. The gap between an 'old' and 'new' study is usually a decade or more, giving historical reach to a re-study. But legacy data may also be revisited fast on the heels of its original creation, where it can be used as a springboard for the development of a new study (Bishop, 2007; Tarrant, 2016; and Anna Tarrant and Kahryn Hughes, Chapter 6).

Community-based re-studies have a venerable history in anthropological ethnographies, and in their sociological counterpart – the field of community studies in large-scale societies (Bell and Newby, 1971; Foster et al., 1979; Burawoy, 2003; Charles and Crow, 2012; Crow, 2012). Lewis (1951) provides a striking example of an anthropological re-study. He visited the Mexican community of Tepoztlan in the 1940s, some 20 years after Redfield (1930) had carried out his original research there. The meticulous field materials gathered by Redfield are preserved in the special collections of the University of Chicago Library. Such materials, along with accompanying sound recordings, represent the core elements of a traditional anthropological dataset. Prior to the post-war development of anthropological methods, fieldnotes were personal and idiosyncratic documents, not produced for sharing. However, they were often inherited by the next generation following the death of the originator, part of the process of 'passing the mantle' (Sanjek, 1990). It is not clear whether Lewis had access to these materials at the time of his study, or how useful they would have been for his purposes, although apparently he made use of them in his subsequent research (Foster et al., 1979: 10).

Lewis's re-study gained notoriety for comprehensively refuting the findings of his predecessor. Where Redfield had found homogeneity, integration and harmony in Tepoztlan society, Lewis uncovered heterogeneity, individualism and conflict. He accused Redfield of adopting, 'the old Rousseauian notion of primitive peoples as noble savages and the corollary that, with civilisation, comes the fall of man' (Lewis, 1951: 435). The stark difference between the findings of these two studies requires some explanation (Bell and Newby, 1971; Crow, 2012). Whether such discrepancies are the result of historical change or changing researcher perceptions and preoccupations, or a mixture of these, is not always clear. But in this case, the differences largely reflected the changing methodological and theoretical orientations of the two researchers rather than any wholesale change in Tepoztlan society. Where Redfield was operating as a sole doctoral researcher, with relatively limited time in the field and dependent on the accounts of only half a dozen key informants, Lewis was much better resourced. He drew on more advanced and systematic fieldwork techniques, mobilised a large, multidisciplinary team of researchers, spent twice as long in the field, and interviewed over 100 individuals.

But perhaps the key difference across these two studies was the shifting theoretical orientations of the researchers (Bell and Newby, 1971: 77). Redfield was working in an anthropological tradition that focused on formal and ritualised social practices (those that tend to express collective values and solidarity), while Lewis prioritised the everyday worlds of the people and their economic and political livelihoods. As Bell and Newby (1971) note, since the questions that drove Lewis's research were quite different from those asked by Redfield, it is hardly surprising that the two studies produced different findings.

With hindsight, it seems that the researchers were tapping into different facets of the dialectical forces of continuity and change, collective and individual values and practices, and harmony and conflict, which co-exist in dynamic and creative tension with each other in any society, at any given time (cf. Gusfield, 1967). There is clearly some wisdom in the old anthropological adage that what we see depends mainly on what we look for (Lubbock, 1892). This suggests the need for researchers to work abductively (moving from the particular to the general, building knowledge from careful observations of the world). Otherwise, their pre-occupations may lead them to miss compelling evidence about social processes.

In recent years, community based re-studies have been characterised increasingly in terms of building on and developing an earlier study, rather than baldly replicating it (Charles, 2012; Crow, 2012). As Heraclitus reminds us, it is not possible to step into the same river twice (Charles and Crow, 2012). This is illustrated in a recent re-study of the classic 'Middletown' community studies (Lynd and Lynd, 1929, 1937), which sought to explore the ethnic composition of the city and document the lives of its African/American inhabitants (Lassiter, 2012). Asking new questions and developing fresh interpretations is intrinsic to qualitative enquiry (Bornat, 2013); in this case, it enabled Lassiter and his colleagues to redress a major gap in the focus of the earlier studies.

4.5.3 Revisiting processual data: Insights through time

A third approach to data revisiting concerns the use of processual or qualitative longitudinal (QL) data, that is, data that are generated through time or through successive visits to the same individuals or groups, to capture 'change in the making' (Bergson 1946 [1903]; Mills, 1959). A QL dataset is built upon the process of revisiting people and events over time, giving the data a distinctive temporal character. Diaries and collections of letters have a serial quality: they prospectively document unfolding lives in an incremental and episodic way, providing a flow of personal reflections on an ever-changing present (Neale, 2019). Similarly, through successive waves of a QL study, narrative and multimedia forms of data are generated in 'real' time, in ways that continually update the past and anticipate the future (for a detailed account see Neale, 2020). Of particular note, since these dynamic forms of data are generated from the same individuals or small collectives (a longitudinal panel of participants), they can offer unique insights into unfolding biographies, and how these intersect with wider processes of historical change.

Revisiting such data enables researchers to explore temporality in a distinctive way: through a *processual* understanding of change and continuity as lives unfold. This generates a description *through* time rather than a bald comparison of two 'snapshots' in time (Howell and Talle, 2012; Neale, 2019). This is particularly the case when QL studies are conducted intensively, over the short to medium term. The process involves turning synchronic (snapshot) readings of data into diachronic (processual) readings, and bringing cases, themes and time into a common conceptual framework (Neale, 2019).

Much like the process of revisiting 'old' data (outlined above), QL researchers look backwards in time, interrogating their legacy data retrospectively from the standpoint of the present day, thereby discerning the seeds of change. And much like the re-studies described above, they build on existing data prospectively to craft one or more return visits to the field, building chronologies of events as they occur. But, working through the stream of time enables those engaged in QL studies and re-studies to take these approaches a stage further: they are able to oscillate between past, present and future to gain a more nuanced understanding of people's unfolding lives and to illuminate how they construct and overwrite their biographies (Neale, 2019). In the process, new themes, insights, conceptual questions and methodological refinements are continually emerging, shaping how data are generated and revisited, and transforming their meaning with every return to the field.

Working with processual data enhances the potential to uncover fluid time, time that is embedded in our daily events and experiences (Neale 2020). Fluid time, as a theoretical and analytical device, can be used to explore turning points and trajectories, to construct chronologies, to trace lives backwards, to oscillate between continuity and change, between past, present and future – in short, to uncover the unpredictable contours, tempos and horizons of unfolding lives (Neale, 2019, 2020; Gray et al., 2013; Geraghty and Gray, 2017; Salter, 2017; Tarrant and Hughes, 2019; see also Jane Gray and Ruth Geraghty, Chapter 11).

Historical time can provide a structure for sampling in the archive (Salter, 2017). The scope to revisit qualitative longitudinal datasets over more extensive time horizons, and to link multiple datasets together, is evident in the work of Elder and Hareven (1992). These researchers explored both qualitative and quantitative longitudinal data in their study of the impact of the Great Depression on family fortunes across the generations. They drew on extensive longitudinal data from the *Berkeley Guidance Study* and the *Oakland and Berkeley Growth Studies*, which had followed the lives of 500 Californian children over a period of 60 years. These were combined with data from Hareven's rich oral historical study of two generations of mill worker families at the Amoskeag Mill in Manchester, New Hampshire. Reading across these different sources of data, both qualitative and quantitative, gathered over the generations, enabled the researchers to reach new understandings of the many factors (including military service) that could lift families out of poverty and enhance their life chances. The methodological challenges and rewards of a mixed-method approach have been explored more recently by Lindsey and colleagues (2015), who drew on longitudinal data from the Mass Observation Archive, the British Household Panel survey and the British Social Attitudes survey to explore the cultures and practices of volunteering.

The potential to revisit processual forms of legacy data has been greatly enhanced in recent years through the work of the long-running Mass Observation Archive (MOA) and related biographical life-writing resources such as the French APA Archive (Lejeune, 2011); the Irish Qualitative Data Archive with its rich holdings of life history data (Gray et al., 2013; Geraghty and Gray, 2017); and the fledgling Timescapes Archive, a digital resource of QL datasets. The longitudinal qualitative datasets held in the MOA are based on a unique national life-writing project that captures aspects of everyday life in Britain. In response to regular directives from the MO project, some 500 observers across the UK produce narratives of their experiences, thoughts and opinions that are then deposited in the Archive. In many cases, the diaries and accounts of every-day life that make up the collection run across decades of change (Salter, 2017). The numerous studies of these data include reconstructions of a single biography from a historical collection of hand-written diaries (e.g., Broad and Fleming, 1981; Salter, 2017); explorations of the changing social fabric of a particular decade, generation, or period of history (the Second World War, for example); and explorations of a variety of changing social and historical values and practices across cases, themes, and/or across time (see, for example, Shaw, 2001 and Savage, 2007). Data in this resource are gradually being digitised to support the process of data discovery and access.

The Timescapes Archive is a fledgling resource of social scientific data that has been under continual development since its launch in 2010 (Neale and Bishop, 2012; Tarrant and Hughes, 2019; see www.timescapes-archive.leeds.ac.uk). New QL datasets are gradually being added to the resource. The original core collection comprises a suite of thematically linked datasets, generated through the national-level *Timescapes Study* that explored the dynamics of family and interpersonal lives across the generations (www.timescapes.leeds.ac.uk). The legacy data held in this resource will grow in historical value as the archive matures. But researchers have already begun to explore new ways to engage with and interrogate 'big' QL data, and create new assemblages of data drawn from the multiple datasets in the resource. Pioneering studies of this sort were conducted as part of the Timescapes Study (Irwin and Winterton, 2011, 2012, 2014; Irwin et al., 2012; Winterton and Irwin, 2011, 2012), and have been developed further since (Tarrant, 2016; Davidson et al., 2018; Tarrant and Hughes, 2019; see www.bigqlr.ncrm.ac.uk) (see also Rosalind Edwards and colleagues, Chapter 5).

It is worth noting here that specialist temporal archives such as MOA and Timescapes are not merely passive stores of knowledge (Tamboukou, 2014; Salter, 2017). They actively curate and organise their collections in ways that are thematically and temporally linked; they mediate between those who deposit data in the archive and those who use the resource; and they facilitate data revisiting in ways that shape and advance the field of temporal research. They are crucial lynchpins in the development of a processual understanding of lives and times.

4.6 Conclusion: Valuing Documents of Lives and Times

The overview presented above has sought to tease out the sometimes subtle differences and similarities between three approaches to revisiting research data, which operate within and give access to different horizons of time. These are not mutually exclusive approaches and may be adapted and combined in varied ways, creating important synergies across different fields of study (for an example of a fusion of these approaches, see the Qualitative Longitudinal re-study of O'Connor and Goodwin, 2010, 2012; also Chapter 10).

Over recent decades, some important epistemological questions have been raised about the status and meaning of legacy datasets, and their value for revisiting. These issues have been extensively debated (see Sarah Irwin, Chapter 2), but some salient points are drawn out here. A core concern revolves around the extent to which such data are embedded in the contexts of their production, and are therefore best mediated through the original researchers with their experiential knowledge of the field. Related to this, there may be a lack of 'fit' between the nature and scope of a legacy dataset and the research questions that drive a new study, leaving the re-analyst with missing or incomplete data that are not robust enough to contribute new knowledge or evidence (Hammersley, 2010; Duncan, 2012). Research data inevitably give us a partial vision of the social world. Seen in historical context, legacy data may be regarded as 'fragments of past occurrences' (Bond, 1990: 287), while archives provide little more than 'traces of the past' (Moore et al., 2017). As Steedman (cited in Tamboukou, 2014: 619) observes, 'you find nothing in the Archive but stories caught halfway through: the middle of things, discontinuities.'

These concerns about context and the fragmented nature of legacy data raise doubts about the viability of transporting these data to another research context, and what (if anything) they may tell us. The idea that a researcher can instrumentally revisit a dataset as if it has independent veracity and existence becomes questionable. These concerns are founded on a tension between realist understandings of data (as fixed texts that are simply 'out there', outside of time), and a narrowly constructionist view that, as embedded, relational texts, data are not transferable because they are jointly produced and their meaning tied to the social, spatial, and temporal contexts of their production (Bond, 1990).

More recently, these concerns have begun to shift ground (see, for example, Mauthner et al., 1998 and Mauthner and Parry, 2013). There is a growing recognition that it is not the re-use of data that creates these challenges of contextual understanding: on the contrary, these are foundational issues for 'primary' researchers that impact on how data are generated and interpreted in the first place. In other words, these issues cross over and confound the 'primary/secondary' divide. It is clear that research data are by no means simply 'out there': they are inevitably constructed and re-constructed (crafted, re-crafted, re-generated, re-purposed) in different social, spatial and historical contexts. Indeed, they are transformed historically simply through the passage of time (Moore, 2007). But this does not mean that the narratives they contain are 'made up' or that they have no integrity or value across different research contexts (Hammersley, 2010; Bornat, 2013). It does suggest, however, that data sources are capable of more than one interpretation, and that their meaning and salience emerge in the moment of their use:

> There is no a-priori privileged moment in time in which we can gain a deeper, more profound, truer insight, than in any other moment … There is never a single authorised reading … It is the multiple viewpoints, taken together, which are the most illuminating. (Brockmeier, 2006; Reissman, 2004; cited in Andrews, 2008: 89)

It is the combination of different readings that offers additional layers of complexity and insight. Historical distance is by no means a disadvantage; it provides a new temporal context, a broader horizon from which to view past times (Duncan, 2012). Lassiter's (2012) re-study of Middletown, for example, reveals the partial insights generated by the 'primary' researchers, and illustrates how contextual issues relating to time, place, and cultural embeddedness can shape very different understandings of the same community; in temporal perspective there is not one Middletown but, potentially, many.

Moreover, whether revisiting temporal data involves stepping into the shoes of an earlier self, or of someone else entirely, this seems to make relatively little difference to the interpretive process. From this point of view, the distinctions between *using* and *re-using* data, or between *primary* and *secondary* use, begin to break down (Bornat, 2005; Moore, 2007; Bishop, 2007; Holland, 2011). The language itself seems to lose its meaning. Re-framing these processes in terms of re-visiting may help to overcome this difficulty. Not least, it does away with the implicit and dubious assumption that, somehow, 'primary' analysis is the privileged lens for analysis, while 'secondary' is merely 'second best' or 'second rate' (Irwin and Winterton, 2012).

The transformative potential of data and the value of multiple temporal readings is nowhere more evident than in the process of generating a QL dataset. Since these data are used and re-used over the time frame of a study, they are always provisional and in the making; their regeneration is a continual and cumulative process (Bond, 1990). The production of new data as a study progresses inevitably reconfigures and recontextualises the dataset as a whole, creating new assemblages of data and opening up new insights from a different contextual standpoint. By their very nature, longitudinal datasets tend to outlive their original research questions, requiring researchers to ask new questions of old data, to maximise the degree of 'fit' between them, to conjure new interpretive frameworks, and thereby to 'breathe new life' into the data (Bond, 1990; Elder and Taylor, 2009).

The status and veracity of research data, then, is not a black and white, either/or issue, but one of recognising the limitations and partial vision of *all* data sources, requiring researchers to appraise the degree of 'fit' and contextual understanding that can be achieved and maintained (Hammersley, 2010; Duncan, 2012; Irwin, 2013). In particular, understanding data through the lens of time reveals that they have no fixed meaning; they do not stand still. Nor do the temporal and social contexts in which they can be understood; these too are not static, fixed or bounded, but perpetually transforming (Moore, 2006). This is vividly conveyed by Ottenberg, reflecting here on his longitudinal ethnography of the Nigerian Afikpo community:

> As anthropological theory has changed, so has the way I look at my written notes ... I am constantly re-interpreting Afikpo, ever looking at my field notes in different ways ... through more than thirty years of using these notes. (Ottenberg, 1990: 146)

In temporal perspective, then, data have no definitive meaning and there are no definitive findings. Longitudinal researchers are acutely mindful of the need to frame their research enterprise in a more modest way: to seek plausible accounts of the social world, generated and regenerated in particular contexts of time and place, which are inherently provisional and in the making (Elliott, 2005; Neale, 2019; Cilliers in Neale 2020).

A decade ago, debates about the use of qualitative datasets were in danger of becoming polarised (Moore, 2007). However, the preoccupations of researchers are beginning to move on. The concern with whether or not qualitative datasets *should* be revisited is giving way to a more productive concern with *how* they should be revisited, not least, how best to work with their inherent and shifting temporality (Neale, 2017). Overall, the 'jackdaw' approach to repurposing documentary and archival sources of data is the very stuff of historical sociology and of social history more generally (Kynaston, 2005), and it has huge and perhaps untapped potential in the task of understanding lives through the stream of time.

4.7 References

Andrews, M. (2008) 'Never the last word: Revisiting data', in M. Andrews, C. Squire and M. Tamboukou (eds), *Doing Narrative Research*. London: Sage. pp. 86–101.

Bell, C. and Newby, H. (1971) *Community Studies*. London: Allen and Unwin.

Bergson, H. (1946 [1903]) 'An introduction to metaphysics', in *The Creative Mind*. New York: Citadel Press.

Bishop, L. (2007) 'A reflexive account of reusing qualitative data: Beyond primary/secondary dualism', *Sociological Research Online*, 12. Available at: www.socresonline.org.uk/12/3/2.html (accessed 23 May 2019).

Bishop, L. (2009) 'Ethical sharing and re-use of qualitative data', *Australian Journal of Social Issues*, 44(3): 255–72.

Bishop, L. and Kuula-Luumi, A. (2017) 'Revisiting qualitative data reuse: A decade on', *SAGE Open*, Jan–March: 1–15.

Bond, G. (1990) 'Fieldnotes: Research in past occurrences', in R. Sanjek (ed.), *Fieldnotes: The Makings of Anthropology*. Ithaca, NY: Cornell University Press. pp. 273–89.

Bornat, J. (2003) 'A second take: Revisiting interviews with a different purpose', *Oral History*, Spring: 47–53.

Bornat, J. (2005) 'Recycling the evidence: Different approaches to the re-analysis of gerontological data', *FQS/Forum: Qualitative Social Research*, 6(1): art. 42.

Bornat, J. (2013) 'Secondary analysis in reflection: Some experiences of re-use from an oral history perspective', *Families, Relationships and Societies*, 2(2): 309–17.

Bornat, J. and Bytheway, B. (2012) 'Working with different temporalities: Archived life history interviews and diaries', *International Journal of Social Research Methodology*, 15(4): 291–99.

Broad, R. and Fleming, S. (1981) *Nella Last's War: A Mother's Diary, 1939–1945*. Bristol: Falling Wall Press.

Burawoy, M. (2003) 'Revisits: An outline of a theory of reflexive ethnography', *American Sociological Review*, 68, October: 645–79.

Charles, N. (2012) 'Families, communities and social change: Then and now', *The Sociological Review*, 60: 438–56.

Charles, N. and Crow, G. (2012) 'Introduction: Community re-studies and social change', Special Issue of *The Sociological Review*, 60: 399–404.

Corti, L., Witzel, A. and Bishop, L. (eds) (2005) 'Secondary analysis of qualitative data', *FQS/Forum Qualitative Social Research*, 6: 1.

Crow, G. (2012) 'Community re-studies: Lessons and prospects', *The Sociological Review*, 60: 405–20.

Crow, G. and Edwards, R. (eds) (2012) 'Editorial Introduction: Perspectives on working with archived textual and visual material in social research', *International Journal of Social Research Methodology*, 15(4): 259–62.

Davidson, E., Edwards, R., Jamieson, L. and Weller, S. (2018) 'Big data, qualitative style: A breadth and depth method for working with large volumes of secondary qualitative data', *Quality and Quantity*, 53(1): 363–76. DOI: 10.1007/s11135-018-0757-y.

Duncan, S. (2012) 'Using elderly data theoretically: Personal life in 1949/50 and individualisation theory', *International Journal of Social Research Methodology*, 15(4): 311–19.

Elder, G. and Hareven, T. (1992) 'Rising above life's disadvantage: From the Great Depression to global war', in J. Modell, G. Elder and R. Parke (eds), *Children in Time and Place: Developmental and Historical Insights*. New York: Cambridge University Press. pp. 47–72. (Reprinted in T. Hareven (ed.) (2000) *Families, History and Social Change*. Oxford: Westview Press.)

Elder, G. and Taylor, M. (2009) 'Linking research questions to data archives', in G. Elder and J. Giele (eds), *The Craft of Life Course Research*. London: Guilford Press. pp. 93–116.

Elliott, J. (2005) *Using Narrative in Social Research: Qualitative and Quantitative Approaches*. London: Sage.

Foster, G., Scudder, T., Colson, E. and Kemper, R. (eds) (1979) *Long-Term Field Research in Social Anthropology*. New York: Academic Press.

Geraghty, R. and Gray, J. (2017) 'Family rhythms: Re-visioning family change in Ireland using qualitative archived data from *Growing Up in Ireland* and *Life Histories and Social Change*', *Irish Journal of Sociology*, 25(2): 207–13.

Gray, J., Geraghty, R. and Ralph, D. (2013) 'Young grandchildren and their grandparents: A secondary analysis of continuity and change across four birth cohorts', *Families, Relationships and Societies*, 2(2): 289–98.

Gusfield, J. (1967) 'Tradition and modernity: Misplaced polarities in the study of social change', *American Journal of Sociology*, 72(4): 351–62.

Hammersley, M. (2010) 'Can we use qualitative data via secondary analysis? Notes on some terminological and substantive issues', *Sociological Research Online*, 15(1): 47–53.

Holland, J. (2011) 'Timescapes: Living a Qualitative Longitudinal study', *FQS/Forum Qualitative Social Research*, 12(3): Art 9.

Howell, S. and Talle, A. (eds) (2012) *Returns to the Field: Multi-temporal Research and Contemporary Anthropology*. Bloomington: Indiana University Press.

Irwin, S. (2013) 'Qualitative secondary analysis in practice: Introduction', *Families, Relationships and Societies*, 2(2): 285–8.

Irwin, S. and Bornat, J. (eds) (2013) 'Qualitative secondary analysis in practice', *Families, Relationships and Societies*, 2(2): 285–8.

Irwin, S. and Winterton, M. (2011) *Timescapes Data and Secondary Analyses: Working Across the Projects*, Timescapes Working Paper 5. Available at: www.timescapes. leeds.ac.uk/publicationsandoutputs (accessed 24 October 2019).

Irwin, S. and Winterton, M. (2012) 'Qualitative secondary analysis and social explanation', *Sociological Research Online*, 17(2). Art. 4.

Irwin, S. and Winterton, M. (2014) 'Gender and work–family conflict: A secondary analysis of Timescapes data', in J. Holland and R. Edwards (eds), *Understanding Families Over Time: Research and Policy*. London: Palgrave Macmillan. pp. 142–58.

Irwin, S., Bornat, J. and Winterton, M. (2012) 'Timescapes Secondary Analysis: Comparison, context and working across datasets', *Qualitative Research*, 12(1): 66–80.

Kynaston, D. (2005) 'The uses of sociology for real-time history', *FQS/Forum Qualitative Social Research*, 6(1): Art 45.

Lassiter, L. (2012) '"To fill in the missing piece of the Middletown puzzle": Lessons from re-studying Middletown', *The Sociological Review*, 60: 421–37.

Lejeune, P. (2011) 'The story of a French life-writing archive: "Association pour l'autobiographie et le patrimoine autobiographique"', *FQS/Forum Qualitative Social Research* 12(3): Art 7.

Lewis, O. (1951) *Life in a Mexican Village: Tepoztlan Revisited*. Urbana: University of Illinois Press.

Lindsey, R., Metcalfe, E. and Edwards, R. (2015) 'Time in mixed methods longitudinal research: Working across written narratives and large-scale panel survey data to investigate attitudes to volunteering', in N. Worth and I. Hardill (eds), *Researching the Life Course: Critical Perspectives from the Social Sciences*. Bristol: Policy Press. pp. 43–62.

Lubbock, J. (1892) *The Beauties of Nature and the Wonders of the World We Live In*. London: Macmillan.

Lynd, R. and Lynd, H. (1929) *Middletown: A Study in Contemporary American Culture*. New York: Harcourt Brace.

Lynd, R. and Lynd, H. (1937) *Middletown in Transition: A Study in Cultural Conflict*. New York: Harcourt Brace.

Mauthner, N. and Parry, O. (2013) 'Open access digital data sharing: Principles, policies and practices', *Social Epistemology*, 27(1): 47–67.

Mauthner, N., Parry, O. and Backett-Milburn. K. (1998) 'The data are out there, or are they? Implications for archiving and revisiting qualitative data', *Sociology*, 32(4): 733–45.

McLeod, J. and Thomson, R. (2009) *Researching Social Change*. London: Sage.

Miller, R. (2000) *Researching Life Stories and Family Histories*. London: Sage.

Mills, C.W. (1959) *The Sociological Imagination*. Oxford: OUP.

Moore, N. (2006) 'The contexts of context: Broadening perspectives in the (re)use of qualitative data', *Methodological Innovations Online*, 1(2): 21–32.

Moore, N. (2007) '(Re)using qualitative data?' *Sociological Research Online*, 12 (3): 1.

Moore, N., Salter, A., Stanley, L. and Tamboukou, M. (2017) *The Archive Project: Archival Research and the Social Sciences*. London: Routledge.

Neale, B. (2015) 'Time and the life course: Perspectives from qualitative longitudinal research', in N. Worth and I. Hardill (eds), *Researching the Life Course: Critical Perspectives from the Social Sciences*. Bristol: Policy Press. pp. 25-41.

Neale, B. (2017) *Research Data as Documents of Life*, Guest-Post no. 13. Available at: http://bigqlr.ncrm.ac.uk/2017/12/04/guest-post-13-prof-bren-neale-research-data-as-documents-of-life/ (accessed 23 May 2019).

Neale, B. (2019) *What is Qualitative Longitudinal Research?* London: Bloomsbury.

Neale, B. (2020 in press) *Qualitative Longitudinal Research: The Craft of Researching Lives through Time*. London: Sage.

Neale, B. and Bishop, L. (2012) 'The Timescapes Archive: A stakeholder approach to archiving qualitative longitudinal data', *Qualitative Research*, 12(1): 53–65.

O'Connor, H. and Goodwin, J. (2010) 'Utilising data from a lost sociological project: Experiences, insights, promises', *Qualitative Research*, 10(3): 283–98.

O'Connor, H. and Goodwin, J. (2012) 'Revisiting Norbert Elias's sociology of community: Learning from the Leicester re-studies', *The Sociological Review*, 60: 476–97.

Ottenberg, S. (1990) 'Thirty years of field notes: Changing relationships to the text', in R. Sanjek (ed.), *Fieldnotes: The Makings of Anthropology*. Ithaca, NY: Cornell University Press. pp. 139–60.

Plummer, K. (2001) *Documents of Life 2: An Invitation to a Critical Humanism*. London: Sage.

Redfield, R. (1930) *Tepoztlan: A Mexican Village*. Chicago: University of Chicago Press.

Salter, A. (2017) 'Reading time backwards: Archival research and temporal order', in N. Moore, A. Salter, L. Stanley and M. Tamboukou (eds), *The Archive Project: Archival Research in the Social Sciences*. London: Routledge. pp. 99–126.

Sanjek, R. (ed.) (1990) *Fieldnotes: The Makings of Anthropology*. Ithaca, NY: Cornell University Press.

Savage, M. (2005a) 'Revisiting classic qualitative studies', *FQS/Forum Qualitative Social Research*, 6(1): Art. 31.

Savage, M. (2005b) 'Working class identities in the 1960s: Revisiting the *Affluent Worker Study*', *Sociology*, 39(5): 929–48.

Savage, M. (2007) 'Changing social class identities in post-war Britain: Perspectives from Mass-Observation', *Sociological Research Online*, 12(3): 6.

Shaw, J. (2001) 'Winning territory: Changing place to change pace', in J. May and N. Thrift (eds), *Timespace: Geographies of Temporality*. New York: Routledge. pp. 120–32.

Stanley, L. (2013) 'Whites writing: Letters and documents of life in a QLR project', in L. Stanley (ed.), *Documents of Life Revisited: Narrative and Biographical Methodology for a 21st Century Critical Humanism*. London: Routledge.

Tamboukou, M. (2014) 'Archival research: Unravelling space/time/matter entanglements and fragments' *Qualitative Research*, 14(5): 617–33.

Tarrant, A. (2016) 'Getting out of the swamp? Methodological reflections on using qualitative secondary analysis to develop research design', *International Journal of Social Research Methodology*, 20(6): 599–611.

Tarrant, A. and Hughes, K (2019) 'Qualitative secondary analysis: Building longitudinal samples to understand men's generational identities in low-income contexts', *Sociology*, 53(3): 599–611.

Thomas, W.I. and Znaniecki, F. (1958 [1918-20]) *The Polish Peasant in Europe and America*. New York: Dover Publications.

Thompson, P. (1981) 'Life histories and the analysis of social change', in. D. Bertaux (ed.), *Biography and Society: The Life History Approach in the Social Sciences*. London: Sage. pp. 289–306.

Valles, M., Corti, L., Tamboukou, M. and Baer, A. (2011) 'Qualitative archives and biographical research methods: An introduction to the FQS special issue', *FQS/Forum Qualitative Social Research*, 12(3).

Winterton, M. and Irwin, S. (2011) 'Youngster's expectations and context: Secondary analysis and interpretation of imagined futures', in M. Winterton, G. Crow and B. Morgan-Brett (eds), *Young Lives and Imagined Futures: Insights from Archived Data*, Timescapes Working Paper 6. Available at: www.timescapes.leeds.ac.uk (accessed 24 October 2019).

Winterton, M. and Irwin, S. (2012) 'Teenage expectations of going to university: The ebb and flow of influence from 14 to 18', *Journal of Youth Studies*, 15(7): 858–74.

Yardley, A. (2008) 'Piecing together – A methodological bricolage', *FQS/Forum Qualitative Social Research*, 9(2): Art 31.

FIVE

SEARCH STRATEGIES: ANALYTIC SEARCHING ACROSS MULTIPLE DATASETS AND WITHIN COMBINED SOURCES

Rosalind Edwards, Susie Weller, Lynn Jamieson and
Emma Davidson

CHAPTER CONTENTS

5.1 Introduction: Why Work Across Multiple Datasets and Combined Sources?

The sharing and re-use of data is vital to accountability and transparency, and judgements of rigour, in qualitative research practice. Moreover, increasingly it is a requirement of receiving funding for primary qualitative research and an element of research funding calls. For example, the UK Economic and Social Research Council obliges researchers to offer datasets to the UK Data Archive and has an ongoing Secondary Data Analysis Initiative funding call (see https://esrc.ukri.org/funding/). Outside the UK too, datasets from qualitative studies are stored in central and local digital repositories and available for re-use, for secondary analysis (Corti, 2017), albeit these are not as extensive as archives of quantitative data. These developments mean that large amounts of qualitative data from multiple projects are now available for re-use and reassemblage to exploit their potential for opening up new questions that qualitative researchers may ask.

In this chapter we will be exploring the potentials and pitfalls of bringing together and conducting search activities across and within one large dataset comprising several sets of digitally archived qualitative data. Such a process involves both 'breadth-and-depth' analytic search strategies, including:

- across and within multiple sets of qualitative data from different archive sources to identify appropriate material for a project;
- the auditing and management of large volumes of data for analytic searches;
- keyword and preliminary thematic analytic searches within the combined corpus of data; and
- engaged analytic searches of selected cases.

Major contemporary online qualitative archival sources established internationally for data preservation and sharing are shown in Table 5.1 (see also the Registry of Research Data Repositories, www.re3data.org).

Table 5.1 Examples of online qualitative archival sources

The UK Data Archive	www.data-archive.ac.uk/
Finnish Social Science Data Archive	www.fsd.uta.fi/en/data/catalogue/quali_archived_by_title.html
Henry A. Murray Research Archive (Harvard)	https://murray.harvard.edu/
Irish Qualitative Data Archive	https://www.maynoothuniversity.ie/social-sciences-institute/research/iqda/
Northern Ireland Qualitative Archive	www.ark.ac.uk/qual/ageism/ www.ark.ac.uk/qual/conflict/

Swiss Data and Research Information Services	http://forscenter.ch/en/data-and-research-information-services/
Swiss Foundation for Research in Social Sciences	www.css.ethz.ch/en/services/datasets.html
Qualitative Data Repository	https://qdr.syr.edu/
Timescapes Qualitative Longitudinal Data Archive	http://timescapes-archive.leeds.ac.uk/

The qualitative materials that are lodged in these and other archives are an underused resource for secondary analysis but, as modern repositories, they have the advantage of including project documentation. This might consist of information about the research aims and findings, the project design and methodology, and the units and kinds of data stored alongside the data itself – in other words, descriptive, structural and administrative 'metadata' about the dataset. Indeed, in the UK the increasing emphasis on the re-use of data means that researchers may have to consider data storage, management, documentation and re-use potential at the research funding application stage.

These archives offer researchers the opportunity to identify and reanalyse a particular qualitative dataset, making it possible to ask questions from different conceptual, substantive and analytic preoccupations to those of the original researcher or research team who deposited it. Social research data archives also offer the possibility of conducting secondary data analysis across several, disparate qualitative studies, with interview transcripts, fieldnotes, etc. drawn from a number of studies merged together into one bespoke secondary qualitative dataset. There are potential gains from working across multiple studies that each provide information on the topic of interest to the secondary researcher. Key benefits include the ability to scope out new research questions that make use of the new possibilities of comparison and new grounds for claims to generalisability.

Advantage can be taken of differences between the studies to ask comparative research questions that could not be answered by the individual projects (Tarrant, 2016; Tarrant and Hughes, 2019). Strategic comparisons can be created using contextual metadata information about each study (see also Section 5.4). Sample characteristics could be the basis of comparison, for example using data gathered from one study of older people's experiences of care homes and data from another study of cared-for young people's experiences of residential care, to undertake a comparison of age-based generational care provision. Or an analytic comparison can be made across disciplinary differences, for example combining a study of experiences of crime using psychoanalytically oriented analysis of biography with another using narrative analysis, and/or with one using life course perspectives or oral history accounts (see also Irwin, Chapter 2).

Merging data from several discrete small-scale qualitative projects into one large dataset can also strengthen the basis of generalising from the data, making wider claims. Multiplying the number of small, unrepresentative samples, of course, will never add up to a representative sample in the empirical sense of the sample being statistically typical of a wider population. It is not this form of claim to generalisability that is a possibility. Rather, increasing the number of small samples and thus diversity of research participants can strengthen theoretical generalisation, in the form of claims that can be made about understanding how social processes work (Mason, 2018). Such generalisability posits that the detailed and holistic analysis that gives insight into how and why a certain process in social life unfolds in one way or another in a particular place and time may help understanding of similar processes in other settings. Further, the possibility of evidence-based generalisation can be built into the design for a merged qualitative dataset, giving the possibility of asking questions that test propositions and alternative argumentation. For example, claims about social change in couple relationships over time could be addressed and tested through undertaking comparison of datasets collected at different points in time, say the 1960s and 2010s, or from merged contemporary studies containing participants from different generations (Tarrant and Hughes, 2019).

In the rest of this chapter we will consider, in turn, the wider context and implications for working with large amounts of qualitative data for secondary analysis, and look at some examples of how other researchers have undertaken such analytic searches, before presenting our own breadth-and-depth strategy for analytic searches across multiple datasets and within combined sources (see also Davidson et al., 2018). We discuss how we merged and worked with all of the projects stored in one particular archive – the Timescapes Archive (http://timescapes-archive. leeds.ac.uk/) – which contains seven core empirical qualitative longitudinal projects documenting change and continuity in significant relationships and identities over time, with each project capturing different aspects of the life course, from childhood and youth, through starting families, to older age. There are caveats to working with large amounts of merged qualitative data from multiple sources and conducting analytic searching in this way, and so finally we will also cover the practical and conceptual implications and cautions.

5.2 Who has Conducted Analytic Searches of Large Amounts of Data Before, and How?

Researchers working with large amounts of qualitative data have undertaken analytic searches using a range of computational tools to conduct forms of analysis such as mapping word frequencies, co-locations and keyness to get a sense of the main themes across a dataset(s). Ken Benoit (e.g., Perry and Benoit, 2017), for example, has analysed large amounts of textual data from political speeches and other texts using R, which is a programming language and software environment for data mining and statistical computing (see www.r-project.org/). Versions of the techniques used, such as looking for 'topics' by constellations of words and comparing usage rates of words across groups of speakers, are more or less available in the many software products developed for textual analysis. Texts can be broken down into different constellations or types of words (e.g., by topic, or negative or positive words), and usage rates of words can be compared (e.g., comparing its appearance in government speeches and opposition speeches, or between ministerial and back-bench positions) (e.g., Perry and Benoit, 2017). Such techniques work with the breadth of the large volume of qualitative data identifying patterns, but do not engage with the depth of nuanced context and detailed process that is the hallmark of conventional qualitative research.

Other researchers have undertaken a more layered approach to dealing with relatively large volumes of qualitative data, edging towards deeper engagement in a two-step process. For example, in their study of the influence of gender, social class, age and illness type in the language of people talking about their experience of illness, Clive Seale and Jonathan Charteris-Black (2010) worked with a corpus of over 1000 transcripts from an existing dataset of interviews about illness and health experiences. They undertook a matched comparison using a sub-sample of 102 interviews where people talked about their experiences of cancer, and ordered them by age and gender to explore the way that men and women of different ages talked about this. Their first step of secondary analysis of these interviews involved an analytic search for keyword patterns in the texts using the WordSmith software (see www.lexically.net/wordsmith/), which was then followed by deeper qualitative analysis of interview transcripts around these patterns. Similarly, in their study of how people talk about poverty, Wendy Olsen and Jamie Morgan (2010) used NVivo for part of their work (see www.qsrinternational.com/nvivo/what-is-nvivo) to undertake a keyword search, subsequently grouping the keywords into sets of discourses each signifying a set of meanings or assumptions about poverty. They then studied these discourses in the interviews as a whole using in-depth methods. We will return to keyword searches and how the 'keyness' of a word can be judged in Section 5.3.3.1, and deep analysis of cases in Section 5.4.

For the most part, in the above instances, the researchers were working with a single dataset rather than analytically searching for and across multiple small-scale qualitative studies. Some years ago, Jennifer Mason identified the need for:

> appropriate qualitative ways to 'scale up' research resources currently generated through multiple small-scale studies, to fully exploit the massive potential that qualitative research offers for making cross-contextual generalisations. (2002: 3)

Working with two disparate datasets from the Timescapes Archive, which help-fully consists of thematically linked projects, has been one step in this direction. Sarah Irwin and Mandy Winterton (2012) worked with two Timescapes projects that carried data on identities and orientations to parenting. Rather than pursuing analytic searching on one combined 'big qual' dataset, these researchers kept the projects separate. They proceeded by reviewing the content of each dataset and reading all the interview transcripts from one set and then the other, and subse-quently pursued selected cases in the first dataset to then undertake comparisons with selected cases from the other set. Similarly, working with another two Times-capes datasets to explore men's care responsibilities in low-income families across generations, Anna Tarrant (2016) retained the separation of the projects before bringing them into conversation (see also Tarrant and Hughes, 2019). In contrast though, she identified a sub-sample from each of the studies (echoing Seale and Charteris-Black) based on certain criteria, developing case histories from multiple readings of the cases and then moving to a framework analysis to bring cases from each project into conversation. There have been other endeavours working across two archived datasets, with Jane Gray and colleagues (2013) identifying two datasets from the Irish Qualitative Data Archive that enabled them to take a gen-erational comparative approach to grandparent–grandchild relationships. They worked backwards and forwards across the different studies to develop a thematic analysis and then examined individual case studies.

A recurrent message emphasising the value of iterative analytic searching is clear from these secondary qualitative data analysis initiatives. But these practices also raise questions about appropriate approaches. Should researchers begin by searching extensively across all the available data before moving into intensive engagement, or should they start intensively from selected data and then move out to extensive analytic searching? And how, if at all, should a researcher move analytically between the different projects involved? Of course, there is no one 'right' way to work across different qualitative datasets: it will depend on the logic of the research questions posed and the type and amount of secondary data. Below we offer an approach to searching and working across more than two small-scale archived qualitative stud-ies that are merged into one large corpus while retaining qualitative integrity – our breadth-and-depth process that aims to meet this challenge.

5.3 Strategies, Examples and Techniques for Analytic Searching Across Multiple Datasets and Combined Sources

Below, we detail a breadth-and-depth process in analytic searching that supports dealing with a volume of qualitative data that exceeds the capacity of researchers to read it all, yet remains true to the principles underpinning the conventional repertoire of techniques of qualitative data analysis. We first cover analytic searching of archives for material to use and then merging and managing it, followed by discussion of the steps in our breadth-and-depth approach. We illustrate these steps by referring to our study, *Working Across Qualitative Longitudinal Studies: A Feasibility Study Looking at Care and Intimacy* (http://bigqlr.ncrm.ac.uk),[1] which worked across six archived empirical projects made available digitally for re-use in the Timescapes Archive. In particular, we draw upon our analysis of the meaning of 'moving home' for caring and intimacy practices across the life course where appropriate.

5.3.1 Identifying appropriate material from archived sources

The first step in our breadth-and-depth approach is exploring the data that are available in an archive or from several archives. It involves the qualitative secondary researcher searching different online archive sources, such as those identified in our introduction, to find appropriate qualitative material for their project. Researchers may be alerted to possible datasets via conversations with colleagues, reading published work on secondary analyses or via external sources, such as the media. The aim of this initial searching is to acquire a precursory understanding of the nature, quality and focus of the available small-scale datasets and their 'fit' with the secondary analytic research topic. This initial element of the process may be wide-ranging, for example, locating datasets on a broad topic area. Alternatively, it may be narrow, focused on searching for data to fit a specific substantive issue and set of research questions. As part of this initial identification of datasets it can also be useful to explore the publications and outputs produced by the original researchers.

Online archives can require researchers to register and sign an agreement or licence before they can access and download datasets. Usually these 'end user' terms and conditions include undertaking not to use the data for commercial purposes; to keep the data secure and only share it with registered users; to preserve confidentiality and not attempt to identify individuals, households or organisations in datasets; and to destroy all copies of the data once registered use is completed.

Different archives will have procedures that require specific ways of searching their databases. For example, the UK Data Service (UKDS) uses the 'Discover'

[1]The project was part of the ESRC National Centre for Research Methods research programme, funded under grant number ES/L008351/1; see www.ncrm.ac.uk/research/

search function for reviewing their data catalogue, filtering for qualitative data sources. The Timescapes Archive has a search function that recommends searching by project, concepts or descriptive word, enabling searches by criteria such as gender, employment status, age group, year of birth, ethnicity, and so on. An issue for most archival search functions though is that they are reliant on the keywords that the original researchers provided when they deposited their dataset, so there may be data that are of interest in archived material that are not returned by a descriptive word search. It also may not be possible to filter for qualitative data, thereby protracting the search strategy. An exception is QualiBank, accessed via the UKDS. In this collection all content can be searched in detail, although at the time of writing it comprises only a small collection of classic social research studies. Using international archives can raise further challenges of searching for terms in different/multiple languages or making appropriate translations.

When searching for and reviewing potential sources for inclusion, the researchers' questions set the criteria, the topic of study, and the geographic or linguistic context. These parameters form the driver for decisions about which datasets, or which parts of multiple small-scale datasets, to include or exclude from the larger, combined dataset to be constructed. We refer to this as our data assemblage. This unique assemblage may be seen as a new dataset, with its own methodological history and the potential to be curated and used by other researchers (see also Bornat, Chapter 8).

In our study, we surveyed the parameters of six of the core datasets deposited in the Timescapes Archive to gain a sense of the scope and nature of the datasets, and then moved on to map the studies, explore the state and volume of the data, view any contextual material and metadata available, log the research tools used and get an overview of the substantive emphasis of each project.

5.3.2 Organising, managing and storing multiple/complex datasets: Retaining context

Undertaking analytic searching of the content of large volumes of qualitative material requires careful organisation and data management. This is also important if an understanding of the context of the data production, or the circumstances in which a dataset was originally generated, is to be retained. Information relating to, for example, the purpose of the original project, the methods used, geographical location, and sample characteristics all provide insight into the context of production. Studying available contextual material not only aids the identification of relevant datasets with which to work but also, as we will discuss in Section 3.3, is valuable in the interpretation of data.

Attending to the context in which data is produced are central to the integrity of rigorous qualitative research, just as it is for quantitative 'big data'. In response to claims that bigger volumes of data offer 'better' or more accurate forms of knowledge, critics (e.g., boyd and Crawford, 2012; Halford and Savage, 2017) have called for the biases within big data to be acknowledged, and in particular for more attention to be paid to the context of its creation and use. For qualitative secondary data, discussion around context has formed part of wider debates between realist and constructivist perspectives regarding the nature of data as, respectively, transferable data representing knowledge that exists separate from its production, or non-transferable data that is tied to deep primary knowledge of its research production (Irwin and Winterton, 2012; Tarrant, 2016), and debates about the implications for primary and secondary researchers (Coltart et al., 2013; Irwin et al., 2014).

Organising, managing and storing multiple and complex datasets is important to enable the retention of context in future analytic searching of the merged dataset. An initial data audit allows for a comprehensive exploration of the volume, nature and type of data available in the selected datasets to lay the groundwork for analytic searching further on in the process. At this point, the data remains in its original datasets. The information recorded will depend on the secondary researchers' approach to sampling, analysis and the study design. Crucially, the amount of delving into the dataset required to uncover this information will depend on the extent and nature of information that the particular data archive (from which the data has been sourced) requires or does not require data depositors to provide, as discussed in Section 3.

In our own project we explored and catalogued the files available in each of our six chosen datasets to record the information on:

- the number and type of files available (i.e., pseudonymised transcriptions, visual material, fieldnotes);
- details of any embargoed materials (i.e., audio files, sensitive material);
- the number and type of cases (i.e., the units of analysis constructed by the original research teams such as individual or family group) and, because our dataset was longitudinal, participation in each wave of data collection;
- the metadata (i.e., descriptive, structural and administrative) and availability of contextual materials (i.e., fieldnotes, project guides or reports);
- sample characteristics including date of birth and gender;
- the geographical spread of the sample; and
- the keywords that the original researcher assigned to their dataset as a whole to enable archival searches.

We also documented the type of files and file names assigned. This part of the process gave us a sense of the state of the data, the nature of the original projects, an understanding of the structure of cases within the archive, and an insight into what our data assemblage might look like. It also revealed anomalies in the data landscape, such as gaps in contextual material, or unusual, misplaced or incorrectly labelled or categorised files. It was important then to manage the data that we were combining from the Timescapes projects through (i) the harmonisation of file names to aid retrieval; and (ii) the reorganisation of files from their original datasets into new groupings based on the substantive focus and chosen unit of analysis for cases.

In the example of our own study, the substantive focus, derived from our areas of interest and expertise, was on exploring the change in caring and intimate identities, relationships and practices by gender and over time. As our starting point we considered the question 'Do gendered vocabularies of care and intimacy change over historical and/or biographical time, and do they do this in different ways for women and for men?', which we developed into more specific questions later in the analysis once we had a sense of the parameters of the data assemblage (see Section 5.3.3.1). This initial phase of data organisation revealed that the majority of the metadata on gender and date of birth had been supplied by the original research teams and were held in the archive. We proceeded by cataloguing this information for each interviewee. It then became possible to reassemble the dataset, shifting from its original structure, which was organised by project, to one organised by age cohort and gender. It was at this point that the individual datasets became one new assemblage, and the basis upon which to undertake our substantive secondary analysis was complete.

So far we have addressed analytic searching to identify qualitative datasets to combine in a new project, and how to manage them – the foundations of working with merged sources. There is then the issue of how to search and deal with large amounts of qualitative data in a way that enables analysis of issues beyond the foci of the constituent parts, to combine extensive coverage with intensive illumination: a breadth-and-depth method.

5.3.3 Conducting keyword and preliminary thematic analytic searches

The entry point to analytic searching of assemblages of qualitative data in our breadth-and-depth method involves using computational text-mining approaches to conduct searches of keywords, or identify key concepts and themes (depending on the tools used) within the combined corpus of data.

5.3.3.1 Keywords and keyness

Keywords and keyness analytic searches are about breadth. They provide a map of the substantive surface of the large, merged, qualitative dataset, and point towards where to conduct preliminary deeper investigations.

Drawing on corpus linguistics, keywords are meaningful words that have particular salience (Baker, 2006). Salience is understood as demonstrated by occurring with higher frequency in the text than the norm, more than just by chance (for that particular corpus). 'Keyness' provides an indicator of the importance of the keyword (i.e., to what extent is it key in its context). Keyword analysis uses computation techniques that involve algorithm-driven sifting and sorting of words in search of associations, covering searches for word frequency, for themes based on word proximity and association, and for matching words to pre-given dictionaries or to an iteratively generated thesaurus of terms. An extensive and growing range of tools are available for this type of analysis. Examples include the programming language 'R' adopted by Benoit for his political text studies, the use of WordSmith by Seale and Charteris-Black in their study of gendered language about cancer, and Olsen and Morgan's use of NVivo in their study of talk about poverty (see Section 5.2).

In order to assess keyness, a benchmark of some kind is required to assess whether or not the keyword occurs with unusual frequency – a reference corpus to be used as the 'norm' against which keyness is calculated. For example, Olsen and Moore compared their dataset to the British National Corpus as a means of identifying the significance of particular words (see www.natcorp.ox.ac.uk), while Seale and Charteris-Black compared their selected sub-sample of accounts of cancer with the whole dataset containing accounts of illness and health experiences generally.

In our own study we used Leximancer (see https://info.leximancer.com/), specialist text-mining software designed to help the researcher find meaning in text. The software uses automated semantic analysis to identify word frequencies and co-occurrence, creating clusters of terms that are inclined to feature together in a text. It is premised on the idea that words relate to one another: that the terms surrounding a given word determine its meaning. Accordingly, Leximancer mines thousands of iterations to see how words 'travel together' through a text or set of texts (Gapp et al., 2013; Kivunja, 2013). From this mining, the package produces two-dimensional visual concept maps, akin to a network map. Working across our entire corpus we produced concept maps for both women and men, and for our gendered cohort groupings. Leximancer organises the key concepts visually into coloured coded themes with hotter colours (i.e., red, orange) relating to the strongest themes and the cooler colours (i.e., blue, green) denoting the least salient. This pointed us towards appropriate places to 'dig deeper' into the data.

The most salient themes were, to some degree, relatively obvious, reflecting the foci of the original projects. We identified 'home' as having significant meaning across the corpus (see Figure 5.1), and followed up on this as relevant to our interest in change in practices of care and intimacy over time, and differences between men and women. On closer inspection the relationship between 'home' and 'moved' seemed particularly important for all women, and even more salient for those born before 1950.

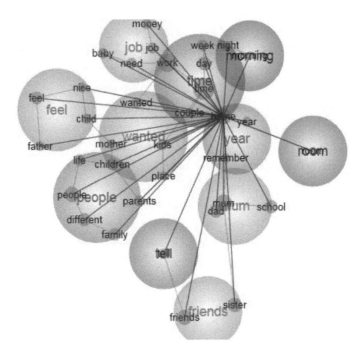

Figure 5.1 The theme and concept 'home' and its relationships to other key concepts (Leximancer screen shot)

Using text mining tools enabled us to conduct searches across a large qualitative volume of data and to identify key concepts and themes, particularly those we had not envisaged and/or had not featured explicitly in the focus of the original projects, such as our example of home.

5.3.3.2 Preliminary thematic searches

Preliminary thematic analytic searches are a step towards depth analysis. Keywords can be followed up and used to sample for further preliminary examination of particular issues to explore whether or not there is anything of interest underlying the keyword in the data. Preliminary thematic searches move on from word counts or word associations to start to identify implicit and explicit ideas within the data. As we argued earlier, working across large amounts of qualitative data from different datasets enables researchers to address a range of comparative research questions or test generalising claims about social processes. Such comparative and/or generalising aims for research mean that researchers need to focus on keywords that help them to fulfil these objectives. Keywords that appear clearly to be identified with the substance or theory of the secondary analysis research project in question are ones to follow up, although it is important not to discard all of those that do not seem directly relevant, because they may be insightful later on, once more in-depth analysis is underway.

Preliminary thematic analytic searching involves reading relatively short extracts from interviews that contain the keyword(s) or concept(s). The size of the extract of interview text in which the keyword appears will vary: enough to provide a clear sense of whether or not the content is related to the secondary analysis project's research questions. As a rough guide in our project we usually identified around 200 words. As the extracts are searched through analytically, some recurring or idiosyncratic themes may emerge, which can then be followed up. In other words, some surface patterns of meaning come through that are important for describing or understanding the issue under investigation.

In our analysis we identified the short extracts of text using Leximancer, though other programs can also perform this function. Differences in the gender and gender cohort-grouping concept maps were identified in relation to the salience afforded to 'home' and the relationship between 'home' and 'moving'. We then used Boolean searches using operator words such as 'AND', 'OR' or 'NOT' to combine keywords using these concepts (discussed further below). This showed us all the instances in our data assemblage where 'home' and 'moving' (including synonyms and stemmed words) appeared together in a two-sentence block. Leximancer's interface enables data extracts to be viewed in context; see Figure 5.2. Reviewing the segments of text surrounding the extracts, we were able to see whether the results of a search were relevant. In line with our interest in changing vocabularies of care and intimacy by gender and over time, we then exported and organised all of the extracts into gender and generation-cohort groupings. Informed by a review of the literature on moving home, we adopted a theoretical approach to sampling that combined our emphasis on exploring similarities and differences between/across cohort generations with a focus not merely on those who had moved home and the implications for caring and intimate relationships, but also on those 'left behind'.

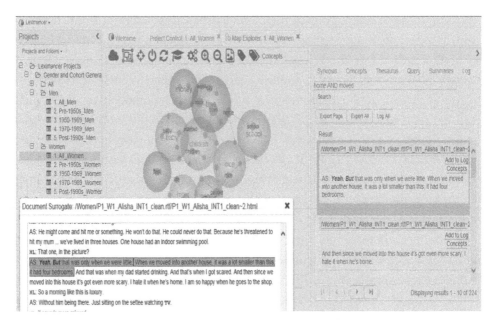

Figure 5.2 A concept map, outcomes of a Boolean query and the data extract-in-context (Leximancer screen shot)

The indications associated with the emergent preliminary themes may mean returning to the keyword identification to look into some others. Alternatively, there may be nothing of interest in the extracts behind the chosen keywords, or they are ambiguous or tangential, and a return to delving into other keywords is required. The breadth-and-depth method is an iterative process.

Once a theme or themes have been settled upon from the preliminary analytic searches, the next step involves several readings of the extracts in order to identify, sample and categorise cases of interest to explore in more depth. There is no exact recipe to follow here; it will depend on the number of extracts generated and the number of readings needed to generate a thematic analysis. In our own thematic analysis of data extracts concerned with moving home or being moved away from, we identified themes such as ambivalence and acceptance, and different temporal motions ranging from 'pendulum' moving back and forwards between homes (such as children or siblings going away to university and returning home every so often, or constant home moves connected with employment), 'conclusive' moving away completely (such as parents getting divorced or grandparents going into a care home), through to 'return' moving away and then back again over a longer period of time (such as adult children moving back to be near to elderly parents). Here is an illustrative data extract, showing the key sentences (in bold) and surrounding text:

Interviewer:	'Cos your family's been at the centre of your life since you've been 16, 17.
Sheila:	Yeah. Since I've been 17.
Interviewer:	So now, you've never really had this phase to think about what else you might want to do.
Sheila:	**I just now, I mean Sarah was the first** [of my children] **to leave home but that weren't too bad because she only moved two doors away. So that was it. And then Katie left.** Er, Steven left home. Anna left home. James left and, er, it just, it's going from eight and it was shrinking. You know what I mean? And I didn't know how I felt about it. I know that I've got to let them go because they're getting older. They need lives of their own. Everybody does. It's just that when I was raising them I never looked at that part. You know, you didn't look that far ahead. And then one day it just smacked you in the face, you know.
Interviewer:	So what do you think you might do?
Sheila:	I don't know. **I haven't got a, like I've said, I've still got three at home but like Louis' moving to** [a city] **soon so that will just leave Michael and Jo.**
Interviewer:	Who are at opposite ends.
Sheila:	Yeah. I don't think he's ever gonna leave home.

(Sheila, born 1961)

5.4 Working In-depth with Cases

The final stage moves fully into depth, from examining extracts of data to engaged analytic searches of selected whole cases or units of analysis. Cases are a unit of analysis that enables a close, detailed exploration of the complexity of a phenomenon under investigation in its various contexts. In the breadth-and-depth method, building on the preliminary thematic analytic search, particular cases are selected as fruitful to pursue in-depth because they hold the promise of insight into specific aspects of the social processes and meanings that are the focus of the secondary analysis project. Cases may comprise individuals and/or groups of connected individuals or other units of analysis, as fits the secondary research analytic focus. The guiding mechanism for decisions about what constitutes a case lies in the rubbing-together of the 'internal' intellectual purpose of the secondary researcher's project and the 'external' empirical parameters of the various sets of qualitative data available to them to create the merged corpus (see Davidson et al., 2018 for a further discussion of cases in the breadth-and-depth method; also Emmel, 2013). Which cases are selected from the data assemblage rests on the previous preliminary thematic analytic search in interaction with the researchers' epistemological and theoretical standpoint, and the substantive research topics and questions. Illuminative cases are not just those that are typical of preliminary analytic findings, but also those that are interesting, unusual or seem especially revealing of a set of understandings and circumstances.

The sort of in-depth interpretive analysis that is undertaken for this case level of analytic searching is a process that the majority of qualitative researchers will recognise, value and be comfortable with. It involves immersion in the data at a scale that uses the strengths of qualitative analysis. It is sensitive to changing context and to multi-layered complexity, and it focuses on rich data to represent intricate social realities and produce nuanced social explanations. There are a diversity of qualitative analytic strategies and in-depth techniques that qualitative researchers use to illuminate, variously, social meanings, subjectivities, activities, processes, constructions and discourses. Familiar methods of qualitative analysis include in-depth thematic analysis (Clarke and Braun, 2016), framework analysis (Ritchie and Lewis, 2003), grounded theory (Charmaz, 2014), narrative analysis (Holstein and Gubrium, 2012), conversation analysis (Sidnell, 2010) and discourse analysis (Fairclough, 2010). Which of these methods of analysis is adopted, or combination of them used, depends on the researchers' philosophical and conceptual approaches, the theoretical and substantive orientation of the research project, and the pragmatics of the forms of data being worked with.

Our own study was conducted from an interpretive epistemological approach. Our broader interest in comparisons of intimacy and care by gender and age cohort led us to focus on individuals and their interview transcripts as our cases. Our points for deeper excavation of the example of 'moving home' that we have been using for in-depth analytic searching in cases were chosen by the clusterings and configurations of keyness and the preliminary thematic analytic search process described above. We selected cases from different age cohorts and genders that enabled us to illuminate staying put and being moved away from, or moving home – whether 'pendulum', 'conclusive' or 'return' – as practices that are embedded in social relations and unfold over time rather than forming discrete events. We undertook a deep analysis of each of the selected cases that involved working with whole transcripts rather than extracts, undertaking in-depth thematic analysis, and then worked across cases to undertake a comparison by gender and age cohort in accounts of moving home.

5.5 The Implications of How You Search: Practicalities, Resources and Findings

Searching analytically across an assemblage of qualitative data from different sources requires a considerable investment of time and other resources across the research process. This means that any bid for funding breadth-and-depth 'big qual' analysis needs to take these into account in building the timetable, budget and case for support. Resources will include search software, some of which may be free such as R, or need to be purchased, such as NVivo or Leximancer. Either way, proficiency in the software is crucial, and investment in training and time to become proficient is crucial. Further, large volumes of qualitative data can require significant storage space, especially if audio and/or visual materials are involved. Many universities now have research file stores. Password-protected files on personal computers are another option. Cloud-based saving can be problematic in terms of data security and may also breach the terms of consent to use agreements for the source archives.

Crucially, the value of documenting all actions through all stages of searching cannot be stressed enough in pursuing a breadth-and-depth method of working. We noted the care that needs to be dedicated to organising, managing and storing multiple and complex datasets in Section 5.3.2. The breadth-and-depth approach to working with large data assemblages is iterative, moving backwards and forwards between stages as required. This means that it is important to document each action along the way meticulously, so that steps can be retrieved and retraced. This recording is necessary from start to finish, encompassing logging searches in the archives for potential component projects, cataloguing files and recording comprehensive information on the parameters of the project datasets, resaving documents where different projects may have saved their documents in different formats, harmonising document labelling, careful recording of keyword and preliminary thematic searches, and so on.

Overall then, working with merged qualitative datasets for secondary analysis is not a quick fix of time and other resources. It is a time-consuming process involving managing and familiarising oneself with a 'deluge of data' (Tarrant, 2016: 607).

5.6 Some Cautions about Analytic Searching

There are worries that the volume and procedures associated with big data create the temptation to dispense with any role for theoretically or substantively driven analysis. This is especially the case where the context for data is absent or difficult to obtain, such as tweets and some other social media, or data that are poorly archived (we could not have undertaken our analysis if data about gender and age cohort had been missing for example). These are caveats that need to be borne in mind when undertaking analytic searches with large amounts of qualitative data too.

Working across differently constituted datasets is likely to be challenging. This is not only because of the need to harmonise the different formats in which documents from distinct sets of projects may be saved, or manage the various types of data that may be involved, from text-based to visual to audio. The different epistemological and conceptual underpinnings of projects also need to be considered as they are brought into engagement. One example would be merging two projects that look at stepfamilies, where one is informed by an understanding of meaning as arising out of social interactions between people (involving interviews that pursue issues of negotiation between step-parents), while the other is rooted in role theory ideas about ascription (following up normative perspectives through questioning).

Reliance on computational text-mining approaches to conduct searches of key-words, or identify key concepts and themes within the combined, large corpus of qualitative data, runs the risk of terms that are not frequent utterances in people's accounts but yet are of huge significance potentially in denoting aspects of their lives being missed analytically, or keywords that do not 'travel together' yet may intersect not being identified, let alone alerts to unspoken issues. Our breadth-and-depth approach, however, goes some way towards mitigating such omissions. The subsequent move from a breadth analysis to in-depth readings of the data means that such solitary, apparently unconnected or muted elements of people's accounts of their lives may be identified.

5.7 Conclusion

Working with a large corpus made up of discrete qualitative datasets merged together is a worthy endeavour in that it offers the possibility of deriving added value from and enhancing the richness of research. Combining and working across multiple small-scale datasets also offers the possibility of new insights into social processes. We regard this way of working as a means of strengthening the use of comparison in qualitative research to extend and aid generalisability.

In this chapter we have aimed to convey how to undertake a 'breadth-and-depth' systematic and rigorous approach to 'big qual' analytic searching in a manner that maintains the integrity of qualitative work, pays attention to the context and richness of qualitative research, and provides the means of handling large volumes of detailed data. We have demonstrated the complex reality of how qualitative researchers can deal with these large volumes and multiple datasets.

As part of this, we have attempted to be mindful not to disregard small-scale qualitative studies; indeed we consider the breadth-and-depth approach explained here as a way of further bringing out the value of these. There is a risk that ideas about big data as 'better' recreate the divide between quantitative and qualitative approaches, and reassert the superiority of quantitative data. It is important that big data developments, and the big qualitative aspect to this created by merged datasets, do not marginalise and diminish small-scale studies. Our breadth-and-depth method seeks to recognise and value them, not least because it is small-scale studies that form the starting point for our analytic searching across and within sets of qualitative data from different archive sources, keyword and preliminary thematic analytic searches within the combined corpus of data, and engaged analytic searches of selected cases.

5.8 Pedagogical Resources

'Big Qual' project website - http://bigqlr.ncrm.ac.uk/   The website for the ESRC National Centre for Research Methods. The *Working Across Qualitative Longitudinal Studies: A Feasibility Study Looking at Care and Intimacy* project contains a number of resources, including a series of thoughtful guest blog posts by key figures in the field.

UK Data Archive - www.ukdataservice.ac.uk/use-data/teaching/teaching-resources/qualitative/   Practical information, exemplars and tips for using archived data in teaching qualitative and mixed methods, including ideas on sharing data with students, teaching resources and teaching case studies.

'Digging Deep' podcast - www.ncrm.ac.uk/resources/podcasts/mp3/NCRM_podcast_Weller2.mp3   The podcast provides an outline of our breadth-and-depth method for working across multiple archived qualitative projects.

Videos from the *Approaches to Analysing Qualitative Data: Archaeology as a Metaphor for Method* event:

Clive Seale - www.youtube.com/watch?v=mKzAA6ShO4E&t=3s

Maria Tamboukou - www.youtube.com/watch?v=nIObCJjKeNo&t=2s

Emma Davidson - www.youtube.com/watch?v=SXI638JhHGQ&t=2s

> Researchers working with different bodies of qualitative materials discuss how they approached their analysis, from a range of methodological perspectives, using the metaphor of archaeology to think about what lies 'underneath' the corpus of material being analysed.

Teaching how to analyse large volumes of secondary qualitative data - www.ncrm.ac.uk/resources/online/teaching_big_qual/   An online resource providing open education to support the development of research methods, teaching on the analysis of large volumes of secondary data, including handouts, podcasts, activities, quick guides and lesson planning patterns.

5.9 References

Baker, P. (2006) *Using Corpora in Discourse Analysis*. London: Continuum.

boyd, d. and Crawford, K. (2012) 'Critical questions for big data', *Information, Communication and Society*, 15(5): 662–79.

Charmaz, K. (2014) *Constructing Grounded Theory*, 2nd edn. London: Sage.

Clarke, V. and Braun, V. (2016) 'Thematic analysis', in E. Lyons and A. Coyle (eds), *Analysing Qualitative Data in Psychology*, 2nd edn. London: Sage. pp. 84–103.

Coltart, C., Henwood, K. and Shirani, F. (2013) 'Qualitative secondary analysis in austere times: Ethical, professional and methodological considerations', *Forum Qualitative Sozialforschung/Forum: Qualitative Social Research*, 14(1): Article 18. Available at: www.qualitative-research.net/index.php/fqs/article/view/1885/3493 (accessed 24 May 2019).

Corti, L. (2017) *A Year of Great Progress in Qualitative Data Archiving and Exchange*, Data Impact blog. Available at: http://blog.ukdataservice.ac.uk/2016-a-year-of-great-progress-in-qualitative-data-archiving-and-exchange (accessed 13 April 2017).

Davidson, E., Edwards, R., Jamieson, L. and Weller, S. (2018) 'Big data, qualitative style: A breadth-and-depth method for working with large amounts of secondary qualitative data', *Quality and Quantity*, 53(1): 363–76. Available at: https://link.springer.com/article/10.1007/s11135-018-0757-y (accessed 24 May 2019).

Emmel, N.D. (2013) *Sampling and Choosing Cases in Qualitative Research*. London: Sage.

Fairclough, N. (2010) *Critical Discourse Analysis: The Critical Study of Language*. Abingdon: Routledge.

Gapp, R., Stewart, H., Harwood, I.A. and Woods, P. (2013) 'Discovering the Value in Using Leximancer for Complex Qualitative Data Analysis', paper presented at the *British Academy of Management Conference (BAM2013)*, 10–12: 1–6. Available at: https://eprints.soton.ac.uk/351475/ (accessed 24 May 2019).

Gray, J., Geraghty, R. and Ralph, D. (2013) 'Young grandchildren and their grandparents: A secondary analysis of continuity and change across four birth cohorts', *Families, Relationships and Societies*, 2(2): 289–99.

Halford, S. and Savage, M. (2017) 'Speaking sociologically with big data: Symphonic social science and the future for big data research', *Sociology*, 51(6): 1132–48.

Holstein, J.A. and Gubrium, J.F. (2012) *Varieties of Narrative Analysis*. London: Sage.

Irwin, S. and Winterton, M. (2012) 'Qualitative secondary analysis and social explanation', *Sociological Research Online* 17(2): Art. 4. Available at http://www.socresonline.org.uk/17/2/4.html (accessed 24 May 2019).

Irwin, S., Bornat, J. and Winterton, M. (2014) 'Qualitative secondary analysis in austere times: A reply to Coltart, Henwood and Shirani', *Forum Qualitative Sozialforschung/Forum: Qualitative Social Research*, 15(1). Available at: www.qualitative-research.net/index.php/fqs/article/view/2100 (accessed 23 October 2019).

Kivunja, C. (2013) 'Qualitative data mining and knowledge discovery using Leximancer digital software', *Lecture Notes on Information Theory*, 1(1): 53–5.

Mason, J. (2002) 'Qualitative Research Resources: A Discussion Paper', prepared for the ESRC Research Resources Board [unpublished, obtained from the author].

Mason, J. (2018) *Qualitative Researching*, 3rd edn. London: Sage.

Olsen, W.K. and Morgan, J. (2010) 'Institutional change from within the informal sector in Indian rural labour relations', *International Review of Sociology*, 20(3): 535–53.

Perry, P.O. and Benoit, K. (2017) *Text with the Class Affinity Model*, London School of Economics and New York University. Available at: https://arxiv.org/abs/1710.08963 (accessed 24 May 2019).

Ritchie, J. and Lewis, J. (2003) *Qualitative Research Practice: A Guide for Social Science Students and Researchers*. London: Sage.

Seale, C. and Charteris-Black, J. (2010) 'Keyword analysis: A new tool for qualitative research', in L. Bourgeault, R. Dingwall and R. De Vries (eds), *The SAGE Handbook of Qualitative Methods in Health Research*. London: Sage. pp. 536–665.

Sidnell, J. (2010) *Conversation Analysis: An Introduction*. West Sussex, UK: Wiley-Blackwell.

Tarrant, A. (2016) 'Getting out of the swamp? Methodological reflections on using qualitative secondary analysis to develop research design', *International Journal of Social Research Methodology*, 20(6): 599–611.

Tarrant, A. and Hughes, K. (2018) 'Qualitative secondary analysis: Building longitudinal samples to understand men's generational identities in low-income contexts', *Sociology*, 53(3): 599–611.

SIX

COLLECTIVE QUALITATIVE SECONDARY ANALYSIS AND DATA SHARING: STRATEGIES, INSIGHTS AND CHALLENGES

Anna Tarrant and Kahryn Hughes

CHAPTER CONTENTS

6.1 Introduction

The increasing requirement of social researchers to archive datasets generated from research, alongside advances in methods of qualitative secondary analysis (or QSA), is creating new opportunities for greater innovation and flexibility in data re-use and approaches to qualitative analysis. One such opportunity is collective secondary data analysis, namely analysis within research teams assembled for the purposes of QSA. Collective QSA facilitated by the new and expanded data landscape described throughout this volume prompts new questions about what the processes in collective QSA might involve, and what the theoretical and methodological implications are of bringing data together via data sharing.

While the analysis of qualitative data in research teams is not uncommon (e.g., Oleson et al., 1994; Fernald and Duclos, 2005; Mauthner and Doucet, 2008) and reports on qualitative research are increasingly multi-authored (Richards and Hemphill, 2017), analytical processes are rarely described in research outputs or reported as a collective endeavour. Methods for conducting analysis in teams, as well as reconciling multiple interpretations of data, are seldom explicated, and research outcomes are usually presented as if all team members have the same perspectives and interpretations. Alternatively, researchers sole-author outputs in order to express their personal intellectual views. Collective approaches to QSA re-emphasise the necessity for reflexive attention to analytic procedure, practice and process in qualitative data analysis more generally (Mauthner and Doucet, 2008).

This chapter offers insight into how and why QSA might be conducted collectively and the opportunities that are opened up in sharing data. It does so via reflection on two data sharing workshops that brought together purposefully assembled teams of researchers and two existing qualitative datasets. The chapter documents advances in collective modes of QSA as follows:

1   a brief overview of key debates on QSA that situates new modes of collective analysis;
2   an overview of emerging collective qualitative secondary analysis activities and data-sharing;
3   worked examples of data sharing workshops run by the authors to facilitate collective secondary analysis, providing a template for future researchers;
4   explanation of the kinds of collective analysis that can be supported by data sharing workshops, including theoretical sampling and guided and critical conversation; and
5   reflections on some of the key challenges of analysing qualitative data collectively.

6.2 Existing Approaches and Interdisciplinary Uses

The data sharing workshops we developed, where we engaged in collective secondary analysis activities, built upon and extended a relatively recent but emerging debate on innovations in qualitative data sharing and collective analysis (Bornat et al., 2008; Elliott et al., 2013; Phoenix et al., 2016). Our approaches are rooted in the now well-established tradition of qualitative longitudinal (QL) research more generally, and also debates on data re-use and qualitative secondary analysis (QSA) both in the UK (Mauthner et al., 1998; Moore, 2007; Thomson et al., 2010, 2012; Irwin and Winterton, 2011a, 2011b; Bornat, 2013) and internationally (Åkerström et al., 2004; Dargentas, 2006; Corti, 2011; Jesser, 2011; Medjedović, 2011; Broom et al., 2012). These debates are characterised by a significant degree of critique and concern about the feasibility of secondary analysis of qualitative data, but they have also fostered the exploration of creative ways of working with archived qualitative data for purposes beyond which they were originally generated (Bishop, 2009; Bornat, Chapter 8). Pushing past the moralistic tones of early debate about whether QSA should even be done, reflections on how existing data might be used 'carefully, revealingly and reflexively' (Mason, 2007) within group settings, highlights an increasing ease with 'investigative epistemology' towards data. Qualitatively inclined researchers can 'be purposefully investigative with and about data, and be creative and interpretive in what they make from them' (2007).

Notably however, the processes and mechanics of, and arguments for, analysing existing qualitative data collectively are less rehearsed. There are clear exceptions, such as those with connections to the developments in QSA methodology under the ESRC-funded Timescapes programme of research (Neale and Bishop, 2012). This work was organised in two ways; meetings between original team members of pairs of projects, and whole-project residential meetings (Bornat et al., 2008; Irwin et al., 2012; see also Sarah Irwin, Chapter 2). Bornat et al. (2008) for example have reported on their pilot of a data sharing meeting between *Men as Fathers* (MAF) and *The Oldest Generation* (TOG) projects, which became the footprint for the subsequent models of data sharing employed by the authors, as Bornat et al. (2008) had intended. This workshop responded to one of the main aims of Timescapes, which was to consider how the linked collection and assembly of archived QL data might facilitate secondary and collaborative analysis activities, and draw out common and overlapping substantive themes (Irwin et al., 2012). Their report on the workshop illustrates both the process of running the workshops and how new interpretations and theorisations (serendipitous and planned) about fathering were developed, facilitated by bringing the two datasets into 'analytical conversation' (Irwin and Winterton, 2011a).

While Bornat et al. (2008) delineate the successes of their earlier workshop, another data sharing workshop between members of the *Intergenerational Exchange* (IGE) and TOG projects demonstrated the limitations of using other studies for the simple purposes of sample boosting. As explained elsewhere (Tarrant and Hughes,

2019), while (superficially at least) both studies researched the same familial generation, namely grandparents, discussions at the workshop confirmed that participants could not be shared between both studies, because of their differing ages. The IGE grandparents were aged 35-55 and the TOG grandparents were over the age of 75. These age differences were linked to the much shorter life expectancy of the IGE population because of their levels of disadvantage (Emmel and Hughes, 2010). Indeed, a key substantive finding of the IGE study was that as a result of the compression of generations in low-income families, linked to the younger age of becoming a parent or grandparent, the generational roles and identities of these kinship grandparents were not the same or even comparable to those of older grandparents. Workshops can therefore be productive in establishing the extent to which datasets can be aligned for the purpose of 'scaling up' through dataset compilation, or identify the epistemological work required to bring datasets into analytic conversation, if at all.

Data sharing workshops involving a purposeful assemblage of researchers with a shared interest in psychosocial methods have also been held to explore analytical opportunities and insights using existing data. Thomson et al. (2012), who include members of the originating research team for the Timescapes study *The Dynamics of Motherhood*, describe a model of data sharing premised on Irwin and Winterton's (2011a) insights, which advances consideration of ethical and epistemological complexities of this approach. Their work involved original project members and new researchers connected to Hollway's (2007, 2008) study *Becoming a Mother*. A key aim was to foreground emotion and affect both in the content of the existing data, and as experienced by the group of researchers working together. Adopting what they describe as a psychosocial method of reading data aloud in a group, they documented how their data was recontextualised in new times and places (in this case within a space of collective analysis), redefining data as both mobile and temporal, as 'travelling data'. Their collective work techniques, employed on observational data with a mother and baby, involved 'affectively attuned' (Thomson et al., 2012: 311) readings of the data, first as a large group, then as smaller groups that focused on specific aspects of the case. This process of data sharing and re-use provided additional weight to arguments 'that temporal processes in research can help reveal the emotional undercurrents that connect researchers, subjects, and the changing times and places of the analytic process' (Thomson et al., 2012: 319). The approach favoured by Thomson and her colleagues privilege group forms of working, recognising in them 'the potential for enhanced creativity, insight and pleasure' (Thomson et al., 2012: 9).

Collaborative workshops have also been held for the purpose of exploring what methodological lessons might be learnt in bringing together datasets generated by two different research teams. Members of the NOVELLA[1] research node offer an example of collective analysis, which they have described and assessed in recently published working examples of group analysis employing narrative approaches (Elliott et al., 2013; Phoenix et al., 2016). They describe their approach as an 'analytic procedure that resulted when two research teams came together to build their research capacity by trying out each other's analytic methods collectively' (Phoenix et al., 2016). Their review of the existing literature draws out six benefits of group analysis. They suggest that:

- analysis is more creative when different interpretations are brought to bear on data;
- the analytical process and researcher reflexivity become more visible, meaning that interpretation is more transparent and accountable;
- political inequalities and social difference can be more easily identified;
- data can be re-rendered as 'strange' to primary analysts thus highlighting alternative interpretations;
- it can support the building of research skills; and finally
- it can enable multi-disciplinary knowledge sharing beyond research teams (Phoenix et al., 2016).

Their reflections on the practical and organisational issues encountered during their own practice of group analysis further highlighted that group analysis rendered the 'art of interpretation' (Denzin, 1994, quoted by Phoenix et al., 2016) more visible as discussion between group members helped to reveal their individual experiential resources as researchers. The process also aided the group in noticing what was originally unnoticed in data (although this can be uncomfortable for primary teams); in processing emotional experiences of research; in confirming the porous boundary between primary and secondary analysis; and in developing a detailed understanding of the case.

6.3 Collective Secondary Analysis and Data Sharing: A Rationale

Rooted in this existing literature about good models of practice and convinced by the possibilities afforded by data sharing, Anna held two workshops for her Leverhulme Trust study *Men, Poverty and Lifetimes of Care* (MPLC) funded under their Early Career Fellowship scheme (October 2014 to June 2018, grant number

[1]NOVELLA stands for 'Narratives of Varied Everyday Lives and Linked Approaches', comprising an interdisciplinary team of researchers funded as part of the ESRC National Centre for Research Methods.

ECF-2014-228). This study sought to investigate men's care responsibilities in low-income families and localities across the life course using a creative mix of qualitative methods, including QSA. Workshop 1 aided in establishing the study, embedding QSA in the research design, and Workshop 2 supported subsequent analytic work for the purpose of substantive advance (see Tarrant, 2016; Tarrant and Hughes, 2019, forthcoming). Transcripts from two datasets in the Timescapes Archive were brought together for discussion at each workshop. These datasets were *Intergenerational Exchange* (IGE) and *Following Young Fathers* (FYF). As above, IGE examined the experiences of grandparents on a low-income urban housing estate in a northern English city. This dataset included the voices of grandfathers who were providing care to grandchildren. However, the experiences of these men had not been the main focus of the original analysis that was conducted and published by the IGE team, thus providing an opportunity for secondary analysis. FYF examined the lives of young and teenage fathers aged 25 and under, ten cases of which were identified by the research team in outputs as socially disadvantaged (Neale et al., 2015). These were theoretically sampled by Anna following Workshop 1 and analysed for the MPLC study. The aim of bringing transcripts from these datasets together was to explore whether it would be possible to examine men's care responsibilities in low-income families from the perspectives of multiple generations, and to consider the extent to which the datasets might be complementary.

Researchers involved in designing and conducting the IGE and FYF studies[2] were invited to participate, all of whom were based at local universities. Prior to the workshops, Anna held conversations with researchers from both teams to gain their insights about the substantive focus and orientation of each study and to establish whether bringing the two datasets together might be a fruitful task. Following these consultations, it was decided that there were opportunities for her to use QSA on the datasets to refine the questions for her MPLC study. Anna decided that data sharing workshops had the potential to enhance the process of familiarisation with the datasets. Further, the workshops could be used to determine the feasibility of establishing meaningful 'analytic conversation' between the two datasets by creating a space for dialogue with and between those who produced them. Anna's early decision to run Workshop 1, in particular, was also informed by her reading of Irwin and Winterton (2011a) who suggest that in order

---

[2]The IGE data originators are Dr Kahryn Hughes and Prof. Nick Emmel (University of Leeds). The FYF data originators are Prof. Bren Neale (University of Leeds), Dr Carmen Lau Clayton (Leeds Trinity University), Dr Laura Davies (Leeds Beckett University), Dr Esmee Hanna (De Montfort University) and Linzi Ladlow (University of Leeds).

to conduct secondary analysis effectively and to make valid and reliable knowledge claims, the following competencies are required and must be developed by those using the data:

- a detailed understanding of the research projects;
- an understanding of the structure of the project data;
- a familiarisation strategy with the project data as a whole; and
- an approach for working *across* datasets that are not directly comparable, but which brings them into 'conversation' in a meaningful way.

The main goal of Workshop 1 was therefore to explore the possibilities of cross-project work involving bringing the two datasets together. In addition, the process of refining the research questions for the MPLC study was initiated and worked alongside a number of other activities designed to clarify the research design and establish access to the field (see Figure 6.1). Workshop 2 aimed to consolidate this work and to explore and confirm theoretical, substantive and methodological issues and outcomes in analysing within and across the datasets.

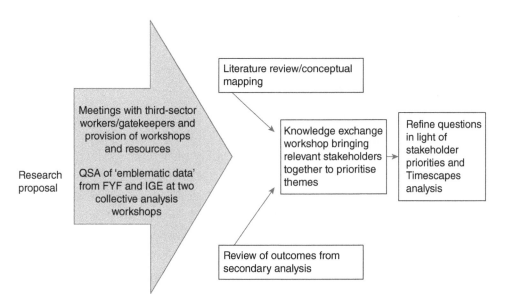

Figure 6.1   Process of refining research questions for MPLC

The two data sharing workshops consequently had shared and distinct rationales. Both had a mutual aim of enhancing the familiarisation process and also to bring together researchers from the two studies to interrogate their data afresh via guided reflections on shared insights from both sets of data. While the two workshops were run as separate events, they were thematically and practically linked and served the various substantive and methodological interests of the group members. They differed in that where Workshop 1 focused on exploring whether or not it would be feasible to bring together data from IGE and FYF, Workshop 2 operated with the knowledge established by Workshop 1 that this was achievable. Workshop 2 was therefore designed to guide researchers to test and confirm ideas using additional cases from each dataset by bringing new lines of enquiry and interpretation to bear on them.

6.4 Collective Secondary Analysis Activities

Each workshop was distinctively structured to generate novel analytical strategies and insights via collective qualitative secondary analysis (QSA). The team members participated in a number of distinct activities that organise this section of the chapter. The first describes the invitation process and the questions posed to the participants to encourage them to engage in theoretical sampling from the IGE and FYF datasets. The second describes how the workshops were run via guided conversation, followed by a third section explaining the new modes of analysis engaged in by the participants, which we define as a process involving 'critical conversation'.

6.4.1 Theoretical sampling

Researchers from IGE and FYF were invited to participate by Anna, prior to each workshop. Meeting requests were sent to each individual, providing an overview of the substantive focus of her research, the aims of the workshop and the requirements of each of the attendees. The composition of each workshop differed according to researcher availability, but all were able to attend at least one workshop. For both workshops, the team members were asked to sample two transcripts from their datasets in advance of the meeting that they considered 'emblematic cases' (Thomson et al., 2014) linking to the overall interests and aims of MPLC. Where team members were not available or able to attend the workshops, they still had some input into the process by being involved in selecting the transcripts. The process of asking the IGE and FYF team members to choose transcripts meant that each of the teams were tasked with theoretically sampling from their datasets prior to the workshops. In this way, they were implicated in the process of assembling the workshop data (in this case transcripts) and creating a small 'sample'.

At this stage, members were also sent a list of open-ended questions to guide their choices and emphasise the focus of the MPLC study on men's care practices in low-income contexts, over the life course. The questions for both workshops asked participants to consider a range of issues including: whether project data (in IGE and FYF) could offer meaningful insights into men's care practices and trajectories; which transcripts in their datasets could do this most effectively; brief notes on decision-making about the choice of transcripts to understand theoretical orientation towards the datasets and the aims of MPLC; and how the data originators were conceptualising care.

Once the transcripts had been selected and received by Anna, approximately two weeks prior to the workshops, they were circulated to the attendees along with a brief description of each case (archived pen portraits made this process quicker). This allowed enough time for each group member to read through those transcripts sampled from the datasets that they were not involved in generating. However, we recommend a longer period of time to engage fully with the data, as identifying and selecting transcripts is both labour intensive and time consuming (Gillies and Edwards, 2005; Wilson, 2014).

6.4.2 Running the workshops: Guided conversation

Workshop 1 was structured around two questions to ensure productive outcomes, and frame and guide the conversations. Anna was Chair, and sought to move between the position of primary and secondary researcher (Tarrant, 2016). This involved asking for clarifications as a secondary researcher about the datasets and choice of transcripts, while seeking to make meaningful conceptual connections between the work for the MPLC study and the two extant studies to inform the next empirical project as a primary researcher. The questions that framed these discussions were as follows:

1   What can we understand about men and care simply from these transcripts?
2   What else do we need to know?

This second question enabled the IGE and FYF researchers to input in ways that may have been unanticipated by the Chair. In asking these questions, we brought a new set of theoretical questions and concerns to bear on these existing datasets. Shared themes were identified, as well as themes that were not followed up in depth as lines of enquiry in either study (see Tarrant, 2016).

Workshop 2 was chaired by both Anna and Kahryn, the MPLC study mentor and second author, for the purposes of interrogating a shared set of questions. The sampling criteria for the workshop transcripts were also guided and framed by the substantive focus of MPLC, which had evolved in part prompted by the discussions in Workshop 1 and subsequent analytical work, to explore gendered routes through poverty over the life course and the roles of familial generations in mediating that process (Tarrant, 2016). Choices were guided too by Kahryn's methodological questions, including:

1   How far do the temporal frames of the young fathers in FYF and the grandparents in IGE mesh?
2   Can the grandparents in IGE stand as 'proxies' for the parents of the young fathers in FYF?
3   What emerges when bringing these datasets into conversation (in relation to new knowledge, insights and understanding of the compatibility of the datasets)?

Kahryn's questions for Workshop 2 were driven by the apparent failure of the workshop between IGE and TOG to provide a pragmatic means of sample boosting, as described earlier, and were more exploratory in their conception, seeking to establish how far *theoretical* samples could be developed by bringing the two datasets together.

Anna recorded the conversations in both workshops in the form of written notes, and made an audio recording of Workshop 2. The audio recording, to which all group members consented, proved particularly helpful because it supported the Chair/s to engage more directly in the conversations. Records of both meetings have also significantly informed later work and analysis.

6.4.3 Critical conversations

We describe the collective mode of analysis in each workshop as a form of critical conversation, characteristic of Mason's (2007) 'investigative epistemology'. These critical conversations supported a process of theory building central to this epistemological approach, enabling us to explore how and why various events and episodes occurred in the data. This was the basis for establishing meaningful analytical conversation across the datasets. Discussion at both workshops moved between focus on specific segments of text within transcripts, to the relevance of the material for conceptual and theoretical development. Therefore, we did not conduct multiple micro-analyses of a specific text, as others have done (Frost et al., 2010; Phoenix et al., 2016). We focused instead on what happens when bringing data together in this way, and the practical affordances and challenges of this sort of group analysis. In bringing datasets together, we also worked both within and across them, exploring patterns and themes within IGE or FYF and then considering the extent to which these were also prevalent in the other dataset. This process enabled interrogation of whether, and how far, meaningful analytical conversation between datasets was possible. The themes identified included: narratives of journeys to 'good' (grand)parenthood; fear in interactions with social services in low-income families; the use of children as weapons within and across generations; and concerns over the micro-management of money (see also Tarrant, 2016). This process prompted additional analytic work beyond the workshops whereby we sought to establish the extent of data linkage and complementarity between both datasets, starting with depth analysis of specific cases then expanding to a wider breadth reading (Tarrant and Hughes, 2019). We have loosely termed this a 'breadth to depth to breadth' approach, where breadth is across two datasets rather than as it is described in Edwards et al. (Chapter 5) across a very much larger aggregation of numerous datasets that comprise 'big qual' data (see also Davidson et al., 2019).

As well as fora for collective analysis, the workshops also provided opportunities for collegial debate in which the IGE and FYF team members defended and clarified the theories shaping their understanding of the data sampled. In so doing, the group acted as 'critical friends', where interchanges were underpinned by 'stakeholder ethics' (Neale, 2013). The pragmatics and application of 'stakeholder ethics' additionally formed the basis of some of the discussion in Workshop 2. The collaborative QSA in these workshops involved a process of negotiation and consent requiring buy-in from all team members, from a specific ethical orientation. These workshops were largely productive and enjoyable, and they facilitated engagement with data for those who were not research active at the time. In working ethically, several of the team members reflected that individual connections to, and understandings of, data are not necessarily subsumed by the shared experience and relational dynamics of the group, but work to illuminate and confirm individual intellectual directions – a key affordance of this methodological approach.

6.5 Implications of Data Sharing and Collective QSA for Research Practice

The workshops provided a number of different analytical opportunities for each of the team members. For Anna, as a researcher with no prior involvement in either the IGE or FYF studies, the conversations informed the research design for MPLC (Tarrant, 2016), which built directly out of the analytical work that took place in Workshop 1. The other group members, who had each been involved with the original studies under Timescapes, were tasked with asking new methodological questions about working with QL data that are oriented to time, by bringing data from a dataset they were involved in generating together with a dataset created by others. This process provided members with opportunities both to explain and defend early analyses of the data while also testing out ideas about previously unexplored substantive areas and lines of enquiry engendered by bringing differently constituted data into analytic conversation. In their orientation to questions posed by MPLC, bringing datasets together 're-rendered strange' (Phoenix et al., 2016) both the IGE and FYF data, and supported alternative interpretations. Although sampling criteria were established prior to the workshops, the process of theoretical sampling thus enabled the broadening and intensification of interpretation for each researcher via reconstruction and recontextualisation (Moore, 2007). In the workshops, this involved recontextualisation via new questions to produce new interpretations; and also by the recontextualisation of data and extant analyses within a newly constituted (albeit modest) dataset, and purposefully assembled research team. These workshops were therefore distinctive in that, unlike other approaches (described in Section 6.2), we did not seek to develop a single group analysis but instead sought to tease out answers to our own questions, identify avenues for new research, and explore afresh long-held interpretations of the data. Subsequent to the workshops and promoted by the discussions, Anna and Kahryn furthered their collaborative analysis as a pair by building on shared substantive interests (Tarrant and Hughes, 2019).

In the process of conducting collective QSA, combining the data and exploring its complementarity we were also able to look at where the 'edges' of our sample might be. This was a process of casing methodology (Emmel and Hughes, 2009), where we brought theory, sample and context into critical dialogue. In our workshops, meaning-making occurred because each team had already sampled according to a set of questions, prompting the sampling of complementary data. However, each researcher's analysis and theoretical 'take' on the analyses as they emerged remained individual. Researchers in effect still have their own stories to tell from research, despite the collective, collaborative and shared meanings they generate. It has been argued that meaning-making processes employed in data analytic sessions by research teams is a hermeneutic practice, which relies on cooperative, embodied and situated practices that are reflexively intersubjective (Meyer and Meier zu Verl, 2013; Phoenix et al., 2016). In other words, the process of collective QSA requires researchers to reflect on who they are in the research process.

We would suggest, however, that while this view of collective analyses may provide an additional analytic resource, it also raises additional challenges for reconciling analyses where data is interpreted in multiple ways by different researchers. Despite the benefits of working as a collective, there was some agreement between group members that this type of analysis is probably most valuable for identifying major themes/structural issues rather than in-depth understandings of individual participants' lived experiences.

The workshops thus represented a new wave of engagement with existing data, in that they involved researchers from the original or 'generating teams' in a process of 'creative scholarship' (Mauthner and Doucet, 2008). This particular assemblage of researchers affirmed the 'fuzzy boundaries' between primary and secondary research teams and contributed to establishing a broader culture of cross-team working, data sharing and creativity in knowledge production (Moore, 2007; Phoenix et al., 2016).

6.6 Cautionary Tales

Overall, we would argue that the investigative and reflexive sensibility adhered to by the participants at the workshops ensured that they were productive in numerous ways. There is still need, however, to remain critical and aware of the impracticalities of collective analysis in data re-use. As Fernald and Duclos (2005) report, a number of issues can occur in the collaborative efforts of research teams that influence team or collective analysis. These include changes in team membership, and differences in the analytical styles, philosophies, training, experience and skills of team members. The collegiate and exploratory stance adopted in our workshops helped to ameliorate some of these issues but are worth addressing early in the process of any collective intellectual endeavour where multiple researchers stake a claim to data. Phoenix et al. (2016, citing Smithson et al., 2015) also reflect that while face-to-face consensus can be built within the context of a data sharing workshop, within group settlements may be contingent. In fact, the process of group analysis is likely to be more emotionally difficult than is apparent in a workshop, linked in part to the hybrid of theoretically informed interpretations it produces. As authors, we spent a great deal of time considering how to write about the workshops, and thinking through the ethics of how to appropriately acknowledge the intellectual property of those who took part, and to distinguish these from our own in subsequent work and publications.

Unsurprisingly, there are few reports on workshops that are unproductive or produce limited output. However, insights from the IGE and TOG workshop were that it is important to interrogate how bringing datasets together may *not* produce the desired outcomes. Interrogating why the studies were not able to sample boost by drawing on each other's participants, enabled greater insight into the socio-economic contexts and histories of those in each study population. Distinct differences between the grandparents in each study, linked to age and class in particular, meant that the datasets did not mesh. Thinking positively, the two projects in combination covered a remarkably wide range of experience of grandparenthood and later life; thinking rather more negatively, there was little overlap in the accounts of the everyday being collected (IGE and TOG workshops report, unpublished). This may work as a cautionary tale, but it points to how different sets of questions may help to establish alternative and more productive lines of enquiry. In the contexts of the workshops discussed in this chapter, the authors have had to do a great deal of subsequent work as individuals and in collaboration to establish how the datasets might be linked. Workshops 1 and 2 predominantly supported relatively superficial lines of enquiry that required much more intensive later work.

Finally, the boundaries between primary and secondary analysis have been questioned in debates about QSA, and are considered to be blurred rather than easily defined (e.g., Moore, 2007). In the workshops, members of the IGE and FYF research teams were able to clarify and explain how their studies were designed and how their chosen transcripts for the workshops sit within the broader study as primary researchers while also testing out new interpretations prompted by insights from the other study. However, our own experience suggests that data sharing workshops may be limited with regards to how much they can achieve without subsequent analytic work. Indeed, a related issue is that data sharing workshops are time and resource intensive and require buy-in from all team members. We were fortunate that at the time of the workshops all of the researchers were working locally and were able to attend at least one workshop (although only two of us were able to attend both; see also Phoenix et al., 2016).

6.7 Conclusion

The reflections in this chapter suggest that data sharing workshops provide a robust yet flexible model for facilitating creativity in data re-use and fostering potentially productive relationships between several researchers as they engage in collective modes of analysis. The existing literature and two workshop examples discussed here highlight that group or collective QSA can be employed for multiple purposes, with benefits for researchers even if they do not have a direct relationship to the data. In contrast to previous researchers, our workshops supported various activities including:

1   New modes of analysis, in which data from multiple datasets were shared, theoretically cased and brought together to establish 'meaningful analytic conversation' (Irwin and Winterton, 2011a);
2   Team members testing out their ideas through the enactment of guided and critical conversations;
3   Multiple interpretations of the same data being confirmed, refined and developed.

In running the workshops, we were able to engage in and elaborate a robust process of QSA via methods of theoretical sampling and guided and 'critical conversation'. This supported us to develop new analytical modes of collective QSA, where we considered both the process of data production – in the original studies, and in our own collaborative work – and the content of the data. This approach to collective QSA also supported us to consider what is distinctive about this methodology as a particular mode of knowledge production and how we might situate it in the broader debate around the usefulness and challenges of QSA more generally.

While requiring considerable time and input from a number of researchers, a key point we would make, also highlighted by several of the group members, is that the substantive and theoretical interests of this diverse group of researchers were not subsumed within the process, but enhanced. The differing standpoints of each researcher on the same data proved informative and allowed new lines of enquiry that were unique to each study to emerge. This finding has implications for teaching, where extracts can be taken from our data and given to students, who may produce new and unexpected interpretations (see Haaker, Chapter 7). This mode of working highlights the importance of multiple perspectives for making sense of data and heightens awareness of how analyses are inevitably dialogic (whether with others collectively, or with oneself over time in the context of a continuously changing academe) rather than naturally occurring.

We would suggest that this adds further weight and justification for archiving data and engaging in data re-use and sharing. Multiple interpretations do not have to happen with the originating team, nor at a given historical point; it unfolds over time, where time itself changes the meaning of the data via historical comparison. Pragmatic and substantive linkages between datasets may enhance the possibility of QSA. For example, of the particular datasets in the Timescapes Archive, six of the empirical studies were conducted simultaneously over several years, seven studies were thematically linked and included shared questions, and participants in each study were explicitly encouraged to reflect on the times through which they lived (see Edwards and Irwin, 2010).

Nevertheless, we emphasise that this reflexive discussion of collective QSA and data sharing both extends, and provides impetus for, further exploratory work and debate about the potential of collective QSA and collaborative modes of working in processes of knowledge production and theoretical refinement.

6.8 Pedagogical Resources

Men, Poverty and Lifetimes of Care blog – http://menandcare.blogs.lincoln.ac.uk

The Timescapes Archive – www.timescapes.leeds.ac.uk/archive/index.html

Tarrant, A. (2018) *Researching Men's Care Responsibilities in Low Income Families Using Qualitative Secondary Analysis*, SAGE Research Methods Case – http://dx.doi.org/10.4135/9781526427526.

Elliott, H., Brannen, J., Phoenix, A., Barlow, A., Morris, P., Smart, C., Smithson, J. and Bauer, E. (2013) *Analysing Qualitative Data in Groups: Process and Practice*, NOVELLA Working Paper: Narrative Research in Action – http://eprints.ncrm.ac.uk/3172/1/jointanalysispaper200813.pdf

6.9 **References**

Åkerström, M., Jacobsson, K. and Wasterfors, D. (2004) 'Re-analysis of previously collected material', in C. Seale, S. Silverman, J.F. Gubrium and G. Gobo (eds), *Qualitative Research Practice*. London: Sage. pp. 314–27.

Bishop, L. (2009) 'Ethical sharing and reuse of qualitative data', *Australian Journal of Social Issues*, 44(3): 255–72.

Bornat, J. (2013) 'Secondary analysis in reflection: Some experiences of re-use from an oral history perspective', *Families, Relationships and Societies*, 2(2): 309–17.

Bornat, J., Bytheway, B. and Henwood, K. (2008) *Report of Meeting between Timescapes' 'Men as Fathers' and 'The Oldest Generation' Projects*, University of Cardiff, 21 July. Available at: www.timescapes.leeds.ac.uk/assets/files/report-fathers-oldest-generation-projects-july08.pdf (accessed 24 May 2019).

Broom, A., Cheshire, L. and Emmison, M. (2012) 'Qualitative researchers' understandings of their practice and the implications for data archiving and sharing', *Sociology*, 43(6): 1163–80.

Corrigan, O. (2003) 'Empty ethics: The problem with informed consent', *Sociology of Health and Illness*, 25(7): 768–92.

Corti, L. (2011) 'The European landscape of qualitative social research archives: Methodological and practical issues', *Forum: Qualitative Social Research*, 12(3): Art. 11. Available at: http://nbn-resolving.de/urn:nbn:de:0114-fqs1103117 (accessed 24 May 2019).

Dargentas, M. (2006) 'Secondary analysis and culture of disputation in European qualitative research', *Forum Qualitative Sozialforschung/Forum: Qualitative Social Research*, 7(4): Art. 9. Available at: www.qualitative-research.net/index.php/fqs/article/view/197/435 (accessed 24 May 2019).

Davidson, E., Edwards, R., Jamieson, L. and Weller, S. (2019) 'Big data, qualitative style: A breadth-and-depth method for working with large amounts of secondary qualitative data', *Quality and Quantity*, 53(1): 363–76.

Edwards, R. and Irwin, S. (2010) 'Lived experience through economic downturn in Britain – Perspectives across time and across the life-course'. *Twenty-First Century Society*, 5(2): 119–24.

Elliott, H., Brannen, J., Phoenix, A., Barlow, A., Morris, P., Smart, C. and Bauer, E. (2013) *Analysing Qualitative Data in Groups: Process and Practice*, NOVELLA Working Paper: Narrative Research in Action: Thomas Coram Research Unit. Available at: http://eprints.ncrm.ac.uk/3172/1/jointanalysispaper200813.pdf (accessed 24 October 2019).

Emmel, N. and Hughes, K. (2009) 'Small-N access cases to refine theories of social exclusion and individuals and access to socially excluded individuals and groups', in D. Byrne and C.C. Ragin (eds), *The SAGE Handbook of Case-based Methods*. London: Sage. pp. 318–30.

Emmel, N. and Hughes, K. (2010) '"Recession, it's all the same to us son": The longitudinal experience (1999–2010) of deprivation', *Twenty-First Century Society*, 5(2): 171–81.

Fernald, D.H. and Duclos, C.W. (2005) 'Enhance your team-based qualitative research', *Annals of Family Medicine*, 3: 360–4.

Frost, N., Nolas, S.M., Brooks-Gordon, B., Esin, C., Holt, A., Mehdizadeh, L. and Shinebourne, P. (2010) 'Pluralism in qualitative research: The impact of different researchers and qualitative approaches on the analysis of qualitative data', *Qualitative Research*, 10(4): 1–20.

Gillies, V. and Edwards, R. (2005) 'Secondary analysis in exploring family and social change: Addressing the issue of context', *Forum: Qualitative Social Research*, 6(1): 44.

Hollway, W. (2007) 'Afterword', *Infant Observation*, 10: 331–6.

Hollway, W. (2008) 'The importance of relational thinking in the practice of psycho-social research: Ontology, epistemology, methodology, and ethics', in S. Clarke, H. Hahn and P. Hoggett (eds), *Object Relations and Social Relations: The Implications of the Relational Turn in Psychoanalysis*. London, UK: Karnac.

Irwin, S. and Winterton, M. (2011a) *Debates in Qualitative Secondary Analysis: Critical Reflections*, Timescapes Working Paper 4. Available at: www.timescapes.leeds.ac.uk/assets/files/WP4-March-2011.pdf (accessed 24 May 2019).

Irwin, S. and Winterton, M. (2011b) *Timescapes Data and Secondary Analysis: Working Across the Projects*, Timescapes Working Paper 5. Available at: www.timescapes.leeds.ac.uk/assets/files/WP5-March-2011.pdf (accessed 24 May 2019).

Irwin, S., Bornat, J. and Winterton, M. (2012) 'Timescapes secondary analysis: Comparison, context and working across datasets', *Qualitative Research*, 12(1): 66–80.

Jesser, A. (2011) 'Archiving qualitative data: Infrastructure, acquisition, documentation, distribution. Experiences from WISDOM, the Austrian Data Archive', *Forum: Qualitative Social Research*, 12(3): Art. 18.

Mason, J. (2007) '"Re-Using" qualitative data: On the merits of investigative epistemology', *Sociological Research Online*, 12(3). Available at: www.socresonline.org.uk/12/3/3.html (accessed 24 May 2019).

Mauthner, N.S. and Doucet, A. (2008) 'Knowledge once divided can be hard to put together again: An epistemological critique of collaborative and team-based research practices', *Sociology*, 42(5): 971–85.

Mauthner, N.S., Parry, O. and Backett-Milburn, K. (1998) 'The data are out there, or are they? Implications for archiving and revisiting qualitative data', *Sociology*, 32(4): 733–45.

Medjedović, I. (2011) 'Secondary analysis of qualitative interview data: Objections and experiences. Results of a German feasibility study', *Forum: Qualitative Social Research*, 12(3): Art. 10. Available at: http://nbn-resolving.de/urn:nbn:de:0114-fqs1103104 (accessed 24 May 2019).

Meyer, C. and Meyer zu Verl, C. (2013) 'Hermeneutische Praxis. Eine ethnomethodologische Rekonstruktion sozialwissenschaftlichen Sinnrekonstruierens', *Sozialersinn*, 14: 207–34.

Moore, N. (2007) '(Re)-using Qualitative data?', *Sociological Research Online*, 12(3): 1. Available at: www.socresonline.org.uk/12/3/1.html (accessed 24 May 2019).

Neale, B. (2013) 'Adding time into the mix: Stakeholder ethics in qualitative longitudinal research', *Methodological Innovations Online*, 8: 6–20.

Neale, B. and Bishop, L. (2012) 'The Timescapes Archive: A stakeholder approach to archiving qualitative longitudinal data', *Qualitative Research*, 12: 53–65.

Neale, B., Lau Clayton, C., Davies, L. and Ladlow, L. (2015) *Researching the Lives of Young Fathers: The Following Young Fathers Study and Dataset*, Briefing Paper no. 8. Available at: https://followingfathers.leeds.ac.uk/wp-content/uploads/sites/79/2015/10/Researching-the-Lives-of-Young-Fathers-updated-Oct-22.pdf (accessed 24 May 2019).

Oleson, V., Droes, N., Hatton, D., Chico, N. and Schatzman, L. (1994) 'Analyzing together: Recollections of a team approach', in A. Bryman and R.G. Burgess (eds), *Qualitative Data Analysis*. London: Routledge. pp. 111–28.

Phoenix, A., Brannen, J., Elliott, H., Smithson, J., Morris, P., Smart, C., Barlow, A. and Bauer, E. (2016) 'Group analysis in practice: Narrative approaches', *Forum: Qualitative Social Research*. Available at: www.qualitative-research.net/index.php/fqs/article/view/2391/3978 (accessed 24 May 2019).

Richards, K.A.R. and Hemphill, M.A. (2017) 'A practical guide to collaborative qualitative data analysis', *Journal of Teaching in Physical Education*, 37(2): 1–20.

Tarrant, A. (2016) 'Getting out of the swamp? Methodological reflections on using qualitative secondary analysis to develop research design', *International Journal of Social Research Methodology*, 20(6): 599–611.

Tarrant, A. and Hughes, K. (2019) 'Qualitative secondary analysis: Building longitudinal samples to understand men's generational identities in low-income contexts', *Sociology*, 53(3): 599–611.

Tarrant, A. and Hughes, K. (forthcoming) *Precarious Families, Marginalised Men: Telling Longitudinal Stories of Low-Income Family Life*. Basingstoke: Palgrave Macmillan.

Thomson, R., Hadfield, L., Kehily, M.J. and Sharpe, S. (2010) 'Family fortunes: An intergenerational perspective on recession', *Twenty-First Century Society*, 5(2): 149–57.

Thomson, R., Hadfield, L., Holland, J., Henwood, K., Moore, N., Stanley, L. and Taylor, R. (2014) *New Frontiers in QLR: Definition, Design and Display*. Technical Report. NCRM. (Unpublished.) Available at: http://eprints.ncrm.ac.uk/3297/ (accessed 23 October 2019).

Wilson, S. (2014) 'Using secondary analysis to maintain a critically reflexive approach to qualitative research', *Sociological Research Online*, 19(3): 1–12.

SEVEN

QUALITATIVE SECONDARY ANALYSIS IN TEACHING

Maureen Haaker

7.1 Introduction

Usually when we think of re-using data, we often think about a secondary analysis project or re-study. However, data re-use projects can include a creative array of possibilities, including re-using data in teaching. This chapter seeks to:

- explore the landscape of data services and the involvement of data services in the education sector;
- signpost to existing teaching resources and the key skills these resources can help develop for students;
- highlight key benefits and considerations for re-using data for teaching.

7.2 The Landscape of Data Services

Archiving data has a rich history dating back to the 1960s, and largely starts with the efforts of survey researchers who wanted to share their data with other researchers. Scheuch (2006) documents this history in detail and credits the start of data services with an initiative by Elmo Roper, one of the founders of survey research. In 1945, Elmo Roper gifted boxes of IBM punch cards from his 1930s surveys to his university library. His day-to-day operations of survey research saw that survey data were a vastly underutilised resource of significant historical value. With this awareness, he encouraged one of his colleagues, George Gallup, to follow suit. With a growing and substantial amount of data available, the library created a separate unit in 1947 to house these collections. In 1957, this section of the library became the Roper Center and was opened to the public. Among those who visited the Center was Erwin Scheuch, who was both inspired by the centre but also daunted by the challenges of re-using data that were archived without a finding aid, inventory, or any other documentation. In 1962, Scheuch collaborated with other survey researchers at the First Conference on Social Science Data Archives in La Napoule and, from that, established the basic principles needed to begin building basic infrastructure for the archiving of research data.

By the 1970s, the movement to build data archives was well under way; however, these efforts were not without objection. The arguments against the archiving and re-use of data claimed that there is insufficient knowledge surrounding the conditions under which data was collected, a lack of contextual knowledge of the social and political context under which data was collected, and no clear finance strategy to fund these efforts. To confront these issues, it was deemed necessary to ensure data services had sufficiently trained staff, resources, and clear cataloguing and documentation so researchers would be able to easily navigate collections. Slowly, an informal network of data services began to form throughout North America and Europe. The approach and funding for data services varied considerably between regions and institutions. Although researchers could visit and use single collections, it was impossible to look across datasets without a clear standardisation of the collections. A key issue for researchers to resolve was that it was nearly impossible to conduct cross-national, cross-cultural, or comparative analysis even when similar data existed across different services.

To tackle this issue, a pioneering network of social scientists, librarians, information technology professionals, and data archivists came together in 1974 to form the International Association of Social Science Information Services and Technology (IASSIST). The primary concern of the group was to create the tools needed to facilitate advanced analysis and, specifically, comparative research. This 'data community' of social scientists and data services began the process of setting out standards for data inventories, manuals of data classification, and information guides for researchers, which eventually allowed researchers to effectively work across datasets and even across institutions (O'Neill Adams, 2006). As data services continued to develop their practices and, in turn, enhance the collections they held, data re-use became a well-established practice, particularly within the quantitative tradition of social science research, as a way to take advantage of the full value of data.

By the mid-1990s, some public research funders in the UK began outlining data-sharing policies which mandated the sharing of data that was conducted using taxpayer-funded grants, including qualitative research projects (Corti et al., forth-coming). To ensure that qualitative data could be archived according to these policies, Louise Corti and Paul Thompson established the Qualidata Resource Centre at the University of Essex in 1994 (Corti and Thompson, 1996). This was among the earliest initiatives to build infrastructure for qualitative, social science data, and it provided a single point of access of information about the extent and availability of qualitative research material deposited in public repositories. As collections for qualitative studies grew, so did the infrastructure for qualitative data. Since the establishment of Qualidata, other qualitative archives (including Timescapes, the Irish Qualitative Data Archive, ARK Qualitative Data Archive, UCL Human Communication Audiovisual Archive, and Australian Qualitative Data Archive) have been established to fulfil the needs of qualitative researchers wanting to share their data. The last ten years, especially, has seen an explosion in the number of archives specialising in qualitative data, the number of requests to re-use qualitative datasets, and the number of publications mentioning secondary analysis of qualitative data (Bishop and Kuula-Luumi, 2016). In 2015, the National Centre for Research Methods formally recognised 'secondary analysis of qualitative data' as a methodology, one of the many developments which cemented the re-use of qualitative data as an important consideration for data services.

While the re-use of qualitative data has been one area of change within data services over the past decade, there continues to be several other developments within data services. One of the most influential changes in recent years has been the framing of research data policies around the Concordat on Open Research Data (UKRI, 2016). Launched in 2016, the Concordat for Open Research Data outlines ten principles to promote the sharing and publication of data. Alongside outlining the call to curate open and citeable data (where it is deemed appropriate to do so), it also specifies that those involved in research need to consider effective research data management strategies. As data sharing policies are reviewed and updated, this Concordat will help to shape and extend policies, and it will likely see data sharing becoming a standard in research practice.

Beyond the policy changes, advances in technology have also changed the face of data services since their inception 70 years ago. Specialist data archives are able to offer expertise in standards in handling and managing a range of different types of data, and initially were set up with a physical capacity to digitise hard copies of data to this standard. Now, however, data is digital from the start of its life cycle. Consequently, new ways of being able to search, catalogue, and, perhaps most importantly, cite data (using persistent identifiers, such as DOIs) have changed the way data services ingest, process, and disseminate data collections. Researchers can now self-publish data in generic repositories, such as Harvard's Dataverse, Figshare, and Open Science Framework, and assign their own persistent identifiers for others to re-use and cite the dataset. New initiatives, like Google's Dataset Search, have aimed to help re-users to find this data no matter where it is published. As long as data is discoverable (that is, it has basic metadata that allows it to be found through a simple search), data can be archived anywhere. Data services will have to carefully consider how this influx of data can be quality checked and – most importantly – how to offer the necessary skills training to ensure that researchers are fully equipped with knowledge of how to meet the standards of data archiving. Looking forward, data services will not only be an end point for researchers looking to deposit data after a project is over, but also be more actively involved with data management from the start of research projects.

Perhaps one of the more interesting changes in data services operation has been their relationship to the education sector and the re-use of data for teaching purposes, particularly for qualitative data. Bishop and Kuula-Luumi (2016: 6) showed that 64% of the downloads of qualitative data at the UK Data Service were re-used for teaching and learning, writing that '[a]lthough there is sometimes a tendency to privilege data re-use for research, the widespread use across several levels of education is clearly enriching teaching by the use of real data.' The relationship between archives and higher education benefits both: teachers who re-used data have commented about how it enhances learning and 'is effective in engaging student interest', and, for archives, the promotion of specific collections within teaching settings has a clear impact on the reach and significance of that dataset (Bishop and Kuula-Luumi, 2016: 6). Although data services were conceived with the idea that they would supply data for 'genuine researchers' to re-use, their role has expanded to allow re-users more scope and creativity in their re-use projects. Some archives have gone as far as to develop specific education strategies, such as the National Archives' (2018) *A Guide to Collaboration between Archives and Higher Education*, which explores methods for further outreach and engagement with undergraduate and postgraduate students. As this pattern of re-use continues, it is likely that more archives will formally recognise their relationship to the education sector.

7.3 The Rise of Research-informed Teaching

Although a pattern of re-use for purposes of teaching has become clearer in recent years, the reciprocal relationship between data services and education is not driven entirely by data services. Higher education, specifically, has its own goal to provide 'research-informed teaching'. Since the 1960s, higher education institutions (HEIs) have sought to show that use of research (and its data) in teaching and success in learning are inextricably linked (Griffiths, 2004). To test this, Hattie and Marsh (1996) conducted a meta-analysis of 58 studies which sought to understand the relationship between research and learning. Their conclusions were mixed: they found nothing to suggest that learning was best done within a research-intensive setting. However, they went on to conclude that they cannot make the claim that *teaching* is not better for involving research. In other words, there may be a benefit to pedagogy for being research-based. Hattie and Marsh (1996: 533) thus concluded, '[U]niversities ought to set as a mission goal the improvement of the nexus between research and teaching ... to increase the circumstances in which teaching and research have occasion to meet.' From the mid-1990s onward, ways to facilitate a research/teaching nexus became a priority for higher education, spurring questions about the best ways to bring data into the classroom.

In the early 2000s, research projects such as Project LINK (Griffiths, 2004) and the Research-led Teaching and Learning Project (Zamorski, 2002) began to systematically explore some of the more innovative ways research was being used in teaching. In 2005, the Higher Education Funding Council for England (HEFCE) introduced grants to support further examination of the teaching/research nexus. Funded by this HEFCE grant, Healey and Jenkins (2009: 7) modelled four types of 'research-informed teaching':

- research-led – learning about research in the discipline;
- research-tutored – engaging in research discussion;
- research-oriented – developing research and inquiry skills;
- research-based – undertaking research and inquiry.

Healey and Jenkins (2009) emphasised that the latter two methods of research-informed teaching encouraged students to actively immerse themselves in research activities, rather than simply being passive recipients of information derived from research.

Equipped with a framework with which to develop teaching strategies, higher education asked institutions to develop their 'research-informed teaching' and ensure data was brought into the classroom. After 2018, this ambition was formally acknowledged with the introduction of the Teaching Excellence Framework (TEF). The framework is aimed at incentivising good pedagogy, using measures such as student satisfaction and employment outcomes. The policy also specifically commends research-informed teaching, as defined by Healey and Jenkins (2009). In the first TEF exercise, completed in 2018, there was a huge variation between institutions on how they evidenced their research-informed teaching. Some universities relied on their scores from the Research Excellence Framework to show that those teaching were also involved in high-quality research, whereas others drew attention to their education strategies and emphasis on 'building research-based and research-led curricula' (Beech, 2018: 24). The traditional way of demonstrating research-informed teaching is to require students to complete a small-scale research project within their mandatory research methods modules. Typically, students are asked to develop a research question, collect a small amount of data, analyse the data, and write a research report which often serves as the final piece of assessment for the module. However, while this method provides hands-on experience and allows for some decision-making within the research process, it is also usually prefaced by an internal, ethical review board. The process can take up valuable class time and place strict conditions on research activities which do not reflect how research is conducted in real life. Recent years has seen a movement toward proportional review of student projects, which aims to streamline the ethical review process and keep requirements realistic to the level at which students are working (Hunter, 2007). There is still variation in the guidelines for a student-friendly ethical framework (see for example Lowney, 2014, for a discussion on ethical consideration for student research projects), highlighting the tension between assessing risk and encouraging students to learn about research by 'doing'. Consequently, there still exists a gap between how a teacher can practically introduce students to the complexities of the research process and how the student can have a personal experience of real-world research.

Moreover, as Elman and colleagues (2015: 39) also point out, 'simply carrying out a research task, isolated from the research design and epistemological justification which motivated it' does not necessarily teach the most important aspects of research and its impact on knowledge creation. Without adequate time and preparation to go through these processes, students can lose out on a nuanced understanding of the very lessons meant to be taught by research-informed teaching. Learning about research needs to expand beyond a rote memorisation of how research is done: it needs to explain why research is done in a particular way. This involves explaining how knowledge is derived from research, how consensus on those conclusions are formed, and how claims can be challenged. It also involves demonstrating how different methods contribute new perspectives. A small, independent research project has its place in helping students understand the research process from start to finish; however, the data allows students to explore the limitations of that knowledge and encourages them to continue their search for alternative perspectives. Re-using data thus not only satisfies the policies and requirement of higher education, but it also unlocks a new potential in students to engage with their learning in a more critical way.

7.4 Existing Infrastructure to Support Research-informed Teaching

Despite the acknowledgement of the benefits of bringing data into the classroom, there are still concerns about the relevance, availability, and accessibility of data to re-use. The proliferation of qualitative-specific archives and increasing numbers of qualitative datasets available, improved standardisation and function of search tools, and easily downloadable, digital-born datasets all align to present new opportunities for re-use. These dramatic improvements in the infrastructure for qualitative data archives are understood to enrich a re-user's consumption and experience of the data and bring people closer to the evidence (Corti and Fielding, 2016: 10). For example, Jo Haynes, a frequent re-user of qualitative data, shared this experience with her postgraduate students. Faced with the task of getting students to do qualitative data analysis as part of a 12-week course, Haynes asked students to undertake a secondary analysis assignment from a selected number of datasets held at the UK Data Service (Haynes, 2011). As part of the assessment, Haynes explained that the students had the choice to either come up with an original research question or find a new way to work with the data. Part of the motivation to have students re-use data, rather than collect their own, was to allow them more time to develop analytical skills.

Additionally, students benefited from having to generate multiple perspectives of their chosen dataset and craft diverse arguments and findings out of the data, sometimes beyond what the original researchers found. Haynes (2011) noted that it was 'also a really good way to engage with research that has already been done and to reach a critical dialogue with the British research'. The module was seen as a success, even resulting in one of Haynes' students publishing her results (Haynes and Jones, 2012). Haynes reflects with Jones on the two analyses produced within this class, as well as the deeper understandings of conducting research that came out of re-using data. Although students were working with just a selected sample curated specifically for learning purposes of a larger, archived dataset, Jones, one of the students, was still able to find similar themes as the original investigator. Her publication expands on the substantive similarities, as well as a few differences, between her analysis and the analysis of the original investigator. Alongside this comparison, two key points about analysing data are also discussed. One conclusion reached was that all interactions with data are mediated and interpreted throughout the research process, and thus critical reflection should be a part of the analysis. Following on from this, the other conclusion was that the two, similar analytic conclusions suggest that qualitative data is not wholly dependent upon the researcher for its conclusion. Rather, data can and does exist independently of the research process, so reflexivity should not only reflect on the conditions of data production from the vantage point of the researcher, but also reflect on the world in which the research took place. In terms of students learning to assess methodological rigour, these points show the value that can be obtained from using the teaching dataset and teaching resources available through data services.

7.4.1 Teaching datasets

Teaching datasets are specially curated datasets and user guides which have gone through a process of data reduction to make the datasets of a more feasible size and scope for students to explore within a limited time frame. The simplified versions of datasets give students both a realistic amount of data to explore and documentation curated to provide straightforward but thorough background to the methods. Where possible, these teaching datasets include a range of material, including video, audio, and more traditional word processing formats. Lastly, these datasets are also created from high-quality collections which provide a glimpse into good practices of qualitative research, and may include not-so-often-seen documentation such as anonymisation plans, transcription guidelines, and interview schedules.

For example, the teaching dataset for the School Leaver Study, available through the UK Data Service, provides data samples from the original 1978 School Leavers

Study as well as a re-study conducted in 2010 by Graham Crow (see Lyon and Crow, Chapter 9). Table 7.1 outlines what is available in these two collections. The left column looks specifically at the original study, noting the many more essays available and the advanced methodological documentation that sits alongside this data. The right column notes the size of the curated sample of the essays, as well as more interactive documentation. The student-friendly documentation also includes more detail on the analysis of the data, opening opportunities for students to explore all stages of the research process in more detail.

Table 7.1 Comparison between School Leavers Study 1978 and the School Leavers Study teaching dataset

School Leavers Study 1978	School Leavers Study teaching dataset, 1978 and 2010
141 essays from 1978	10 essays from 1978
Documentation: processing notes	10 essays from 2010
Documentation: article and book chapter on methodology	Methodology video presented by Graham Crow explaining the advantages and disadvantages of the method used, specifically made for student level
	Coding frame from analysis
	Transcription guidelines
	Reference list of related publications

This teaching dataset is not restricted for use in the classroom, however. QSR International have re-used this dataset for training materials of their NVivo products. The diversity of file formats, the size of the essays, and the availability of the coding frame made it ideal to demonstrate the analytic capabilities of NVivo analysis software packages.

The diversity of data available to re-use for teaching – whether it is already curated or re-users have curated their own sample to meet the needs of their classroom – exemplifies the analytical possibilities. Data in the form of focus group transcripts, interview transcripts, short essays, fieldnotes, and visual materials is available to show students the range of methodological tools available. Students can also learn to assess datasets to better understand methodological integrity or evaluate the relevance of datasets to explore what data collection questions are needed to answer research questions. If re-using the data to teach critical analysis skills, students can compare their results to results of the previous study, as was done in the case of Haynes and Jones (2012), or try a new analytic strategy. Social inquiry can also be stimulated by having students ask new questions or focus on new topics arising from the data that are different from that of the original researcher. Teaching datasets are flexible to the needs to lessons being taught and pose opportunities to develop a range of critical skills.

7.4.2 Teaching resources

In addition to teaching datasets, there are a number of resources which target learning about concepts, theories, and methods. Haaker and Morgan-Brett (2017) detail their experiences of using these resources in the classroom, and how they were received by students. They point out that these resources not only present new information to students but also can help them to build their own research and analytical skills. For example, students can use real interviews and interview schedules to see how researchers build rapport and how research questions build up to answer larger research questions. In one specific example, they detail a teaching resource derived from Hollway and Jefferson's (2003a) 1995 study *Gender Difference, Anxiety and the Fear of Crime*. In this resource, they are guided through the pilot interview schedule and compare this to the final interview schedule. Students can see how the researchers' initial style of interviewing did not lead to the results they had anticipated (Hollway and Jefferson, 2003a). They found that participants displayed defence mechanisms when discussing sensitive issues and that a standard interviewing style was not the best way to explore these issues. From this pilot they developed the Free Association Narrative Interviewing Method, which was a unique and highly successful way of accessing these more difficult and emotional stories (Hollway and Jefferson, 2000). Within the resource, students are asked to read further into this new interviewing style and make connections between the theory and subsequent research method. The resource not only explores the final publications resulting from the study, but also engages students in the original aims and objectives of the study, noting that:

> In psychoanalytic theory, anxiety precipitates defenses against the threats that it poses to the self, such that ideas and feelings which arouse anxiety are lost to conscious thought. This proposition has profound implications for method. We aimed to develop an appropriate interview method (which at the beginning we called 'quasi-clinical'). Our development of the 'narrative interview method' is probably the most important outcome of this project, because of its widespread implications for social science research. (Hollway and Jefferson, 2003b: 6)

Through highlighting the trials and errors of their original method, and demonstrating their redevelopment of the interviewing technique, this resource based on Hollway and Jefferson 1995 study documents the often-disordered nature of doing qualitative research and how this can lead to some of the most important research outcomes. The resource thus takes a more guided approach to these realisations than teaching datasets but is nonetheless just as effective.

Data archives already provide a range of similar teaching resources. The Timescapes Archive, for example, has developed numerous guides and multi-media resources, including the Timescapes Methods Guide series, which explains methodological debates and basic research skills as explored through the curation and re-use of its qualitative, longitudinal data (Timescapes, 2012). These resources aim to address specific research skills, such as how to formulate interview ques-tions and how to use time lines and relational maps to visualise time. The Irish Qualitative Data Archive also has a series of resources for students, and makes available audio and text extracts from life-history interviews to help students learn key sociological concepts and how these are represented within real-world research (IQDA, 2015). Finally, the UK Data Service provides a range of qualitative teach-ing resources, which vary from self-led resources with 'activity stops' to tutor-led teaching packs. One of their most recent additions, for example, is *Dissertations and their Data*, a collection of resources to aid basic data management of an under-graduate research project. The pack provides students with a basic checklist of research data management points and templates for informed consent, transcrip-tion approaches, and anonymisation plans (UK Data Service, 2018). Case studies published by the UK Data Service (2015b) demonstrate some examples of how teachers have used these resources in the classroom and in assignments. All of these resources are freely available and offer new opportunities to make teaching truly research-informed.

Beyond guided teaching resources, there are also interactive tools which can help students explore qualitative research data. For example, QualiBank is an online tool which allows users to search, browse, and cite qualitative data. While most database search engines, including Google Dataset Search and many archival catalogues, search through structured metadata about the dataset (which might include anything from more expansive abstracts to simple fields filled in about the methodology of the study), QualiBank searches through the data itself, bringing back search results where keywords are actually mentioned by participants. This not only allows students to think more about the importance of the participant's voice in research, but also stresses the importance of 'getting into the data' to really understand the qualitative dataset. QualiBank additionally allows users to cite the data line by line. The reference generated by QualiBank creates a persistent identifier which can be traced back to the specific line in the data that was being referenced. Often the significance of citations is unrealised, as it requires further work to track down the item cited to understand how it was used. Sometimes, it is not even clear whether the citation is a supportive, challenging, or even a tangen-tial idea to the point being made. Using a tool like QualiBank allows students the opportunity to quickly retrieve and closely inspect the evidence used, and further elaborate on what role the reference is playing within their work. It also allows teachers scope to explain the significance of citation within academia. Beyond interactive tools like QualiBank, archives also offer a more traditional range of face-to-face workshops, webinars, and video tutorials (UK Data Service, 2015a). All of these resources can help enrich the student experience and bring classroom lessons to life.

7.5 Cultural differences between higher education and data services

Despite the recent coordination between higher education and data services, there still exists a cultural gap between the processes and vision of the two sectors. Many of the existing resources required the collaboration of people working together from across higher education and the data services over a sustained period of time. Commonly cited barriers to this kind of collaboration are often based in resource allocation, the familiarity with archive services and discoverability of relevant, archived material, and attitudes toward risk of re-using data for teaching, particularly when it applies to qualitative data (National Archives, 2018). While not insurmountable, there is scope for both the education sector and data services to better understand how each other work which will better utilise the value of the data held within archives.

7.5.1 Allocation of resources

Creating teaching resources and curating teaching datasets takes time and money. To assess what gets allocated further resources, data services regularly collect information to produce statistics which align with the Chartered Institute of Public Finance and Accountancy (CIPFA) statistics. This involves basic tracking of how many people have used which resources and what number of times. It is this data that Bishop and Kuula-Luumi (2016) analysed to better understand how qualitative research data was being re-used. Based on this, further resources can be allocated to ensure archives are responding to the needs and wants of what re-users are using. In this instance, citation is a key factor in ensuring that data services know how many are using teaching resources and for what purposes. Conversely, higher education, however, is assessed through assessment frameworks like TEF and REF, which look at factors like impact, outputs, and student satisfaction. Re-using data for teaching can still aid HEIs needing to abide to these frameworks by evidencing pedagogical practice through impact case studies of data re-use or supplying evaluation and feedback from data-services users (including students) on those resources. When teaching resources are created, these can also be published through archive websites, creating not only another output, but also potential for further evidence of how it is re-used, by whom, and how often. As HEIs and data services continue to build on their collaborative efforts to share out allocation of resources, both sectors will be able to benefit from the harmonisation.

7.5.2 Familiarity and knowledge

Getting to know a dataset well enough to create a teaching resource imposes on teaching staff who may simply not have time to explore datasets in this kind of detail. Conversely, archive staff hold an intimate familiarity of the material held, including material which is uncatalogued or undigitised, but may not know what kind of resources teachers want. These are issues that are easily solved through coordination, but sometimes the limitations are not always obvious. For example, in 2014, Bethany Morgan-Brett stumbled upon a previously undigitised collection of Stan Cohen, *Mods and Rockers*. Initially, the goal was to digitise this quickly degrading, paper-based collection because of its importance to criminology. Seeing an opportunity, Morgan-Brett decided to make a teaching resource based on the collection which guided students through the original study all the way through Cohen's theories on deviance and moral panics. However, much of this collection depended on news clippings, which were still under copyright on the newspapers in which they were published. Working with the archive on the teaching resource immediately addressed the issue of copyright and put forward a plan to ensure enough material was available to complete the resource. The restrictions of copyright made it impossible to make the entire collection available through the archive; however Morgan-Brett was able to contact the newspapers holding the copyright on the selected sample of newspaper clippings to ask permission for those specific articles to be re-published online within this resource. In the end, the teaching resource was published through the UK Data Service website, which not only raises awareness of the existence of this previously undigitised material, but also allows for students to see how such prominent theories were developed. Data services can provide expertise on what is available and any restrictions on reproducing these materials for teaching resources.

7.5.3 Attitudes of risk toward re-use

The arguments against making data available for re-use detailed at the beginning of this chapter – including insufficient knowledge surrounding the conditions under which data was collected, a lack of contextual knowledge of the social and political context under which data was collected, and no clear finance strategy to fund these efforts – continue to be debated as re-uses for data become more creative. The re-use of data by students, in particular, can raise doubts about whether students have enough methodological knowledge to really understand and re-use the data 'well enough'.

Although few in number, some data depositors also specify that data can only be re-used for non-profit research purposes, and not teaching purposes. Data services' assessment of risk in this type of re-use may be different from that of educators and researchers. As this area of re-use continues to grow, some of these issues can be addressed in the design and implementation of the teaching resources. As data sharing and re-use becomes more of a norm, it is likely that different ideas of risk will begin to synchronise. Nonetheless, it is important to check with data depositors or the licensing agreement to see if such restrictions have been placed on the collection before time and effort is put into developing a teaching dataset or teaching resource.

7.6 Conclusion

Re-using data for teaching inspires the dynamic discussion, investigation, and evaluation of research design and facilitates the 'pedagogical culture' (Wagner et al., 2010). The selection of teaching resources available reflects the years of engagement between education and data services and explores an expansive value that data holds for research-informed teaching. Namely, these resources can scope out new analytical possibilities of data, develop a fuller range of research skills in students, and raise the profile and impact of educators. With the increasing call for research-informed teaching and innovative practices, particularly within higher education, re-using data in teaching offers the potential to demonstrate this creativity and convergence between teaching and research. Moreover, re-using data for teaching enhances the value of archived data and can benefit both the education sector and data services.

7.7 References

Bishop, L. and Kuula-Luumi, A. (2016) 'Revisiting qualitative data reuse: A decade on', *SAGE Open*, 7(1). DOI 10.1177/2158244016685136.

Beech, D. (2018) *Going for gold: lessons from the TEF provider submissions*, Higher Education Policy Institute. Available at: https://www.hepi.ac.uk/wp-content/

uploads/2017/10/FINAL-HEPI-Going-for-Gold-Report-99-04_10_17-Screen.pdf (accessed 8 July 2019).

Corti, L., Van den Eyden, V., Bishop, L., and Woollard, M. (forthcoming) *Managing and Sharing Research Data: A Guide to Good Practice*. London: Sage.

Corti, L. and Fielding, N. (2016) 'Opportunities from the digital revolution: Implications for researching, publishing, and consuming qualitative research', *SAGE Open*. DOI 10.1177/2158244016678912.

Corti, L. and Thompson, P. (1996) 'Qualidata', *Sociological Research Online*. Available at: www.socresonline.org.uk/1/3/qualidata.html (accessed 24 May 2019).

Elman, C., Kapiszewski, D. and Kirilova, D. (2015) 'Learning through research: Using data to train undergraduates in qualitative methods', *PS – Political Science & Politics*, 48(1): 39–43.

Griffiths, R. (2004) 'Knowledge production and the research–teaching nexus: The case of the built environment and disciplines', *Studies in Higher Education*, 29(6): 709–26.

Haaker, M. and Morgan-Brett, B. (2017) 'Developing research-led teaching: Two cases of practical data reuse in the classroom', *SAGE Open*, 7(2). DOI 10.1177/2158244017701800.

Hattie, J. and Marsh, H.W. (1996) 'The relationship between research and teaching: A meta-analysis', *Review of Educational Research*, 66(4): 507–42. DOI 10.3102/00346543066004507.

Haynes, J. (2011) *Teaching Case Study: Getting Students to do Data Analysis in a 12-week Unit*, UK Data Service. Available at: http://ukdataservice.ac.uk/use-data/data-in-use/case-study/?id=22 (accessed 24 May 2019).

Haynes, J. and Jones, D. (2012) 'A tale of two analyses: The use of archived qualitative data', *Sociological Research Online*, 17(2). Available at: http://www.socresonline.org.uk/17/2/1.html (accessed 24 May 2019).

Healey, M. and Jenkins, A. (2009) *Developing Undergraduate Research and Inquiry*. York: Higher Education Academy.

Hollway, W. and Jefferson, T. (2000) *Doing Qualitative Research Differently: Free Association, Narrative and the Interview Method*. London: Sage.

Hollway, W. and Jefferson, T. (2003a) *Gender Difference, Anxiety and the Fear of Crime, 1995* [data collection], UK Data Service, SN: 4581. DOI 10.5255/UKDA-SN-4581-1.

Hollway, W. and Jefferson (2003b) *User Guide: Gender Difference, Anxiety and the Fear of Crime, 1995* [data collection], UK Data Service, SN: 4581. Available at: http://doc.ukdataservice.ac.uk/doc/4581/mrdoc/pdf/q4581uguide.pdf (accessed 24 October 2019).

Hunter, D. (2007) 'Proportional ethical review and the identification of ethical issues', *Journal of Medical Ethics*, 33(4): 241–5.

IQDA (2015) *IQDA Resources for Students*, Irish Qualitative Data Archive, University of Maynooth. Available at: www.maynoothuniversity.ie/iqda/data-resources/resources-students (accessed 24 May 2019).

Lowney, K.S. (2014) 'Ask *Teaching Sociology*: What should faculty consider before having students conduct research in a class?', *Teaching Sociology*, 42(3): 240–4.

The National Archives (TNA) (2018) *Guide to Collaboration between the Archive and Higher Education Sectors*, the National Archives and Research Libraries UK. Available at: www.nationalarchives.gov.uk/documents/Guide_for_archives_to_collaborate_with_Higher_Education.pdf (accessed 24 May 2019).

O'Neill Adams, M. (2006) 'The origins and early years of IASSIST', *IASSIST Quarterly*, 5(14): 5–13.

Scheuch, E.K. (2006) 'History and visions for the development of data services for the social sciences', *International Social Science Journal*, 53(4): 384–99.

Timescapes (2012) *Timescapes Methods Guide Series*, Timescapes, University of Leeds. Available at: www.timescapes.leeds.ac.uk/about/timescapes-methods-guide-series.html (accessed 24 May 2019).

UK Data Service (2015a) *Teaching Resources: Qualitative and Mixed Methods Data*. Available at: www.ukdataservice.ac.uk/use-data/teaching/teaching-resources/qualitative.aspx (accessed 24 May 2019).

UK Data Service (2015b) *Case Studies*. Available at: https://beta.ukdataservice.ac.uk/impact/case-studies/ (accessed 24 May 2019).

UK Data Service (2018) *Dissertations and their Data: Promoting Research Integrity in Undergraduate Projects*. Available at: www.ukdataservice.ac.uk/media/622144/dissertations_and_their_data_promoting_research_integrity.pdf (accessed 24 May 2019).

UK Research and Innovation (UKRI) (2016) *Concordat on Open Research Data*. Available at: www.ukri.org/files/legacy/documents/concordatonopenresearchdata-pdf/ (accessed 24 May 2019).

Wagner, C., Garner, M. and Kawulich, B. (2010) 'The state of the art of teaching research methods in the social sciences: Towards a pedagogical culture', *Studies in Higher Education*, 36(1): 75–88.

Zamorski, B. (2002) 'Research-led teaching and learning in higher education: A case', *Teaching in Higher Education*, 7(4): 411–27.

III
METHODS OF QUALITATIVE SECONDARY ANALYSIS WITH NON-INTERVIEW DATA

EIGHT

LOOKING BACK, LOOKING FORWARD: WORKING WITH ARCHIVED ORAL HISTORY INTERVIEWS

Joanna Bornat

CHAPTER CONTENTS

8.1 **Introduction**

As a recognised discipline with its own literature, oral history has drawn on research and observation for several decades (Thompson and Bornat, 2017). An invitation to contribute to this collection offers an opportunity to consider similar territory with QSA research. There is much to be learned from the sharing of methodological experiences and in this chapter I want to focus on a key aspect of oral history which I feel should be of interest to QSA researchers: time. Oral history's use of memory to research the past centralises time and temporality as issues in interviewing and in analysing interview data. However, the preservation, archiving and sharing of interviews raises questions about future time. The UK historian Raphael Samuel pointed out in the early years of UK oral history that archiving is, or should be, an embedded part of oral history practice:

> The collector of the spoken word ... is the creator ... of his [*sic*] own archives ... His role ... is that of archivist, as well as historian, retrieving and storing priceless information which would otherwise be lost ... his greatest contribution may well be in the collecting and safe preservation of his material rather than in the use he can immediately find for it. (1971: 22)

Almost 50 years and many hours of interviewing later, we are looking at a huge data resource of oral history recordings offering the possibility of making connections across generations and space, opening up 'a wealth of oral history material for time periods for which conducting new interviews is impossible' (Freund, 2009: 27). These many thousands of hours of oral history interviews deposited in large and small, national and local archives across the world present a potentially rich resource for researchers. What may have been an unremarked sharing of archived interviews not so long ago is now subjected to closer critical scrutiny, recognised as a resource. Indeed funders now expect researchers to consider existing data sources located in archives, both physical and virtual, set up for this very purpose. And, of course, re-use may be a useful strategy in an age of austerity and underfunding, its utility being what it offers as a cheaper alternative to primary research.

Temporality and its implications will be a theme running through this chapter as it explores some of the challenges and opportunities that archived oral history interviews present. From considering aspects of shared experience between QSA and oral history, the chapter moves on to identify specific insights from an oral history approach, on the way considering context, serendipity, temporality, intersubjectivity and ethical issues.

8.2 Oral History and QSA - Sharing Experience

Interpreting qualitative data not generated by the original researcher requires what the sociologist Hammersley calls 'an informal and intuitive element' (1997: 138). All of this is further complicated in oral history interviews where not only the intersubjectivity of the interview relationship becomes part of the data, but also memory, with its many qualities, is the source and basis of narration – an object in itself (Thompson and Bornat, 2017). In exploring the links between interpretation and memory I want to consider three areas where oral historians and QSA share territory: context, serendipity and sensitivity.

8.2.1 Context

Corti (2011), in a wide-ranging overview and taking a European perspective, identifies the significance of changes over time in relation to the context of social research methods. This was something which Evans and Thane (2006) encountered when they revisited the 116 interviews reconstructed from notes and memory by the sociologist Dennis Marsden in the 1960s. Oral history emerged in the late 1960s and early 1970s, in part because changing technology allowed for the immediate capture of interview exchanges with light and portable recording machines. Note-taking from the memory of the researcher, once a highly valued skill, became side-lined in favour of instant verbatim spoken accounts. Recordings have become a rich resource of direct access to interviewees' own perspectives without the intermediary of the researcher with notebook and skills of recall. The result is descriptive historical information, providing historical perspective with changes in forms of expression and language use as well as clues to modes of social interaction between interviewer and interviewee. All these are invaluable as a part of the process of contextual immersion in a topic or aspect of research (Bornat, 2005; Gillies and Edwards, 2012; Bishop, 2007).

Context is perhaps the issue most frequently raised by those concerned about the usability of archived interviews with re-use drawing us towards the practices of previous researchers as well as the time they were researching in (Mauthner et al., 1998; Parry and Mauthner, 2004: see Irwin, Chapter 2). An example of re-use from a large oral historian collection shows how these various factors can be brought into play. The Millennium Memory Bank (MMB) (1999), deposited at the British Library, comprises 6069 interviews and is the largest oral history collection in Europe. To commemorate and mark the Millennium, a collaboration between the British Library, and the BBC led to all 36 local radio stations across the UK carrying out themed interviews which were then edited into half-hour documentary programmes broadcast during the autumn of 1999. The documentaries as well as the unedited interviews are listed in the British Library catalogue and can be accessed, though not all have been transcribed. In her use of the MMB interviews, Gallwey (2013) was struck by the absence of direct questions relating to class and gender in what she heard. However she was able to discuss the generation of the interview topics with people who had planned the research, as others have also benefited in developing QSA investigations (Tarrant, 2016; Tarrant and Hughes, 2019; see Tarrant and Hughes, Chapter 6). Gallwey could reconstruct the context directly but from contact with one of the original team decided that an absence of references to class and gender in the MMB collection was a product of a late 1990s turn to 'the third way', towards culture and away from 'classical accounts of class as a determinant' (2013: 46). In fact, the structuring of the interviews around themes such as 'Where we live', 'House and Home', 'Crime and the Law', 'Belonging' and 'Money' (British Library, 1998) was an attempt by the team to avoid the standard narrative structuring of mid-century British life in terms of pre- and post-war and to encourage people to talk in terms of topics rather than sticking to questions likely to generate predictable chronologies of life stages. We (and as one of the progenitors of the project, I can say 'we') assumed that the very wide net being cast across the UK, regionally and socially, would introduce differences of class and gender, as in fact it did. Gallwey is quite right to suggest that the MMB, as any other archived set of interviews, is a product of its own particular moment in time (see Tureby and Johansson, 2016, for a discussion of the archive as historical context), and of course her theorising has its own time frame. She goes on to point out that although the MMB interviews did not, for example, invite people to talk about the Women's Liberation Movement during the 1960s and 1970s 'the fact that these topics were muted within the project's research design made the interviewees' vocalization of class and gender within the life histories, all the more pertinent' (Gallwey, 2013: 46). Her exploration of context while immersing herself in the transcriptions revealed new layers of potential interpretation. She goes on to illustrate from the interviews how 'without being questioned directly about issues of class and gender ... The life stories of interviewees in the MMB spoke for themselves' (Gallwey, 2013: 40–41) thus generating unintended emergent theoretical insights.

Gallwey's final comment raises an interesting dilemma for researchers and especially those for whom memory is a key source. Moore (2006) argues that the activity of secondary analysis means that archived data changes: 'the data are ... being constructed in the process of a new research project.' She points to a tension in any research activity as a researcher engages with existing data, producing new evidence within new frameworks of understanding and meaning. As she rightly points out, this process involves change. The point however is to acknowledge what the change is and what it contributes to knowledge (Tarrant, 2016). In finding that the MMB life stories 'spoke for themselves', Gallwey (2013) echoes Hammersley when he argues that 'the data must in some ways constrain what inferences we make and the conclusions we reach, rather than being freely constructed in and through our inferences. And this implies that they must, in some sense, exist prior to and independently of the research process' (Hammersley, 2010: para 4.3).

8.2.2 Serendipity

Secondary analysis offers opportunities for serendipity in research with the discovery of evidence which was not the focus of the original enquiry. In some cases this may be the result of a deliberate attempt at using data for new purposes. Bishop (2007) visited Blaxter's (2004) and Thompson and Lummis's (2006) datasets which were the bases of their two respective studies, *Mothers and Daughters* (Blaxter and Paterson, 1982) and *The Edwardians* (Thompson, 1975). Her aim was to find out about 'individuated eating' and her approach was to use 'convenience food as a probe' (2007: para 2.1). She drew up a list of questions and used these to find mentions of tinned food and whether people ate meals together. The Blaxter and Thompson data took her back several decades into the twentieth century and, with the help of accompanying documentation for both projects, she was able to recontextualise the original project work and broaden out her interpretation of what she found (Bishop, 2007). Her approach was carefully planned and her re-use carried out in line with her project objectives, a form of planned serendipity.

An example of an area of investigation emerged by chance in my own research from reading another researcher's interviews. Professor Margot Jefferys had interviewed men and women doctors, almost exclusively white European in origin, who had pioneered the development of geriatric medicine in the years following the inception of the NHS (Jefferys, 2000). As I was editing proofs of a chapter she had written, I noticed that the summaries of the interviews she cited included references to 'Indians' or 'my Indians', or to junior doctors who were overseas trained and specifically from the Indian sub-continent (Bornat et al., 2012). The coming-together of people from two marginalised groups, frail older people and South Asian doctors, suggested intriguing research questions. These were later to be investigated in a funded project which showed the significant roles these doctors had played in the development of the geriatric specialty and in the NHS, a contribution which had until then been overlooked (Raghuram et al., 2010; Bornat et al., 2016).

When it was underway, the South Asian geriatricians' research revealed yet another unexpected reward from secondary analysis. The project involved the creation of 60 interviews with mainly South Asian doctors, retired or serving.

Reading the two sets of interviews in parallel with one another, Jefferys' and our own, we were able to see the colonial and postcolonial connections between the UK and the Indian sub-continent. It became evident that some of the doctors interviewed by Jefferys had either been born on the sub-continent or had worked there at earlier points in their careers (Bornat et al., 2012). Between them, the two datasets had prompted a conversation, which generated a reinterpretation of the old data. Once again, emergent practice in oral history research matches developments in QSA when datasets are brought into contact with one another.

Sets of interviews created for an unrelated purpose may provide data that have an independence in a way that is fruitful. As a practice and source, oral history attracts researchers in varied and unrelated disciplines. Thus, Roller, a dialectologist, interrogated the Millennium Memory Bank interviews to explore the use and perception of non-standard Welsh–English grammar (Roller, 2015). She transcribed MMB interviews from Wales and also carried out a questionnaire-based study of her own. The MMB interviews were suitable for her research owing to the wide range of Welsh regions, socio-economic groups, and ages included. Using secondary analysis she was able to select speakers whose contributions were appropriate for her research investigation: 'the use and perception of non-standard grammatical features in Welsh–English'. The MMB interviews brought a significant advantage to her study of dialect in that the original interviews were not aimed at any kind of linguistic investigation. They were about everyday life and so were naturalistic, with no concern about how people sounded (Roller, 2015). In her case the different basis of the original study made it valuable to her.

8.2.3 Sensitivity

Secondary analysis may bring into closer view topics that are socially and historically sensitive. Gallwey (2013) had considered the MMB interviews suitable for a doctoral thesis investigating single motherhood in post-1945 England. She planned to interview members of the generation of older women who had been single at that time. This proved not to be possible. Women were unwilling to come forward and she realised that the shame attached to being unmarried and a mother, or divorced, still endured for these women. She turned to secondary analysis as an alternative strategy, eventually discovering the MMB interviews. Searching the catalogue and interview summaries, she encountered an 'unanticipated reward', what she calls 'classificatory summaries'. The words used to describe single mothers in day-to-day parlance gave her insight into their social status (Gallwey, 2013). Similarly sociologists have turned to secondary analysis to explore areas which may be painful for interviewees to return to, or which are perhaps taboo in some way. Fielding and Fielding's research into the psychological survival of long-term prisoners was informed by earlier research carried out by Cohen and Taylor with prisoners in Durham jail (Cohen and Taylor, 1972). With access to data from the original study – documents which included the prisoners' contributions and with comments from Stan Cohen during their research – Fielding and Fielding carried out their secondary analysis, aiming to situate the prisoners as individuals with prior and ongoing life histories. This was an aspect which they felt had been under-emphasised in Cohen and Taylor's study (Fielding and Fielding, 2000).

8.3 Oral History and Insights for QSA

In what follows I explore how a focus on time helps to elaborate intersubjectivity in an interview and in its re-use, and in ethical issues arising from re-use with an extract from an interview, one of five carried out in 1992 to accompany a study of the lives of older women (Bornat, 1993). Each interview took the form of a life story, and though I already knew three of the women, two of whom had already taken part in a community oral history project I had run, Ray Jones was not known to me (having been recommended by a mutual friend). We met for the first time, face to face, when I interviewed her in the living room of her council flat in Halifax, West Yorkshire. There were just the two of us present.

This brief extract is from an interview that lasted more than two hours. As you read, you might like to make notes of your first impressions of what Ray is conveying, her style, her meanings, and what elements of context and sense of temporality might be needed in order that her account might be meaningfully interpreted. Finally, what evidence is there of intersubjectivity between Ray and myself which might be determining the nature of the encounter?

> ... that's really how I became friends with Elsie. My mother knew the family. And we went to school together. But she went on to the grammar school, because they were, they'd just her, you see, and she had a brother who was a lot older, and married. And her dad, he had a decent job, he was a wire drawer. But, so that's where she went. I'll tell you something funny now. This is going back again. You'll have to cut all these bits out, that I keep back tracking on. But in the '30s, during the depressions when everybody was poor. And this Elsie's dad, he worked in Huddersfield, and he worked in a wire mill. And he used to come home on the bus with his workmates, and they lived, you see, on Huddersfield Road, by the Calder and Hebble. And there was a gang of them used to sit upstairs on the bus, and it was winter. And on, just before you get into Huddersfield there's some very big houses, they'll be let off into rooms now I think. But they were really wealthy people who lived there. And there was one house in particular. And they never had the curtains drawn. You could see right in, they'd the lights on. And when the fellows were coming home from work it'd be about seven o'clock or so when they were on the bus. And this huge dining table was always set for dinner. And it had the

silver salvers, and candelabra, and all this. Really posh. And the men, they never said anything to each other, but they always looked. They all looked, those that were on that side of the bus. They always looked in that window, you know, to see how the other half lived. And one night they were coming home, and the curtains were drawn, and they couldn't see in. Nobody said a word. And a man from the back said: 'Kippers for tea lads!' And I thought that's one of the funniest – that's a true story is that! [*laughter*] I thought it was really funny that. That was in the '30s.

Yes, yes. So I mean, people saw those differences. People often–

Yes, Oh, yes, you couldn't help it really.

So, I mean, when you look back through your life, was there a time when you – when's the time when you felt you were best off, you know?

After the war, when, in the 1950s, when before Jessie left home, we went on a holiday. First holiday we'd ever had. And we went on a boat on the River Severn in Avon. On a launch, you know, a cabin cruiser. And that was nice. And then I suppose we were working and then I used to go down to my friends in Bognor. But then you see, when our parents were poorly, and there was only me working, well we started going backwards way. And then, to be quite candid, in the last ten years, since this government came in, it's just gone down and down. And it has for a lot of people.

Ray Jones, 1992

A story of friendship becomes an illustration of social class differences and how these were encountered and commented on in this brief interview extract. From school to work, the boundaries and observations marking social and economic distance in industrial West Yorkshire are neatly delineated in Ray's memories and through a story of 'something funny', which she retells. Ray and Elsie knew each other from primary school, but Elsie 'went on to grammar school'. We have to suppose that this was because she passed the scholarship exam, unlike Ray. But then Ray is suggesting that Elsie's different trajectory was more due to economic circumstances. It may have been that Ray's family could not afford for her to go to the grammar school. This was common enough during the 1930s, carrying on into the post-war era. She explains that Elsie was effectively an only child, as her sole sibling was an elder brother who had married and presumably left home. Moreover her father had 'a decent job'. Things were not the same for Ray, she is suggesting. Even so it seems that a story which Elsie's father told was evocative enough in its references, and indicative of inequality in so many ways, that it was meaningful across a broadly working-class experience.

8.4 Intersubjectivity and Temporality

Ray's account is many layered in terms of temporalities. The now of the interview, her encounter with me in 1992, is underpinned by her memory of a girlhood friendship – her recalling a particular road between Halifax and Huddersfield on the outskirts of the urban areas where houses were much larger and people travelled together between home and factory on the top of a bus. She draws a difference between then and now, pointing out that houses of that size would not be occupied by sole families by 1992. Wealth in West Yorkshire had moved on from the time when it might be displayed – 'really posh', in the way she describes. Within her narrative there is an additional layer of temporality. The story is second hand, told by Elsie's father to his family and somehow to Elsie. She owns it by retelling it in a context which is far removed from the '30s and to someone of a different social class and, presumably, background to her own.

These many temporalities (elsewhere distinguished as 'retrospective time', 'formatted time' and 'told time' – Bornat and Bytheway, 2012: 295) are linked through Ray's remembering; her use of memory is both subjective and collective. Her sense of self emerges in her responses to further questioning, her survival through changes of fortune, and her choice of ways of commenting on what she has lived through. Her recall can also be seen in terms of its socio-cultural references. It has a collectivist feel with what feels like a sense of social class solidarity, told through the story of 'Kippers for tea' but also through her counterposing of individual opportunity and family responsibility. She might not have gone to the grammar school because her family was not so well off, then later in life family responsibility weighs on her shoulders and choices are again limited, this time because she has become the main provider. The structuring of what she recalls plays out the tensions between how she expresses her sense of self and how she presents that self surviving in socio-cultural terms (Cubitt, 2007: 78). Revisiting an oral history transcript opens up these possibilities for interpretation and contextual analysis over time and within time boundaries.

Accounts such as Ray's also provide opportunities to explore the past by means of the scenes which she evokes. An account of 'lads' travelling home from work on the top of a bus, looking down into well-lit windows, evokes memories in a listener of a certain age but the rich depiction she uses helps to transcend further. Ray is performing for her audience of one, but presumably has used this story at other times, because she knows that it will work well.

The particular conditions of our intersubjectivity are set up when she announces a digression: 'I'll tell you something funny now.' Abrams draws on Goffman when she identifies his use of 'keying' a performance. As she puts it, a performance goes beyond 'everyday speech' and is signalled by 'the performance frame, a set of guidelines that signal to the audience that they are about to hear a performance' (2016: 134). She goes on to say that a performance, especially one that involves a joke, only works if it is recognisable and also appropriate within the context of a particular exchange. With 'Kippers for tea', Ray was performing for the interviewer, me, drawing me into the socio-historical context in which she was learning about class differences. At the same time, she is performing collective solidarity, situating herself in a particular social context (Abrams, 2016: 135–7). Her use of an anecdote indicates subversion, 'a rejection of hegemonic values' (Kirk and Wall, 2011: 208–24) at various temporal levels, as she retells the story and in the context of the story as told. She is setting norms, 'what *matters* to people' (Kirk and Wall, 2011: 233, their emphasis), which (rightly as it turns out) she is expecting me to accept.

In transcript form her performance works well; with audio it might tell us even more. What a transcript can only hint at – though in Ray's case the transcriber does make an indication with '[*laughter*]' – is what emotions are being expressed. The US oral historian Michael Frisch writes about oral history's 'deep dark secret' (cited by High, 2016: 557), arguing that oral history lost the connection with sound and orality at an early stage when transcription took over as a way to preserve, communicate and of course share the results of interviews. The result is that many hours of sound are archived; voices are recorded but rarely heard. It might be supposed that digitisation would offer ways to overcome this apparent barrier with sound. Although progress is being made through the development of voice recognition and sound editing software, it is still the case that from a methodological and interpretive perspective, reading, searching and sharing written transcripts is a great deal easier and faster than listening to audio recordings.

Without sound however, much is lost, as Thomas, cited by Hamilton (2016: 110), points out: 'too many historians still lazily mine oral histories (or preferably transcripts of them) for content alone … ignoring the ambience of the tape, the theatrics of the interview and the particularities of the medium, all of which affect the evidential value.' Portelli (1991: 63), the Italian oral historian, had earlier taken a less pejoratively worded perspective on the effect of transcribing: 'No matter how we talk about ourselves as "oral" historians, the very technology of our work is to turn the oral into the written word, to freeze fluid material at an arbitrary point in time.' He goes on to suggest that rather than judging the practice, oral historians should perhaps 'be at least aware that this is what we do'.

Going back to Ray's interview, it is certainly the case that we can't hear her Halifax accent, nor can we hear the way she leads into and tells the 'funniest … true story'. At other points in her interview when she remembers less happy events, someone re-using that interview cannot share her emotion in the way I could, at the time as her interviewer.

A turn to the emotions in the humanities, particularly in history, is leading to a new focus for interpretation, offering interesting opportunities for secondary analysis. Harding (2014: 95) argues that traditionally to be 'emotional' was associated with 'being irrational', and this meant disqualifying those who are 'usually black, working-class female' rather than 'white, middle-class male'. Secondary analysts from whatever discipline, when they work with archived interview data now and in the future, have the possibility to pursue and identify differences and requalify groups and individuals with the help of insights from these advancing methodological contributions.

Harding's work on emotions draws on the work of Raymond Williams and his idea of 'structures of feeling' what he identifies as 'a particular sense of life, a particular community of experience' and he goes on to elaborate this idea in relation to culture. Using his framework of 'levels of culture', he expands possibilities for going back to earlier archived interviews, changing focus to identify expressions of feeling and an awareness of self in the context of sources such as newspapers, magazines, films and other cultural forms, providing context. Such a rethink opens up new possibilities for understanding archived interviews, as I myself found out when I returned to an interview of my own. Looking at a wider range of secondary literature than I had previously consulted, I was able to see the social and psychological significance of music in the life of the inhabitants of a West Yorkshire village, and had to acknowledge what I had missed. To deny or exclude emotion is to narrow the range of possible interpretive contexts (Bornat, 2010). Secondary analysis encourages us to revisit interviews with a differently informed perspective. Even so, Williams emphasises the need for awareness of 'selective tradition'. What we understand to be the past will have been filtered by the perspectives of those living at that time (Williams, 1965: 65–6).

We have already recognised that research practices may change and that re-use will often require an understanding of approaches that might not meet today's ethical standards (Gillies and Edwards, 2012). However, research practice is only a part of our awareness of an earlier researcher's presence. Who that interviewer was and their context and background are also relevant. In connection with this, Hammersley raises the issue of a researcher's 'cultural *habitus*', acquired 'over time in fieldwork'. He is discussing the social anthropologist's fieldnotes which, he argues, are a product of 'first-hand experience'. And he goes on to say, 'much the same problem arises with other forms of data, even with listening to audio-tapes ... that someone else has produced' (Hammersley, 1997: 138–9). He is pointing out what he sees as some limits to using another researcher's data, and though (coming later) we might have to accept that we can only know a part of what fed into the observations and decisions which determined the results, we can make attempts at understanding. The context in which that earlier researcher lived, was influenced, collaborated, worked and what they produced should to some extent be accessible to us and form a part of how our re-use is informed. In this way we will at least be 'walking alongside' not only the research subject (Henderson et al., 2006) but the original researcher too.

8.5 Future Proofing for Ethics

Visiting archived collections of oral history interviews can be a revelation, and whether online, digitised or traditionally catalogued, it soon becomes evident that standards vary and access to material is dependent to a large extent on the degree to which depositors and archivists have taken a longer-term view of accessibility and re-use. Perhaps one can forgive those who were depositing data for not being able to predict what form the future would take. After all, analogue or tape recording lasted for over 40 years once it became available for general use, though MiniDisc recording came and went in ten years. Could any of those earlier users have predicted digitisation and its impact on recording and preserving sound, and how quickly and totally what we now call the 'digital revolution' would take over? Noting this change, and so far as re-use is concerned, there are two main issues which we might want to consider: how we make our material available for future users and what ethical issues arise from this.

Looking at the first question (future proofing) Thompson – making a case for secondary analysis – argues that:

> the most valuable qualitative datasets for future re-analysis are likely to have three qualities: firstly, the interviewees have been chosen on a convincing sample bases [sic]; secondly, the interviews are free-flowing but follow a life story form, rather than focusing narrowly on the researcher's immediate themes; and thirdly, when practicable re-contact is not ruled out. (Thompson, 2000: para 43)

His prescription perhaps errs idealistically. Oral histories vary in scope and size of given survivor rates, types of topic as well as the disciplinary background of the original researcher. The notion of a 'convincing sample' can mean different things to the sociologist, the anthropologist and the historian. The extent to which an interview may be 'free-flowing' is likely to be affected by the generosity and conditions of the funder. The UK's Heritage Lottery Fund had, by 2017 and since the 1990s, contributed over £4m towards projects with an oral history component. These have largely been short-term and community based and were preceded in the 1980s by an earlier wave of funding under the auspices of the Manpower Services Commission (Thompson and Bornat, 2017: 59). Later researchers seeking access to this extensive investment in oral history are likely to find a wide variety of interview strategies, often strictly targeted on local topics and dependent on the skills of newly trained volunteer interviewers, with project managers providing varied documentation (Freund, 2009). Thompson's final condition, re-contact, is again problematic and by no means universally obtainable, though it is an aspect which is more likely to be addressed with current future-proofing strategies including digitisation and the creation of online repositories and requirements for deposit being written into research strategies (Freund, 2009: 27; Neale et al., 2016; Unlocking Our Sound Heritage, 2019).

The readability of a collection of interviews is only one part of planning for future access and their longevity. By far the most important is something which Thompson alludes to with the third of his preconditions: 'when practicable re-contact is not ruled out' (2000: para 43). Contact with an interviewer, or with a close relative, may be possible; however if an interview does not include permission for re-use – agreed with an interviewee, protecting their interests and within a recognised legal and ethical framework – then it is not going to be usable by a later researcher.

Future-proofing interviews is not simply a matter of keeping copies of transcripts and audiotapes in an accessible archive. Without documentation, a signed recording agreement which ensures that copyright in the interview has been assigned by the interviewee to an archive, and including any restrictions requested by the interviewee, the interview cannot be re-used (see Hughes and Tarrant, Chapter 3). Space does not allow a full explanation here of the responsibilities and obligations which attach to the most up-to-date rules concerning the preservation and legal accessibility of interviews, but there are always online sources which will provide such information (see Oral History Society, 2012; UK Data Service, n.d.).

However honest and open an interviewer is about the destination of the recording, digitisation raises ethical issues, which Gluck (2013: 38) had noted even before the arrival of digital archives with online access:

> when I spoke with the women whose transcribed oral histories I edited for my *Rosie the Riveter Revisited* book, I was surprised when one of them commented that she was upset about the passage where she mentioned using a diaphragm. 'But Marie', I said, 'you approved that in your transcript'. 'Yes, but a book is different!' she replied. Indeed. And placing oral history on the web is a quantum leap in distribution that has implications for our work.

Gluck goes on to cite examples of interviews where political contexts have changed and with it the security of the interviewee. She contrasts the time of an interview with a Palestinian woman in 1998, when there was a 'spirit of hopefulness and a sense of community during the first *intifada*', with more recent times, and asks herself if she would be being fair to the 'spirit' and original 'intention' if the interview were later to be donated to the Birzeit University digital Palestinian Archive. She asks whether 'the assumptions we make about honouring the spirit of the interview and our relationship (can) continue in perpetuity' (Gluck, 2014). Changing times and the honouring of commitments resulted in a *cause célèbre* with the case of the Boston tapes when recordings made with IRA activists were archived with assurances that these would not be publicly available. When the

Northern Ireland Police Service successfully challenged this closure in the case of one particular case it was clear that there were implications for all archives (Oral History Society, 2014).

Gluck – with her concern about ethics and responsibilities in data sharing presented by the 'quantum leap' yet 'democratic promise' of putting oral history interviews on the web – could be posing a fundamental challenge not just to re-use but also to how oral historians, and others, practise in relation to the interviewees and the recording and preservation of their words. Hers is a necessary reminder of the need for additional watchfulness and sensitivity when data is made available to all.

8.6 Conclusion

This chapter has looked at aspects of re-using archived interview data from the perspective of an oral historian. With memory as the key source, time and temporality have been at the heart of a discussion which has considered the methodological implications of context, serendipity and sensitivity issues shared by re-use in oral history and in QSA research. Digging deeper with the help of a revisited interview extract, time and temporality again revealed the complexities of intersubjectivity before moving on to draw out the implications for future users of archived interviews.

Studs Terkel, the US oral historian of twentieth-century life and times, recalls that when he met Bertrand Russell, whose uncle the 1st Earl Russell met Napoleon then exiled in Elba, he felt he 'was about to shake the hand of the man who shook the hand of the man who shook the hand of Napoleon' (Terkel, 1986: 64). He was connecting across time and, in doing so, passing on his experience to unknown audiences. In evoking chains of contact he created a metaphor for the relationships and connections, known and unknown, which re-use engenders. There are many lessons to be learned from re-using data but perhaps the most important are those which cause us to examine our own practice and our relationships with interviewees, and how this will be perceived and used in a future which we can only partly imagine and cannot control.

8.7 Pedagogical Resources

British Library, Directory of UK Sounds Collection - www.bl.uk/projects/uk-sound-directory

Oral History Society providing information and publications relating to oral history activity and research - www.ohs.org.uk

Oral History, journal of the Oral History Society.

Timescapes programme archive, including knowledge bank for QL research – www.
timescapes.leeds.ac.uk/index.html

UK Data Service, archiving and providing access to UK government-funded data
sources – www.ukdataservice.ac.uk

8.8 References

Abrams, L. (2016) *Oral History Theory*, 2nd edn. Abingdon: Routledge.

Bishop, L. (2007) 'A reflexive account of reusing qualitative data: Beyond primary/
secondary dualism', *Sociological Research Online*, 12(3).

Blaxter, M. (2004) *Mothers and Daughters: Accounts of Health in the Grandmother
Generation, 1945–1978* [data collection], UK Data Service, SN: 4943. Available at:
http://doi.org/10.5255/UKDA-SN-4943-1 (accessed 24 October 2019).

Blaxter, M. and Paterson, E. (1982) *Mothers and Daughters: A Three-generational Study of
Health Attitudes and Behaviour*. London: Heinemann Educational Books.

Bornat, J. (1993) 'Life experience', in M. Bernard and K. Meade (eds), *Women Come of
Age: Perspectives on the Lives of Older Women*. London: Edward Arnold. pp. 23–42.

Bornat, J. (2005) 'Recycling the evidence: Different approaches to the reanalysis of
gerontological data', *Forum Qualitative Sozialforschung/Forum: Qualitative Social
Research*, 6(1).

Bornat, J. (2010) 'Remembering and reworking emotions: The reanalysis of emotion
in an interview', *Oral History*, 38(2): 43–52.

Bornat, J. and Bytheway, B. (2012) 'Working with different temporalities: Archived
interviews and diaries', *International Journal of Social Research Methodology*, 15(4): 291–9.

Bornat, J., Henry, L. and Raghuram, P. (2012) 'Revisiting the archives – Opportunities
and challenges: A case study from the history of geriatric medicine', *Sociological
Research Online*, 17(2): 1–12.

Bornat, J., Raghuram, P. and Henry, L. (2016) '"Without racism there would be no
geriatrics": South Asian overseas-trained doctors and the development of geriatric
medicine in the United Kingdom, 1950–2000', in L. Monnais and D. Wright (eds),
*Doctors Beyond Borders: The Transnational Migration of Physicians in the Twentieth
Century*. Toronto: University of Toronto Press. pp. 185–207.

British Library, BBC (1998) *The Century Speaks – BBC Millennium Oral History Project:
Research Guide*. London: British Library/BBC.

Cohen, S. and Taylor, L. (1972) *Psychological Survival: The Effects of Long-Term
Imprisonment*. London: Allen Lane.

Corti, L. (2011) 'The European landscape of qualitative social research archives:
Methodological and practical issues', *Forum Qualitative Sozialforschung/Forum:
Qualitative Social Research*, 12(3).

Cubitt, G. (2007) *History and Memory*. Manchester: Manchester University Press.

Evans, T. and Thane, P. (2006) 'Secondary analysis of Dennis Marsden *Mothers Alone*',
Methodological Innovations Online, 1(2): 78–82.

Fielding, N.G. and Fielding, J.L. (2000) 'Resistance and adaptation to criminal identity: Using secondary analysis to evaluate classic studies of crime and deviance', *Sociology*, 34(4): 671–89.

Freund, A. (2009) 'Oral history as process-generated data', *Historical Social Research*, 34(1): 22–48.

Gallwey, A. (2013) 'The rewards of using archived oral histories in research: The case of the Millennium Memory Bank', *Oral History*, 41(1): 37–50.

Gillies, V. and Edwards, R. (2012) 'Working with archived classic and community studies: Illuminating past and present conventions around acceptable research practice', *International Journal of Social Research Methodology*, 15(4): 321–30.

Gluck, S.B. (2013) 'From California to Kufr Nameh and back: Reflections on 40 years of feminist oral history', in A. Sheftel and S. Zembryzicki (eds), *Oral History off the Record: Toward an Ethnography of Practice*. Basingstoke: Palgrave Macmillan. pp. 25–42.

Gluck, S.B. (2014) 'Reflecting on the quantum leap: Promises and perils of oral history on the web', *Oral History Review*, 41(2): 244–45.

Hamilton, P. (2016) 'Oral history and the senses', in R. Perks and A. Thomson (eds), *The Oral History Reader*. Oxford: Oxford University Press. pp. 104–16.

Hammersley, M. (1997) 'Qualitative data archiving: Some reflections on its prospects and problems', *Sociology*, 31(1): 131–42.

Hammersley, M. (2010) 'Can we re-use qualitative data via secondary analysis? Notes on some terminological and substantive issues', *Sociological Research Online*, 15(1): 47–53.

Harding, J. (2014) 'Looking for trouble: Emotion, memory and public sociology', *Oral History*, 42(2): 94–104.

Henderson, S., Holland, J. and Thomson, R. (2006) 'Making the long view: Perspectives on context from a qualitative longitudinal study', *Methodological Innovations Online*, 1(2): 47–63.

High, S. (2016) 'Mapping memories of displacement: Oral history, memoryscapes and mobile methodologies', in R. Perks and A. Thomson (eds), *The Oral History Reader*, 2nd edn. Oxford: Oxford University Press. pp. 556–68.

Jefferys, M. (2000) 'Recollections of the pioneers of the geriatric specialty', in J. Bornat, R. Perks, P. Thompson and J. Walmsley (eds), *Oral History, Health and Welfare*. London: Routledge. pp. 75–97.

Jones, R. (1992) Interview with Joanna Bornat, Halifax. In process of being archived, 2018.

Kirk, J. and Wall, C. (2011) *Work and Identity: Historical and Cultural Contexts*. London: Palgrave Macmillan.

Millennium Memory Bank (1999) British Library: Millennium Memory Bank. Available at: http://bufvc.ac.uk/gateway/index.php/site/1230 (accessed 15 Jun 2019).

Mauthner, N., Parry, O. and Backett-Milburn, K. (1998) 'The data are out there, or are they? Implications for archiving and revisiting qualitative data', *Sociology*, 32(4): 733–45.

Moore, N. (2006) 'The contexts of context: Broadening perspectives in the (re)use of qualitative data', *Methodological Innovations Online*, 1(2): 21–32.

Neale, B., Proudfoot, R., Hughes, K. and Phillips, B. (2016) *Managing Qualitative Longitudinal Data: A Practical Guide*. Available at: https://timescapes-archive.leeds.ac.uk (accessed 15 June 2019).

Oral History Society (2012) *Is Your Oral History Legal and Ethical?* Available at: www.ohs.org.uk/advice/ethical-and-legal/ (accessed 30 October 2018).

Oral History Society (2014) *Oral History Society Statement on the Boston College Belfast Project*. Available at: www.ohs.org.uk/documents/OHS_Statement_Boston_College_Belfast_Project_May2014.pdf (accessed 25 May 2019).

Parry, O. and Mauthner, N.S. (2004) 'Whose data are they anyway? Practical, legal and ethical issues in archiving qualitative research data', *Sociology*, 38(1): 139–52.

Portelli, A. (1991) *The Death of Luigi Trastulli and Other Stories: Form and Meaning in Oral History*. Albany: State University of New York.

Raghuram, P., Bornat, J. and Henry, L. (2010) 'Difference and distinction? Non-migrant and migrant networks', *Sociology*, 44(4): 623–41.

Raphael, S. (1971) 'Perils of the transcript', *Oral History*, 1(2): 19–22.

Roller, K. (2015) 'Towards the "oral" in oral history: Using historical narratives in linguistics', *Oral History*, 43(1): 73–84.

Tarrant, A. (2016) 'Getting out of the swamp? Methodological reflections on using qualitative secondary analysis to develop research design', *International Journal of Social Research Methodology*, 20(6): 599–611.

Tarrant, A. and Hughes, K. (2019) 'Qualitative secondary analysis: Building longitudinal samples to understand men's generational identities in low-income contexts', *Sociology*, 53(3): 599–611.

Terkel, S. (1986) *Talking to Myself: A Memoir of My Time*. London: Harrap.

Thompson, P. (1975) *The Edwardians: The Remaking of British Society*. London: Routledge.

Thompson, P. (2000) 'Re-using qualitative research data: A personal account', *Forum Qualitative Sozialforschung/Forum: Qualitative Social Research*, 1(3): Art. 27.

Thompson, P. and Bornat, J. (2017) *The Voice of the Past*, 4th edn. Oxford: Oxford University Press.

Thompson, P. and Lummis, T. (2006) *Family Life and Work Experience Before 1918, 1870–1973* [computer file]. Colchester: UK Data Archive [distributor], May 2009, SN: 2000. Available at: https://beta.ukdataservice.ac.uk/datacatalogue/doi/?id=2000#!#1, (accessed 15 June 2019).

Tureby, M.T. and Johansson, J. (2016) 'Narratives from multi-cultural Sweden: Positioning and identification in immigrant collections at the archive of the Nordic Museum 1970–2015', *Oral History*, 44(2): 81–90.

UK Data Service (n.d.) *Prepare and Manage Data*. Available at: www.ukdataservice.ac.uk/manage-data (accessed 30 October 2018).

Unlocking Our Sound Heritage (2019) London: British Library. Available at: https://www.bl.uk/projects/unlocking-our-sound-heritage (accessed 15 June 2019).

Williams, R. (1965) *The Long Revolution*. Harmondsworth: Penguin.

NINE

DOING QUALITATIVE SECONDARY ANALYSIS: REVISITING YOUNG PEOPLE'S IMAGINED FUTURES IN RAY PAHL'S SHEPPEY STUDIES

Dawn Lyon and Graham Crow

--- **CHAPTER CONTENTS** ---

9.1 **Introduction**

On a visit to Qualidata, part of the UK Data Archive at the University of Essex, in 2008 to explore the archive of the Sheppey Studies, we were curious to see the materials that corresponded to some of the catalogue descriptions. An entry described as 'School Leavers Study' which referred to 'a collection of essays written by school children from the Isle of Sheppey in 1978' was especially tantalising. It comprised a set of essays that sociologist Ray Pahl had collected as part of the extensive research he conducted (with others) on the Isle of Sheppey in Kent in the late 1970s and early 1980s (Crow and Ellis, 2017). The essays were written by school leavers in 1978 imagining their futures as if they were already past. Crow was familiar with the short piece Pahl had published in *New Society* in 1978 entitled, 'Living without a job: How school leavers see their future' which discussed the essay-writers' inventiveness in relation to their future work and family lives. However, reading the accounts for ourselves, we were astounded by their depth, creativity and insight. They were moving and mature, occasionally silly and often sad. They documented the injustices of class, gender and geography through small instances of the everyday and projections across a lifetime. They made us want to know more about young people's future orientations and how these stances matter for the ways in which futures unfold. And so our story begins.

This chapter describes how we went about doing qualitative secondary analysis of these essays as part of the *Living and Working on Sheppey*[1] project (2009–11) which revisited some of Pahl's materials from his decade-long study on the Isle of Sheppey. In the first part of the discussion, the chapter considers the status of these 'documents of life' (Plummer, 2001) and the ways in which we sought to make sense of them through our own reanalysis. We read them as powerful statements of the 'spirit of the times' in which these young people lived, documenting how their hopes and expectations were inflected by the class, gender and other social relations of the day. In addition, we explored how they carry the 'imprint' of other times as the legacy of the closure of the Royal Dockyard in Sheerness on the Isle of the Sheppey in 1960 resonated down the years with implications for opportunities to live and work well (Misztal, 2003: 84–5).

---

[1]The *Living and Working on Sheppey* project was funded by the HEFCE-financed South East Coastal Communities Programme. The project team included academics from sociology and arts at the Universities of Kent and Southampton, staff from the UK Data Archive, University of Essex, the artists group *Tea*, and members (staff and community volunteers) of the Blue Town Heritage Centre, an information, resource and visitor centre on the history of Blue Town and the Isle of Sheppey. Until his death in June 2011, Ray Pahl was an informal consultant to the project.

We sought to further our understanding of these accounts through comparative analysis with a new collection of essays gathered as part of the *Living and Working on Sheppey* project written by young people in similar circumstances on the Isle of Sheppey just over 30 years later in 2010. Our comparative analysis is the focus of the second part of the chapter where we critically discuss the gains and methodological restrictions of replication.

The chapter then charts the course of our Sheppey research as we took a third step to explore the future orientations of young people by departing from the essay format and making use of tools from arts practice – improvisation and making. This subsequent research project, *Imagine Sheppey*[2] (2013–14), involved working directly with young people and artists. We chose this approach to counter some of the tendencies of working with biographies and the 'illusions' that such narratives can produce (Bourdieu, 1986). In addition, we were keen to adopt visual and performative methods that might be attractive to young people and chime with how they experience the world. This project offered further opportunity for comparison across quite different materials and for reflection on the methodological assumptions and implications of using qualitative secondary analysis as a platform for new forms of inquiry. Across the discussion in this chapter, we explore the scope of qualitative secondary analysis and the possibilities of working with existing material in three ways: reanalysing the archived data, generating more material in the present day using the same methods as previously, and generating new material on the same themes using innovative methods.

9.2 Reanalysis of Existing Data

In May 1978 the sociologist Ray Pahl arranged for classes of mainly 16-year-olds on the Isle of Sheppey in Kent to write essays imagining their futures. One hundred and forty-one pupils (89 boys and 52 girls) took part in the essay-writing exercise in their English lessons, imagining themselves towards the end of their lives, looking back and recounting what had happened. The ostensible purpose of the exercise was modest and part of Pahl's efforts to understand how the chronic economic challenges of the period were affecting ordinary people's everyday lives

---

[2]*Imagine Sheppey* was part of a large Connected Communities research grant from an AHRC/ESRC joint initiative on Community Engagement and Mobilisation. The larger project is 'The social, historical, cultural and democratic context of civic engagement: Imagining different communities and making them happen' – or *Imagine* for short – grant no ES/K002686/1.

locally. Pahl was in the early stages of what was to become a major project on Sheppey that would last a decade, with outputs that included his influential 1984 monograph *Divisions of Labour*. Fascinated by the essay-writing technique which he had read about at the time (Himmelweit et al., 1952; Veness, 1962), he undertook this project in the spirit of exploration – 'sort of a pilot thing' as he later put it in an interview with us (July 2009).

Our early encounter with the essays in the archive shaped the way the *Living and Working on Sheppey* project developed and the subsequent work it stimulated. In this section of the chapter, we discuss how we returned to the archive to read and make sense of the collection of essays from 30 years earlier (at the time of undertaking this work). We consider the possibilities and limits of qualitative secondary analysis which inevitably involves researchers working with datasets they did not design, and whose concerns they may not wholly share. We show how we went about making sense of these essays, including through drawing on the archived notes of Pahl's preliminary analysis and our own interviews with Pahl about his research process.

The essays were deposited by Pahl in the UK Data Archive at the University of Essex explicitly for subsequent researchers to access. As part of our early explorations into restudying some strands of Pahl's research on the Isle of Sheppey, we visited the archive (by appointment) and found ourselves in a temperature-controlled (and rather chilly) storage space with a large number of boxes filling the shelves. At the time, documentation on the content of the collection had been prepared but work was ongoing to organise and digitise materials from Pahl's projects. We were given gloves and asked to handle items with care. When we found the essays – which we had been particularly keen to see – we were able to take them into a small study room (just as cool) and write notes about them (only pencils allowed). The essays were handwritten on lined paper from old school exercise books and even smelled of another time.

It was impossible to read all the essays in a single setting. Most were not long – one or two paragraphs on the page – but they took time to absorb and react to as we wrote our notes about what they evoked and how this made us feel. We wanted to be able to read, reread and contemplate them without time pressure. The archive wanted to digitise them. So once we secured funding for the project, we were able to collaborate in this process and the essays were transcribed and anonymised. We refrained from 'tidying them up' in terms of grammar, spelling and punctuation, preferring the personal and visceral qualities of their original expression (see Lyon et al., 2012 for a more detailed discussion). They were made available to us as Word documents and digitised for the Qualidata collection. This helped a great deal in terms of practically working with the data.

At the same time, another vital dimension of the project was to familiarise ourselves with its context. The Isle of Sheppey is situated along the north

Kent coast in the Thames Estuary around 50 miles to the east of London, and is joined to the mainland by two bridges (including a railway line). It has an important maritime and industrial history with, until 1960, a significant Royal Naval Dockyard at Sheerness, now a commercial port. The island has struggled in times of recession and austerity (in the 1980s and from the 2000s) and scores highly on indices of social deprivation. The 1978 essay writers were facing a bleak future as the labour market which they were set to join was characterised by historically high and rising unemployment, concentrated disproportionately among young adults. Although we have no information about the social characteristics of the essay writers themselves, and no details of their family or class backgrounds, we know they were all attending the same comprehensive school on the island and were all living on Sheppey and imagining their futures from this context. We can infer that they were predominantly working class – although some might be regarded as part of a 'middle mass' bridging the traditional working-class/middle-class divide (Pahl, 1984). In this sense, their geographical and social concentration is a strength even if we cannot make any claims to the sample being representative of a broader local or national population of young people. The shared context does nevertheless provide the opportunity for us to understand how everyday life and social change are manifest and experienced in a particular place and time. This felt within reach for one of us (Crow) by virtue of growing up nearby and being only five years older than the essay writers. Lyon was a few years younger than the essay writers and grew up closer to London. However, visiting the island and reading and hearing about it through Pahl's accounts as well as in the oral history interviews we also collected (not discussed here but see Lyon, 2017) went some way to bridge this distance.

Whilst Pahl made use of the essays to inform *Divisions of Labour*, there was more to say about them, as he remarked at the time, and as we felt when we rediscovered them. Indeed, his 1978 article was just four pages long and so inevitably only touched the surface of a very extensive body of material. He acknowledges that his analysis there does not do full justice to the essay material, writing: '[They] would be extremely hard to interpret without some knowledge of the local context. As this improves, I may wish to modify my present interpretation' (1978: 262). In addition to our close reading of the essays with an interest in work and family life which we shared with Pahl, we brought some different questions to the study, for instance about 'turning points' (Abbott, 2001) and 'projectivity' as a neglected aspect of agency (Mische, 2009). This meant that our reanalysis could both re-tread familiar ground and redirect sociological attention. We were able to generate new insights about old data, and to make sense of these data differently. We were also more systematic in our analysis, both in our coding of themes and our preparedness to quantify the data relating to such variables as projected educational achievement and anticipated marital status (Lyon et al., 2012).

Our appreciation of time, temporality and 'projectivity' informed our thinking about research design (Abbott, 2001; Brannen and Nilsen, 2002; Archer, 2007; Mische 2009 – and see also Neale, 2018: Chapter 4) and the status of the essays, which was different from Pahl's own understanding. We recognised this exercise as a present-day exploration of the past imagination of the future. Jane Elliott has argued that such essays 'provide insights into children's understandings of the social world and their place within it' (2010: 1082). Although we did not read them as 'predictive, or constituting a type of plan that they expected to work towards', we did see their narratives, following Sanders and Munford, 'as expressing their understanding of their present time worlds and the possibilities they see for girls and young women [as well as boys and young men] like themselves' (2008: 331). This may well be significant for how they go on to live. As such, these reflective essays are a 'questioning exploration' which shed light on how young people may make their way through the world (Archer, 2007: 73, 65) and support the notion of 'projectivity' as a neglected aspect of agency (Mische, 2009). They are also revealing of how the world looks to a person aged 16, for example through their references to people of 50 as 'old'!

For many of the essay writers, the timing of the exercise just ahead of leaving school meant they had a heightened awareness that their lives were about to change and were evidently grappling with what this might mean. These future-as-past accounts reveal the transmission of everyday cultures of life, work and community and a sense of one's place in the world – geographically, socially, and symbolically. The analysis of the essays revealed just how much the young people's horizons were shaped by what people in their community regarded as achievements: working for oneself, owning one's own home, travelling in the wider world rather than 'staying put' on the Island. The essays are thus 'multi-voiced texts' hinting at others' values and aspirations for the essay writer as repertoires and critical resources for sense-making (Hall and Jefferson, 1976). In several essays, anticipated achievements follow imagined encouragement from a relative or friend to make the most of their opportunities.

The legacies of the Island's past also shaped the way that futures were imagined. In the context of the closure of the Dockyard as the sole significant and centuries-old employer, we can glean the workings of the 'half-life of de-industrialisation' (Linkon, 2018) in the psyches of young islanders who have grown up in the shadow of the former dockyard and the ruins of associated industries. In the 1970s, Pahl was already interested in how Sheppey came to be the place that the young essay writers experience even if they were not aware of some of its histories and traditions. These, Pahl writes, nevertheless make themselves felt through people's 'latent beliefs and values that have emerged out of their own and their parents', and perhaps grandparents', experiences' (Pahl, 1984: 185). In the context of economic recession, awareness of opportunities no longer available to the current generation meant that in several essays, horizons were shrinking rather than expanding. As researchers we were aware that such downbeat narratives in the essays had a saddening effect on us, in contrast to the buoying effect of essays in which the writers anticipated economic and social success despite such outcomes being against the odds.

The archived material of the original project includes 'behind the scenes' (McLeod and Thomson, 2009: 125) memos amongst the research team, 'marginalia' such as notes and comments on the data, odds and ends gathered in ways that can no longer be traced such as photos and small objects, and the data itself in the form of tapes, transcripts, and hand-written essays. The paradata were too fragmentary to be amenable to the same analysis as the main dataset, as Goodwin and O'Connor argue they should be (2015; see also Chapter 10) (although see Lyon et al., 2012 for a more detailed discussion). This means that we did not treat them as data in the same sense as the essays themselves. We pulled together and read all the notes we found and discussed them, first, as insights into Pahl's research process and, second, in relation to specific extracts from the essays.

Overall, this gave us glimpses into the methodological inspiration of these strands of the original project and the thinking and interests of the research team as the study developed. We came across hand-written notes by Pahl, recorded on cards in the box with the 1978 essays. 'Total fantasy', says one (about essay 8); 'totally unrealistic idea of what he earns and what he gets – own house, car etc.' says another (about essay 38). These are fascinating insights into Pahl's thinking through the data, both in terms of his authoritative stance based on his 'superior' socio-economic position and understanding of the allocation of opportunities, and in terms of themes that sparked his interest. In his *New Society* publication too he shares his own reaction to the essays where he calls 'the general level of awareness and introspection impressive and alarming' (1978: 60) – impressive for the sociological perceptiveness of the young people who wrote them, but alarming for the awareness of the constraining nature of their environment.

We have come to appreciate just how much of a pioneer Pahl was in his preparedness not only to collect but also to archive all manner of materials during the Sheppey studies. Making such material available to later generations of scholars does open a researcher up to critical scrutiny regarding the rigour of their research practices (Savage, 2010). In particular, marginal notes reveal something of the researcher's personal values, and much can also be learned about the researcher and their research practice from archived material that was not used in any publications but which nevertheless forms part of the research process, as Elliott and

Lawrence's (2017) analysis of one particular household case study on Sheppey reveals. The 1978 essays are merely a small part of a vast array of materials collected by Pahl and his colleagues during a decade of fieldwork, and making sense of them and of Pahl's interpretation of them would have been far harder without the materials that give clues to how he practised reflexivity at a time when it was much less widely acknowledged and discussed than it is today. It remains the case that not all researchers are prepared to share their personal record of the research process, but such records are an important point of reference when judging the 'trustworthiness' of qualitative research projects. Furthermore, transparency about the accuracy and care of data and directions taken in analysis by the original researcher(s) offers restudy researchers opportunities to work 'in dialogue' with their predecessors through these materials.

There is of course some personal or subjective judgement on the part of the researcher when interpreting the essay writer's intended meaning. In some instances this was at the most basic level of deciphering handwriting, and some words remained ones which we could only guess at. Even with legible handwriting there were words and phrases that were open to interpretation about whether they were the best choice to convey the author's meaning, or whether they were being used ironically or with intended humour. Our process of understanding was helped greatly by the fact that there were several of us reading the essays and comparing our interpretations. We were also aided by discussion of particular points with a local community partner in the project who was able to provide context for what some of the essay writers had written, such as the local tradition for boys of joining the navy as a career. In addition, the fact that there were 141 essays allowed us to draw out some descriptive statistics about the frequency with which particular jobs or careers were identified, or particular family trajectories envisaged, although the variability of the essays in terms of what they included or simply did not mention meant that our interpretation of these figures needed to be sensitive to the extensive 'missing data' (Lyon and Crow, 2012).

9.3 Replication and Comparative Analysis

Inspired by Pahl's material, as well as by other research using similar techniques to explore young people's aspirations, hopes, and dreams (Rex and Moore, 1967; Jahoda et al., 2002; Thomson and Holland, 2002; Bulbeck, 2005; Elliott, 2010; McDonald et al., 2011), we replicated the essay-writing exercise in 2009–10[3] in

---

[3]For simplicity, from now on, we refer to the 2010 essay writers instead of 2009-10.

order to undertake comparative analysis. The question of the extent to which researchers should change their research instruments over time is a familiar one in longitudinal research. On the one hand, using different research tools diminishes the scope for comparative analysis; on the other, it allows the research team to devise techniques that are most appropriate for the context and participant groups of the new study. This section presents our research process of collecting and analysing this material and discusses the implications of working with pre-existing data for comparative research designs.

In the interests of generating comparable data, we sought to replicate the essay-writing exercise as closely as possible, notwithstanding our awareness that engaging with young people in the twenty-first century might be better pursued with more creative methods (Thomson, 2008; Heath et al., 2009). Any documentation detailing the original instructions was lost so we wrote our own after discussing with Pahl how the 1978 exercise took place. We were very fortunate in having access to the original researcher, given his readiness to discuss the research process in which he had been involved 'warts and all'. We talked with him informally, invited him to project dissemination and community events, and participated in panel discussions with him at other events. We met with him to discuss the project and formally interviewed him twice, and we made use of other interviews he had given about his work.[4] His view of research as inevitably involving mistakes made him a valuable companion in our revisiting of his study, and his death in 2011 provided a stark reminder that the opportunity to draw on the experience of original researchers is time limited.

We followed Pahl in broad terms by asking participants to 'Imagine that you are towards the end of your life. Look back over your life and say what happened to you.' In a similar strategy to that used by Pahl, we approached teachers as collaborators to set the essay-writing task and worked with youth groups visiting the Blue Town Heritage Centre, an information, resource and visitor centre on the history of Blue Town and the Isle of Sheppey with which we collaborated. In line with current ethical research practice, we gained consent first from teachers where this exercise was undertaken in the classroom, and from the essay writers themselves. These new data collected then meant we had two sets of young people's accounts[5] written 30 years apart but marked by similar circumstances of global economic crisis.

---

[4]Notably for the Pioneers of Social Research Project at the UK Data Service: www.ukdataservice.ac.uk/teaching-resources/pioneers/pioneer-detail?id=pioneer_people_pahl

[5]In the 1978 collection, n = 141 (89 boys, 52 girls); in the 2009-10 study, n = 110 (52 girls, 55 boys, 3 unknown).

In practice, the collection of essays from young people in 2010 was a considerable challenge! Although the 1978 essays were written by 16-year-olds, in 2010, the relevant age group of the population of young people about to leave school also included 17- and 18-year-olds. It was difficult to find willing participants within or beyond the classroom, which meant that the period of data collection extended over most of the school year. This meant there was less consistency in our sample than there was with the essays collected by Pahl, which were written 'about ten days before they [pupils] were due to leave school' (Pahl, 1978: 259). An apparent reticence to express themselves in written form meant that the 2010 essays also tended to be shorter than those written in 1978. The socio-economic context of recession in 2010 following the 2008 global financial crisis offered more similarity than we anticipated when first considering the restudy however – an advantage for the research design if not for the young people whose lives were negatively affected. We had anticipated significant contrasts between the two groups of participants due to the pace and extent of social change in the intervening period and we discussed these in our regular team meetings. Nevertheless, the happenstance of both data collection processes falling at a time of economic recession allowed us to reflect on continuity as well as change in our analysis and writing.

Despite these limitations, the 2010 essays offer a rich resource for accessing some of the hopes and concerns of young people and for exploring how these differ from their counterparts 30 years previously. Some of the 2010 essays were already typed up by the young people and we transcribed the others in a similar way to match the 1978 dataset. We decided to code the essays using SPSS to explore patterns in the data, especially by cohort and gender (although current versions of qualitative software would now allow us to do this). The first step in our analysis was to consider at the level of content not only what was present but also what was absent from their accounts (see Lyon and Crow, 2012). This was a simple but powerful way of getting at the taken-for-granted elements of the stories produced at two points in time, and proved very revealing of the operation of class and gender in the local context of Sheppey, which may also have a broader salience.

The central finding that emerged from the comparison was the convergence of imagined futures between boys and girls, notably with respect to education and family formation (see Lyon and Crow, 2012). Work was still deeply gendered although imagined quite differently and with much greater variety in 2010 than in 1978. It is particularly striking that there is less emphasis on 'chronologised milestones' in 2010 compared to 1978, for instance in the proportion of essay writers who refer to the (imagined) dates of their marriages and the birth of their children. However, we do find evidence of considerable 'clarity' (Mische, 2009), that is, the degree of detail in which young people imagine their lives, including 'hyper-planning' (Hockey, 2009: 228) in the face of uncertainty. This may reflect the 'persistence of modernist age-based temporal structures' amongst a minority of both young men and women and supports the argument that young people from less-privileged backgrounds are more reflexive in their planning than their middle-class peers (Bryant and Ellard, 2015; Laughland-Booÿ et al., 2015), a topic of ongoing debate.

A striking device for story-telling in the essays is the young writers' use of a third person through which to emphasise what we might think of as their 'escape' from class destiny. In the two examples below from young men, one in 1978 and one in 2010, both juxtapose their success with the struggles of a peer, already recognising how 'little actions affect you in time' (M57/2010), and the burden of decisions and directions they face at their stage of life. In imagination they can already feel the fragility of their own trajectories expressing how else life might be.

> But now, I've made a lot of money and I've no need to work for the rest of my days, but money isn't everything, sometimes I wonder what would've happened if I hadn't been lucky in business, if I didn't make the money I had now. Would I be like my school friend Mark who is still working at the factory job he found when he was sixteen, and how lucky I thought he was to take home £40 a week although we're probably equally as happy now. [...] But my children will never have to graft like I did, at least I've got the money to give them and thats one thing Marks children will never have. (M15/1978)

> My friend rodger was one of those pieces [treasures] left uncovered, left in the dark, forgotten with no education, no job, nothing......Just writing about him makes me feel sad, but that was his own faultality not mine, I could not change the way he thought and behaved, yes, I helped hime, yes I did, but he ignored and I was left shocked. If Rodger had listened to his family, teacher and even me he could of improved how he lives now, but he chose to ignore me and now I'm retired and living right, with my grandchildren and family, while rodger chose to blow away his future to drugs and is now in sheltered accommodation. Strange how little actions affect you in time and in which become drastic ... (M57/2010)

Returning to archived qualitative material is useful not only for what it can reveal about people's lives at points in the past but also for the framework it provides to gauge social change. If researchers ask present-day respondents the same questions as were asked of previous generations, a sense can be gained of patterns of continuity and change in the interim. In our case we were able to gain a strong sense of how the world seemed to young people today compared to the perceptions of young people a generation before, even though shifting markers such as the age of leaving full-time education and training presented a challenge to the achievement of precise comparison. This is a common problem for researchers undertaking re-studies, although the value of comparisons across time has encouraged the development of innovative solutions to this and related challenges, to the extent that re-studies have become reinvigorated (Charles and Crow, 2012; Crow, 2018: 64–5). This revival will be further facilitated as archiving of material from studies becomes a norm for researchers.

9.4 Inspiration for New Research

As we hope to have shown, reading and making sense of young people's imagined-futures essays was fascinating and illuminating. It exposed their taken-for-granted dreams and expectations and the operation of class, gender and the role of place in their future orientations. At the same time, we were frustrated by some of the limitations of the essay-writing technique. Perhaps it was the reliance on text – rather than image – that led to the brevity of the essays produced in 2010. And the insistence on a single authorial voice did not create space to recognise interaction in the process of future-imagining. In this section, we discuss how we used the essays as a platform for developing and designing a subsequent research project.

In our follow-on project *Imagine Sheppey* (2013–14), we sought to engage with young people in ways that might more freely elicit their different orientations to the future. If the overstated claims of agency and empowerment in using creative methods made us wary of adopting them, at the same time we were attracted by their potential especially in relation to our earlier text-based approach, and because of the capacity of arts practice to work with imagination to produce more embodied ways of knowing (see Lyon and Carabelli, 2016 for a full discussion of this). We (Dawn, along with research associate, Giulia Carabelli) worked with a group of artists, *Tea*, who had also been involved in the *Living and Working on Sheppey* project but in a less central role[6] and a group of young people we came to know through the Blue Town Heritage Centre. We were keen to understand how they were grappling with their imagined futures in a context of limited opportunity and unfavourable public representations, as Sheppey is something of a stigmatised location within and beyond Kent. Indeed, this became apparent in this project as young people often engaged in discussion about their futures through the notion of 'value' as we discuss below.

Our approach was open-ended and experimental. If, as Mische argues (following Dewey), human action needs to be understood as 'constructed within an imaginative horizon of multiple plans and possibilities'; experience is inherently experimental, and characterised by projection (2009: 696–7). We first selected specific sites to explore some similar themes to those present in the essay writers' imaginations: work, home, and public space. *Tea* then devised immersive workshops to take place on these sites, which involved interaction and improvisation to both stimulate and reveal future orientations. We sought to intervene in each space at

---

[6]*Tea* produced a visual and aural montage of a journey along Blue Town High Street through time, drawing on memories and imaginations of people across different ages. *Back and Forth on High Street Blue Town* is at: www.livingandworkingonsheppey.co.uk/blue-town-high-street-a-video-by-tea/.

different levels: temporal, material, and symbolic. We recorded improvised performances that we hoped captured stances towards the future that could not be articulated in language alone. In addition to the audio-visual recordings of all the workshops, we wrote extensive notes and reflections on the activities. Our reports were part of the process of analysis as from one workshop to the next we began to identify significant dimensions and themes (e.g., value). These informed the content of the final project video and in turn we viewed the audio-visual material to stimulate new directions of analysis.

As well as reading this material for future orientations, we also made use of selected images from the workshops for elicitation in focus groups with a wider group of young people. In effect, our research came full circle at this point. Whilst we had engaged with arts practice in an attempt to sidestep an overreliance on talk and text (our criticism of the imagined essays approach), we were then frustrated by the difficulties in getting young people to both show their future orientations in performative and embodied ways, and to talk about them! However, the images from the workshops turned out to be a very rich source for eliciting discussion in the focus groups and (we believe) gave rise to some open and imaginative discussions as we show below.

The relative lack of material and symbolic resources possessed by working-class young people, and the context of class-based antagonisms and direct hostility towards the working class in the UK, mean that they may approach the future with more uncertainty than their middle-class counterparts, in terms of the positions they may occupy and the subjects they may become (Bryant and Ellard, 2015; Laughland-Booÿ et al., 2015). This then intensifies the 'injunction to anticipate' (Adkins, 2011: 350).

In our focus groups, young participants strongly expressed the importance of achieving a future that counts – one that has value (Skeggs and Loveday, 2012). One starting point for this discussion was in relation to Figure 9.1, which was from our workshop on 'home' (including street spaces). We gave participants copies of a selection of images and asked them to write down words that came to mind about them and then discuss them. Figure 9.1 provoked much curiosity and comments such as: 'Looks like he is stuck in a bin. Don't know how to get out.' This stimulated a discussion about their sense of constraint in relation to the future but more specifically fear and concerns about how the future might unravel. These images made possible the articulation of future thinking in more creative ways than the form and space of the essays allowed.

Value is evidently understood by the focus group participants as something which circulates rather than being a 'permanent property of the person' (Skeggs and Loveday, 2012: 472, 480). The fear of not counting was never far from the surface of their remarks. Work offers an opportunity to achieve value and

Figure 9.1 'Stuck in a bin?' – an image used for focus group elicitation

demonstrate worth but this is less true for what participants describe as a 'rubbish job' which may be intended literally: 'if you're a garbage man, it makes you look a complete poor person living on the streets', states Alex. Ambition was valued for its promise of rescuing the future: 'You gotta have an ambition to do something … you don't want to be a Mr Nobody for the rest of your life, do yer', Tom asserts. But the fear of being positioned at the bottom of social hierarchies and economic opportunities was stark: in Charlie's words, 'in the end we're going to have to clean the sewers because everyone else is higher up than us. So we're just going to get nowhere in life really.'

9.5 Conclusion: Future Directions

This chapter has sought to provide readers with a keen sense of our experience of doing qualitative secondary analysis with material from Ray Pahl's School Leavers Study on the Isle of Sheppey in Kent. We have offered a practical guide for those interested in working with existing qualitative data either to generate new insights with existing data, or to undertake new research to replicate the original or as a platform for the development of alternative approaches. We have critically discussed our own research design and analysis in the three modes in which we engaged with this material: through reanalysis of the original data, for replication and comparative analysis, and as inspiration for a new approach to some similar questions.

The process of revisiting an existing study doesn't easily come to an end. Indeed, at the time of writing, we are (once again) trying to follow up the 1978 essay writers with a view to making a short documentary film about remembering, belonging (or not), and the trajectories of deindustrialisation as they have made themselves felt in these biographies. In 2009–10, we attempted to trace them through numerous appeals in local newspapers, notice boards, and via informal channels but with no success. Perhaps having a role in a film will be more attractive than participating in a sociological interview! Similar tracing of participants in other projects has produced interesting results (see Williamson, 2004; Goodwin and O'Connor, 2015; Oakley, 2016), including rethinking the claims made by researchers in the original project. Pahl (1984: 4) himself noted this point about another classic study being revisited that raised doubts about some of the main findings of the original research, in that case because those findings reproduced cultural stereotypes rather than challenging them.

There is also another sense in which this research stays live. Just as we brought new perspectives to some of Pahl's research data which were different from the ideas through which he sought to make sense of the young people's stories (at the time of our original research ten years ago), our grasp of the materials we have added to this collection is renewed as we continue to encounter different ideas through which to explore it. As notions of half-life (Linkon, 2018), 'haunting' (Gordon, 2008), and 'affective history' (Walkerdine, 2015, 2016) have gained prominence in recent years, we have come to think more explicitly about the temporalities young people inhabit. The Royal Dockyard at Sheerness was closed in 1960 before the teenage essay writers contemplating their futures in 1978 were even born, and is an even more distant presence for the 2010 essay writers. Yet to some extent their lives – both lived and imagined – continue to unfold in its shadow.

9.6 Pedagogical Resources

Ray Pahl's *School Leavers Study* (1978) is available from the UK Data Service – https://beta.ukdataservice.ac.uk/datacatalogue/studies/study?id=4867

Several audio-files of the essays can be accessed on the *Living and Working on Sheppey* project website – www.livingandworkingonsheppey.co.uk/living-and-working-on-sheppey/young-people-and-the-future/

See also SAGE Research Methods: Tarrant, A. (2018) 'Researching men's care responsibilities in low-income families using qualitative secondary analysis' – http://methods.sagepub.com/case/mens-care-responsibilities-in-low-income-families-qualitative-analysis

9.7 **References**

Abbott, A. (2001) *Time Matters: On Theory and Method*. Chicago: University of Chicago Press.

Adkins, L. (2011) 'Practice as Temporalisation: Bourdieu and Economic Crisis', in S. Susen and B.S. Turner (eds), *The Legacy of Pierre Bourdieu: Critical Essays*. London: Anthem Press.

Archer, M. (2007) *Making our Way through the World*. Cambridge: Cambridge University Press.

Bourdieu, P. (1986) 'L'illusion bibliographique', *Actes de la Recherche*, 62/63: 69–72.

Brannen, J. and Nilsen, A. (2002) 'Young people's time perspectives: From youth to adulthood', *Sociology*, 36(3): 513–37.

Bryant, J. and Ellard, J. (2015) 'Hope as a form of agency in the future thinking of disenfranchised young people', *Journal of Youth Studies* 18(4): 485–499.

Bulbeck, C. (2005) 'Schemes and dreams: Young Australians imagine their future', *Hecate*, 31(1): 73–84.

Charles, N. and Crow, G. (2012) 'Community re-studies and social change', special issue of *Sociological Review*, 60(3): 399–404.

Crow, G. (2018) *What are Community Studies?* London: Bloomsbury Academic.

Crow, G. and Ellis, J. (2017) *Revisiting Divisions of Labour*. Manchester: Manchester University Press.

Elliott, J. (2010) 'Imagining a gendered future: Children's essays from the National Child Development Study in 1969', *Sociology*, 44(6): 1073–90.

Elliott, J. and Lawrence, J. (2017) 'Narrative, time and intimacy in social research: Linda and Jim revisited', in G. Crow and J. Ellis (eds), *Revisiting Divisions of Labour*. Manchester: Manchester University Press. pp. 189–204.

Goodwin, J. and O'Connor, H. (2015) *Norbert Elias's Lost Research: Revisiting the Young Worker Project*. Farnham: Ashgate.

Gordon, A. (2008) *Ghostly Matters: Haunting and the Sociological Imagination*. Minneapolis: University of Minnesota Press.

Hall, S. and Jefferson, T. (eds) (1976) *Resistance through Rituals: Youth Subcultures in Post-war Britain*. London: Hutchinson.

Heath, S., Brooks, R., Cleaver, E. and Ireland, E. (2009) *Researching Young People's Lives*. London: Sage.

Himmelweit, H., Halsey, A.H. and Oppenheim, A.N. (1952) 'The views of adolescents on some aspects of the social class structure', *British Journal of Sociology*, 3(2): 148–72.

Hockey, J. (2009) 'The life course anticipated: Gender and chronologisation among young people', *Journal of Youth Studies*, 12(2): 227–41.

Jahoda, M., Lazarsfeld, P. and Zeisel, H. (2002) *Marienthal: The Sociography of an Unemployed Community*. New Brunswick, NJ: Transaction Books.

Laughland-Booÿ, J., Mayall, M. and Skrbiš, Z. (2015) 'Whose choice? Young people, career choices and reflexivity re-examined', *Current Sociology*, 63(4): 586–603.

Linkon, S. (2018) *The Half-Life of Deindustrialisation*. Ann Arbor: University of Michigan Press.

Lyon, D. (2017) 'Time and place in memory and imagination on the Isle of Sheppey', in G. Crow and J. Ellis (eds), *Revisiting Divisions of Labour*. Manchester: Manchester University Press.

Lyon, D. and Carabelli, G. (2016) 'Researching young people's orientations to the future: The methodological challenges of using arts practice', *Qualitative Research*, 16(4): 430–45.

Lyon, D. and Crow, G. (2012) 'The challenges and opportunities of re-studying community on Sheppey: young people's imagined futures', *Sociological Review* 60: 498–517.

Lyon, D., Morgan, B. and Crow, G. (2012) 'Working with material from the Sheppey archive', *International Journal of Social Research Methodology*, 15(4): 301–9.

McDonald, P., Pini, B., Bailey, J. and Price, R. (2011) 'Young people's aspirations for education, work, family and leisure', *Work, Employment and Society*, 25(1): 68–84.

McLeod, J. and Thomson, R. (2009) *Researching Social Change: Qualitative Approaches*. London: Sage.

Mische, A. (2009) 'Projects and possibilities: Researching futures in action', *Sociological Forum*, 24(3): 694–704.

Misztal, B. (2003) *Theories of Social Remembering*. Maidenhead: Open University Press.

Neale, B. (2018) *What is Qualitative Longitudinal Research?* London: Bloomsbury Academic.

Oakley, A. (2016) 'Interviewing women again: Power, time and the gift', *Sociology*, 50(1): 195–213.

Pahl, R.E. (1978) 'Living without a job: How school leavers see the future', *New Society*, 2 November: 259–62.

Pahl, R.E. (1984) *Divisions of Labour*. Oxford: Basil Blackwell.

Plummer, K. (2001) *Documents of Life 2*. London: Sage.

Rex, J. and Moore, R. (1967) *Race, Community and Conflict: A Study of Sparkbrook*. Oxford: Oxford University Press.

Sanders, J. and Munford, R. (2008) 'Losing self to the future? Young women's strategic responses to adulthood transitions', *Journal of Youth Studies*, 11(3): 331–46.

Savage, M. (2010) *Identities and Social Change in Britain since 1940*. Oxford: Oxford University Press.

Skeggs, B. and Loveday, V. (2012) 'Struggles for value: Value practices, injustice, judgment, affect and the idea of class', *British Journal of Sociology*, 63(3): 472–90.

Thomson, P. (ed.) (2008) *Doing Visual Research with Children and Young People*. London: Routledge.

Thomson, R. and Holland, J. (2002) 'Imagined adulthood: Resources, plans and contradictions', *Gender and Education*, 14(4): 337–50.

Veness, T. (1962) *School Leavers: Their Aspirations and Expectations*. London: Methuen.

Walkerdine, V. (2015) 'Affective history, working-class communities and self-determination', *Sociological Review*, 62: 699–714.

Walkerdine, V. (2016) 'Transmitting class across generations', *Theory & Psychology*, 25(2): 167–83.

Williamson, H. (2004) *The Milltown Boys Revisited*. Oxford: Berg.

TEN

IMAGINATION AND THE ANALYTICAL POTENTIAL OF WORKING WITH NON-INTERVIEW OR UNUSUAL DATA

John Goodwin and Henrietta O'Connor

CHAPTER CONTENTS

10.1 Introduction

Why is it that in the social sciences we seem to prioritise some forms of data over other forms of data? Why do we champion in-depth interviews undertaken as part of primary data collection over the secondary analysis of the 'flotsam and jetsam' (Stanley, 2016: 3) or the 'life ephemera' that endures the trials and tribulations of complex lives? In this chapter we aim to explore our approach to using non-interview or unusual data in qualitative research, and we illustrate our orientation and approach drawing upon over 20 years of experience and using examples from our revisits to earlier school-to-work transition projects: our work on Pearl Jephcott, C. Wright Mills and the *Return to Winston Parva*. While these projects were undertaken as restudies or as research work to understand the auto/biographical history and contribution of specific sociologists, our examples will be of interest to anyone seeking to understand what has gone before and the immense analytical and explanatory potential of unusual data such as notebooks and personal research ephemera. Indeed, the examples we have included tend to be those where the extraneous data and archived materials have yielded both significant insights and lessons too for our own sociological imagination/practices.

We also hope to reveal something of the implications of our approach for research practice as well as some cautionary notes for those wanting to adopt this orientation to research. The examples we offer here do not appear in chronological research order but instead build upon what we see to be the four key lessons: i) Starting Points – 'Find the Files'; ii) Read the Supporting Materials; iii) Reimagine Drawings, Pictures and Maps; and iv) Don't Forget about Ephemera. We begin with a brief discussion of 'data' and the need for creativity and imagination before outlining our data and the key lessons we want to highlight.

10.2 Be Imaginative - What is Data Anyway?

The social sciences are strewn with textbooks on research methods written from a whole variety of perspectives and approaches ranging from a general 'consideration of procedure' to detailed explorations of particular techniques. General books on research design tend to follow a routine, standardised and often somewhat uninteresting format. They begin with discussions of the philosophy of social science; tracts on epistemology and ontology, subjectivity and objectivity; and considerations of whether the social sciences are really scientific at all, before moving on to the particular applications of methods in the field. We are asked to consider debates that are typically presented along the primary versus secondary, qualitative versus quantitative binary divides. Actual data collection methods are considered, and these are usually the same standard set ones that one would expect in any social researcher's toolkit from interviews (in all their forms) and surveys (in all their forms) through to observational design and perhaps even experimental methods. Following some basics on quantitative or qualitative analysis there is often a conclusion about the future direction of travel for this standard stock of methods. Books on specific methods tend not to deviate from this pattern. Although they are usually more detailed considerations of the specific application of a technique or design, they tend to be the *same* specific methods and approaches undertaken in the *same* way they always have been, leading to the *same* usual data – a good grounding but hardly inspiring. Although our characterisation is, perhaps, a little harsh, such a standardised approach to research design is actually underpinned by preoccupation with what can't be done rather than what can be done. The impact of this approach, the impact of this obsession with 'epistemological rules', of 'correct procedures' and of strict adherence to set formulations, is to preclude alternatives and to potentially stifle creativity, innovation and imagination, seemingly in order to maintain a semblance of 'scientific rigour', 'standardisation' and 'replication'. Of course, these are important broad concerns that we should all be mindful of – but not if this 'closes off', to social science practice, a whole wealth of data, analytical possibilities and orientations not considered usual. As Livingston (1949: 1) wrote to C. Wright Mills: 'it is my belief that a University is a place where people of diverse disciplines may get together to exchange ideas ... this I have found, the east side of the block is surprised to discover that the west side of the block is concerned with anything except equations.' Having other concerns, developing alternative approaches, and dealing with different techniques and unusual forms of data *have* to be worthwhile in stimulating in Millsean terms the 'sociological imagination'. Yet despite this call we continue to be methodologically conservative, use limited ranges of data and techniques, write for implied audiences and remain blinkered to different approaches and potentialities.

This is wasteful, canonical and partisan, enabling methodological fetishism and the avoidance of engagement beyond the standard approaches to 'valid knowledge' creation. Another form of what Miliband (1962) suggested always angered Mills, that is, the 'sophisticated apologetics for the inexcusable, social scientists as shields of orthodoxy and bellboys of authority' (Miliband, 1962: 17). Methods texts protect and project standard research orthodoxies. Or as Mills (1959) himself wrote in *The Sociological Imagination*, 'every time intellectuals have the chance to speak yet do not speak, they join the forces that train men [and women] not to be able to think and imagine and feel in morally and politically adequate ways' (1959: 134). Mills's (1959) attack on bureaucratic research, abstracted empiricism or grand theory still resonates as a call for continued creativity and greater imagination to enable the creation of reality-congruent knowledge so we may know something of 'what is going on in the world'. Despite being written over 60 years ago *The Sociological Imagination* demands imagination – which for us is resourceful, ingenious, original and inventive approaches to data and data collection. As Mills (1959: 120) states, the 'social analyst has avoided any rigid set of procedures: he [*sic*] has sought to develop and to use in his work the sociological imagination ... not inhibited by method and technique; the classic way has been the way of the intellectual crafts-man.' Be inspired by a wide variety of data and approaches, don't limit yourself to rigidity and be open to the opportunities that all materials may offer. Follow your own path, think for yourself and engage with data as you see fit.

> Let every man [*sic*] be his own methodologist; let every man be his own theorist; let theory and method again become part of the practice of a craft. Stand for the primacy of the individual scholar; stand opposed to the ascendancy of research teams of tech-nicians. Be one mind that is on its own confronting the problems of man and society. (Mills, 1959: 245–6)

To this end, in over 20 or so years of research, for us this has manifested itself not in the direct interest with the 'formal data' collected as part of past research projects, but instead with an obsession for the unusual, often secondary, ephem-eral or even discarded materials that existed around the more formalised data collection procedures. The handwritten notes on the interview schedule reveal-ing an intimate glimpse of a person or process as opposed to the data captured by the carefully crafted questions on the interview schedule itself. This 'glimpse' of a person is as important to our understanding and in making the connec-tions between the micro, meso and macro – or in Millsean terms, linking history with biographies – as the formalised data the research was designed to collect. Those glimpses add together as the nexus relationships that tell us much about the changes and transformations in the social world. Our starting point is not abstract theoretical or methodological models nor is this a hierarchy of 'value' (this data is better than that) but a matter of how one orientates oneself as a researcher to the material available and their analytical potentialities. As Gouds-blom (1977: 6) suggests, 'unfortunately it is not superfluous to remind ourselves that in sociology we are dealing with people', and people are not always best understood or explored via rigid research designs or via the reliance on only certain types of data. It is data 'in the round' which is of interest to us.

We have contributed to this argument elsewhere (see Hughes and Goodwin, 2014; Hughes et al., 2016; see also Edwards et al., 2017) in relation to Norbert Elias's sociological practice of analysing society in long-term perspective and 'whether medieval manners texts; literature and art works; and, by extension, latter-day equivalents – television, film, social media, blogs, etc. – can be treated and approached as "reliable informants" on the social universe' (Hughes et al., 2016: 123). Conventional methodological standards place limitations on the use of such materials. Yet if, as researchers, we orientate ourselves differently to such materials rather than seeing them as 'problematic', these become empirical resources that when analysed can offer significant insight into unfolding relationships, human interdependencies and broader social conditions (Hughes et al., 2016) or again, what Mills refers to as the intersections of history and biography. In this sense 'data' can include anything or everything (see Neale, Chapter 4). Why limit data collection analysis based on philosophical epistemological proclivities written in the late nineteenth century? Data is everything and anything that points to the stories of people, their relationships and how those relationships change or remain the same spatially or temporally. As such we could use a discarded building brick from a derelict colliery site, stamped in the 1960s with the initials of the UK National Coal Board, and read this as data to tell the story of the decline of mining in the UK. The brick represents more than the clay it is made from; it is symbolic of a way of life. Alternatively, we could consider the discarded cotton bobbins left unused in since-demolished Leicester factories as a long-forgotten artefact of globalisation (see Goodwin, 2016). Or what about the 'sticker bombs' which decorate the street furniture in most contemporary cities, and which speak to tribal localities, identity politics, fandom or protest? The 'everything' also includes the wider range of ephemera created by researchers. As we suggest elsewhere:

> Our starting point was not with technical definitions of the data or method and we did not create a hierarchy of data privileging one form or type of data or material over another. Instead, we focused on what these materials could tell us … So, we would define fieldnotes, marginalia and paradata quite broadly … For us it was/remains all those materials collected as part of supporting or in addition to the research process, annotations, augmentations revealed through the analysis of original documents, by-products, non-standard data, ephemera, letters, pictures and notes. In short, everything that had been collected was viewed by us as a potential source of data suitable for secondary analysis. (O'Connor and Goodwin, 2017: 94; see also Bornat, Chapter 8).

Such materials provide glimpses into both the lives of those being studied and the lives, working practices, orientations, biases, and preoccupation of those working in the field collecting the data or designing schemes of research. Using such ephemeral, non-standard or unusual data for analysis, to see what we can learn, adds value to our discipline. As such, as well as any substantive findings the formal data may reveal, these additional sources are important for understanding both the history of the social sciences and that it is only through having an appreciation of these that one can understand how we have come to be as a discipline, the context of what the authors were writing and the changing nature of research practices.

10.3 Our Sources of 'Data'

For this chapter we are drawing upon data collected during research undertaken over the last 20 years by the authors collectively or by one of the authors as part of a joint research enterprise with the other associated projects. Since 2001 we have been very fortunate to have the opportunity to revisit 'lost' and/or underutilised school-to-work transition projects. These, in many ways, were the starting point for us with the fascination with data from 'around' research projects as opposed to the formal data itself. For example, in our reworking of *The Adjustment of Young Workers to Work Situations and Adult Roles*, we were initially attracted by the quality of the fieldnotes that accompanied the interview schedule. It was while working on the archive relating to this project that we had a chance encounter with Pearl Jephcott. The reference was to her book *Married Women Working* (1962) and a collaboration between some of the Leicester research team and colleagues at the London School of Economics. This chance encounter transformed into an academic 'obsession' and ongoing research project to document and explore all aspects of Jephcott's life and sociological work (see Goodwin, 2018). This included numerous archival trips which revealed Pearl's skills and her abilities and creativity as a researcher – a researcher not afraid to be imaginative, take epistemological risks and bend methodological rules (see Goodwin and O'Connor, 2015a; Goodwin, 2018).

Following the fiftieth anniversary in 2012 of the death of sociologist C. Wright Mills there has been an increased interest Mills's works (see, for example, Aronowitz, 2012). Mills has been a longstanding research interest of Goodwin and to coincide with the anniversary of Mills's death, he visited the Dolph Briscoe Center for American History at the University of Texas, Austin, to seek out and visit the repositories of Mills's archived materials and unpublished writings. Goodwin had no initial outcome in mind for these trips beyond engaging and interacting with Mills's original materials. However, they did prompt detailed reflection at length on Mills's unique legacy for the practice of sociology – how sociologists learn, perform and refine their craft. Finally, we draw upon our experiences with the second Elias restudy that we have been involved with – *Return to Winston Parva*, 'Winston Parva' being the pseudonym for a Leicester community where the research was conducted for Elias and Scotson's *The Established and the Outsiders* (1965). We have been working on the restudy for some time but our initial efforts were hampered by limited archived materials, a missing thesis upon which the book was based and the premature death of John Scotson. Following our earlier work (see O'Connor and Goodwin, 2012), friends of the research team were contacted by John Scotson's estate. They offered what was described as 'a bundle of papers' belonging to John Scotson which turned out to be the most complete set of background materials and research ephemera relating to his original thesis – *A Comparative Study of Two Neighbourhood Communities in South Wigston* – and, in turn, the basis of the origins of *The Established and the Outsiders* (for a fuller account see Goodwin et al., 2016).

10.4 Working with Non-Interview or Unusual Data in Four Lessons

There are very few texts which deal with the type of research we have undertaken. No specific textbook which could tell us how to conduct a restudy or replication of *Adjustment of Young Workers to Work Situations and Adult Roles* or *The Established and the Outsiders* (indeed there is no standard definition of what a restudy actually is). There are few books aimed at sociologists specially, or social scientists more broadly, about working in archives. There are books on archival research, for sure, but very few which offer insights into the practicalities or realities of undertaking this research or how to frame it sociologically (see Moore et al., 2016). Until we wrote about the issue (see Goodwin and O'Connor, 2006) there was no sustained discussion about the validity of treating fieldnotes or interviewer notes as 'secondary data' in their own right as so little of this type of material has ever been subject to secondary analysis (there are exceptions, e.g., Savage, 2005). Often locked away in filing cabinets, hidden in the attics of retired researchers or (more simply) lost, fieldnotes and research ephemera are so important for our understanding yet rarely feature in analysis. As such, anyone wanting to engage with unusual data may well benefit from our research process and the lessons we have learned along the way.

10.4.1 Lesson One: Starting Points – 'Find the Files'

> Mills' notion of the sociological imagination is mentioned in virtually every introductory textbook and reader on the market today – and with good reason, considering it accurately captures the uniqueness of the sociological perspective. (Kaufman, 1997: 309)

Researchers, typically, generate a substantial amount of material as they research and write. However, a significant proportion is rarely analysed or treated as 'data'. These additional materials may be largely incidental to the research and writing process *or* they might be part of a sustained set of practices. For example, whatever the research or writing project, Mills (1959) famously instructs, sociologists should 'start a file' to capture observations, fringe thoughts or snippets of conversation so as to sustain the 'sociological imagination'. In Mills's calls 'on intellectual craftsmanship', he provides a blueprint for those who want to be social scientists. He provides an outline of the skills required to undertake the sociologist's craft, and keeping a file of material is central to this. He suggests:

> set up a file, which is, I suppose, a sociologist's way of saying: keep a journal. Many creative writers keep journals; the sociologist's need for systematic reflection demands it. In such a file as I am going to describe, there is the joined personal experience and professional activities, studies under way and studies planned. In this file, you, as an intellectual craftsman [sic], will try to get together what you are doing intellectually and what you are experiencing as a person ... It also encourages you to capture 'fringe-thoughts': various ideas which may be by-products of everyday life, snatches of conversation overheard on the street, or, for that matter, dreams. (Mills, 1959: 196)

Mills certainly practised what he preached. He describes his note-taking process in his letter and biographical writings (see Mills and Mills) and his files contain a vast wealth of material with each file hand-labelled and curated for a particular project or purpose (see Figure 10.1).

Figure 10.1   Example of a 'Millsean' file: Mills, Charles Wright, Papers 1934–1965, Box: 4B379. Folder: Theory of the Cuban Revolution. Photograph by John Goodwin

In each file there is a combination of Mills's notes on legal yellow pads, combined (sometimes seemingly randomly) with typescripts and drafts; notes, notebooks and journals; research reports by Mills and others; survey instruments and tables of survey results; and correspondence and reviews. The collection includes type-scripts and mimeographed drafts of his books in various stages of completion, as well as drafts of articles, speeches and reviews. Other items include statistical reports, seminar papers, magazine and journal articles, and classroom materials for courses taught by Mills and others. These research and project files also contain scattered correspondence, notes and literary productions by Mills. The bulk of the collection consists of newspaper and magazine clippings organised by subject or by project, many with underlining, written comments or annotations by Mills himself. Engaging directly with Mills's files reveals them to be eccentric and eclectic about the archived documents, with a mixed logic of their own combining academic work, personal reflections, word play and very personal comments (for example, '[I] *always seems to choke with women*'). Where formal archives relating to the work of Pearl Jephcott exist, most notably the University of Glasgow, we see the same attention to detail as in Mills's files. Like Mills, Jephcott continually recorded and reflected on the social world around her. This means she accumulated a massive amount of material, and from that which is formally archived it is clear she had 'retained everything in these archives going way beyond what most retain including an eclectic mix of extensive correspondence, rich methodological notes, particulars of procedures, details of sampling, response/non response rates, extensive photographs and drawings' (Goodwin, 2018: 4).

> The past is over and gone. What remains are small fragmentary traces, the flotsam and jetsam of past lives and events. These traces have their existence now and are made sense of in the present. They are the basis of what I term the 'now/past' ... The trace, what remains, has an afterlife of a kind. But this is not a residue of the past, for this makes it sound like it's a part of something being re-assembled. And nor is it a clue, for this situates it too much in terms of 'now' and its investigations. The trace is instead the essence of the 'now/past': there is a trace of what once was back then, although this is but faintly seen, and it can only be understood in terms of now. (Stanley, 2016: 3)

Yet these are not complete – in the sense that they do not reflect the sum total of Jephcott's or Mills's work. They only reflect that which was formally archived. Yet the formally archived materials contain hints, suggestions and links to the possibility of connected materials hidden elsewhere in offices, filing cabinets, personal collections, lofts, sheds or informal archives: what Stanley (2016) refers to as 'the trace'. We need to follow the trace. A good example here is the Jephcott research. Goodwin approached every archive, grant awarding body and university that had any association with Jephcott – from Jamaica to Hong Kong via Aberystwyth, Glasgow, Nottingham and Reading. What this provided was snippets of information about her research, but it remained 'incomplete'. Yet there were pointers to other materials, hints at other research work, publications and research collaborations. These traces were located up via genealogical research and the location of Jephcott's relatives in Australia. Picking up on the clues, the close reading of any materials we had meant that the remnants of her personal research archive – personal journals and notebooks on Hong Kong, Australia and Eastern Europe – were discovered and could be used to valuably supplement the formally archived materials relating to Jephcott. By following the trace, what we end up with is a richly detailed and evocative collection.

A few observations are useful at this point. First, as a starting point for creative engagement with data in its broadest sense, the advice that Mills offers is sound. As the above quotation reveals, keeping the sociological imagination alive does not rely solely on traditional forms of data but, as Mills advocates, snippets of conversations, dreams, overheard points of view and so forth. All of these are then reflected upon systematically – observe, record, reflect, repeat. It is here that the imagination is stimulated and kept alive. Mills took inspiration from everyday life, everyday objects, and everyday pieces of conversation, then systematically considered them in the file, moved them around, reflected upon them, and 'played' with the ideas to keep his imagination alive. This is good practice to stimulate the imagination. Second, if others followed the practical advice of Mills then there should be scores of 'files' created, curated and maintained, and significant amounts of data should exist alongside formally created materials. So what is in these files? Where are these files? How can we get access to these files in order that we may subject materials to secondary analysis to aid our understanding, deepen our knowledge, and define the glimpses of the individuals (researchers and researched)? Finally, recognise that finding and accessing this material requires time, patience and commitment. It requires a willingness to devote a substantial amount of effort to hunting, searching, following up leads, closing of 'dead ends' and requesting access. The trace can be time consuming, but the intellectual rewards can be substantial.

In summary, the first lesson is not only to create your own files to help with your imagination but also to trace the files of others. Scour the archives, formal and informal, for materials relating to your areas of interest.

10.4.2 Lesson Two: Read the Supporting Materials

Our first encounter with 'supporting materials' was during *Adjustment of Young Workers to Work Situations and Adult Roles*. It was while carrying out this research that we came to realise the importance of the material that exists 'around' research projects and that this material should be treated as data and analysed in its own right. Project descriptions, correspondence and letters (see Goodwin and Hughes, 2011), draft papers and research notes all became key to our understanding of the evolution and the fate of the original project. Central to our approach was the assertion that to meaningfully interpret the data on youth transitions collected as part of the original research, we must re-examine the research and data collection processes as detailed in the extensive interviewer notes that accompanied the interview schedule. For us this was based on three main reasons. First, interviewer notes provide essential contextual information required for the secondary analysis of the data. Second, interviewer notes provide a rare insight into the experiences of those collecting data in the field. Third, a secondary analysis of the interviewer notes may reveal factors that could have affected the data collection process. Without attempting to understand the thoughts, feelings, ideas, and experiences of the interviewer it would be difficult for the secondary analyst to fully understand the data. Offering a fascinating snapshot into the lived lives of those who participated in the project, the data also revealed a great deal about past research practice (Goodwin and O'Connor, 2003, 2015b).

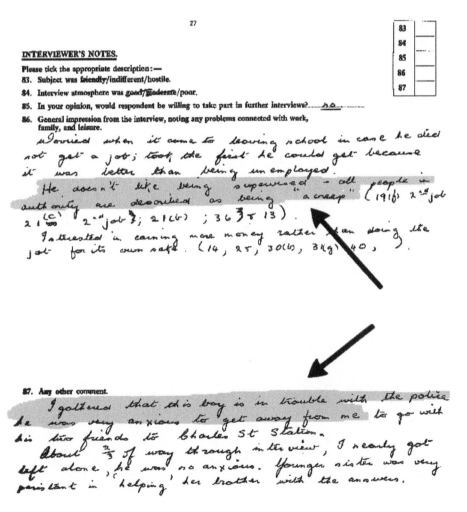

Figure 10.2 Interviewer notes section – *Adjustment of Young Workers to Work Situations and Adult Roles 1962-1964*

In Figure 10.2 we see the interviewers' reflections on the interview and the additional information they have gleaned either through the interview or from other sources. 'I gather that this boy is in trouble with the police and was anxious to get away' is an insight into the life of the respondent that would not have been evident from the more formal interview questions. The respondent's anti-authoritarianism is also revealed here with 'anyone in power being described as a creep'. In another interview, the interviewer wrote:

> The boy to use his own phrase was rather 'miserable faced' but friendly. He came from a large family who lived in one of the decrepit slum dwellings in ******. The front room was filthy dirty, smelt, and wallpaper was peeling off or had already been torn off. There was no carpet and very little furniture apart from a large T.V. set standing in the corner. The children were filthy dirty, but the mother was a very pleasant woman, shabbily dressed. The boy seemed to imply that he had 2 fathers, and it seems probable that one of them has left home and the other moved in ... A rather sad case of a boy with a poor home surroundings and who had experienced being out of work himself and had seen his father unemployed.

A great deal of information is revealed in these interviewer notes about the respondent, their family, their financial circumstances and so forth. One also gets

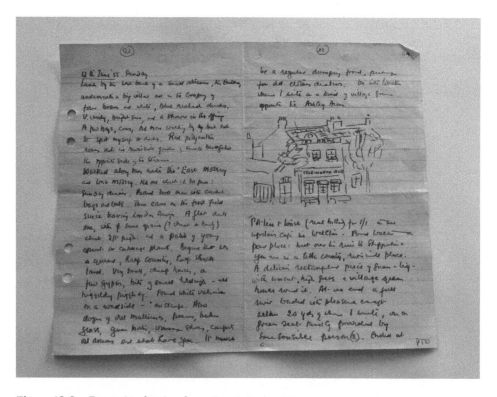

Figure 10.3   Example of notes from Pearl Jephcott's personal notebooks, June 1955. Courtesy of the Estate of Pearl Jephcott. Photograph by John Goodwin

a sense of the interviewer here, and their own values and perspectives. Given the above, it is easy to see why the interviewer notes held our fascination and why we felt that a secondary analysis of this material specifically would add value and aide our understanding.

Research notes written in personal research journals were also a key feature of Pearl Jephcott's research practice. She meticulously recorded the world around her, and the notes underscore the extent of her 'craft'; like Mills she observed, recorded and reflected upon everything and anything of interest. Figure 10.3 is an extract from her personal research journals (dated 1955). In it she records what she sees, documents the people she encounters, and draws a picture of a public house. The notes contain detail of flowers seen, people encountered, and a brief description of a gypsy [sic] camp and their smallholdings. The notes are a pointer to a past way of life, a snapshot of English rural life in the 1950s. They are evocative and suggestive of the key themes that were of concern in her research.

Lesson two suggests that a great deal of additional information can be gleaned by treating supporting materials as data, and subjecting them to a process of analysis.

10.4.3 Lesson Three: Reimagine Drawings, Pictures and Maps

The files that we uncovered have rarely been wholly text-based. Instead, they have contained maps, images, pictures, drawings, greetings cards, postcards, photographs and photographic negatives. Again, it is often the case that these images are created and/or collected 'around' the research in order to document research sites and locations, and depict localities, people and situations. The files have contained supplementary artwork and photographs not finally used in the writer's publications or research. They contain artwork by individuals themselves; Mills's papers, for example, would include drawings of houses, building plans or photographs that he had taken. Likewise, Jephcott's files and notebooks are richly illustrated by herself, so much so that it is clear that drawing was central to Jephcott's sociological craft (see Figure 10.4).

These drawings, doodles, sketches, maps and plans reveal something of the research process, the research locations, and the practice of the researcher. As such they can be analysed as data in their own right. We are mindful that there are many approaches to analysing or interpreting images, but we adopted Akeret's (1973) 'photoanalysis' as it represents a straightforward, 'pragmatic' approach to image analysis, both practical and easy to apply. Akeret (1973) advises going over the images again and again and prompts us to asks questions such as:

1   What do you see?
2   Who is in the picture?

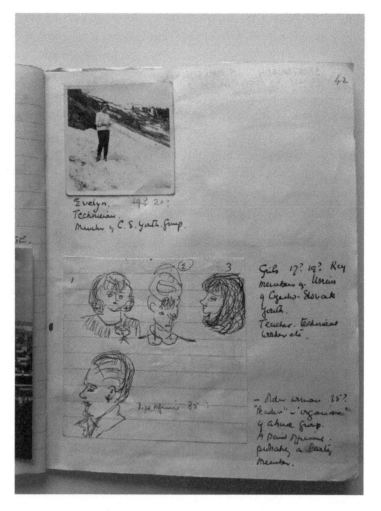

Figure 10.4   Example of drawings from Pearl Jephcott's Czechoslovakia notebook, 1966. Courtesy of the Estate of Pearl Jephcott. Photograph by John Goodwin

3   Where was it taken?

4   How are they dressed?

5   What are the relationships between those in the picture?

6   What can be inferred about their emotions? Does it contain signifiers of class, income, ethnicity, education, occupation?

7   Who created the image and is there evidence of manipulation?

8   What was the intended audience for the 'picture'?

Such questions, while seemingly straightforward, are sociologically pertinent and point to the symbolic and analytical value of the image in terms of what can be revealed through a very 'close reading'. We need to reimagine the images and read them as 'text', and explore the relational clues they contain and the further traces that they may reveal. So, in the case of Jephcott's work presented in Figure 10.4, what do we see? There is a combination of photographic images and pencil drawings all depicting people and annotated with brief descriptions. She has an obsession for detail, a desire to capture 'character', age, dress and the mundane. She draws the individual and records their occupation, organisation and association, perhaps as an aide-memoire for future contacts or research. We can see 'Evelyn' stood on a snow-covered slope. She is a technician and member of a youth group. Yet Pearl is unclear on Evelyn's age as the later pencil annotations show. One page with five images that point to further 'traces' and which emphasise Jephcott's substantive interests and her practice.

As we have discussed elsewhere, the discovery of images can also prompt the creation of new images. In 2012 we wrote about 'walking the field' (O'Connor and Goodwin) using old photographs from *The Established and the Outsiders* research site (Winston Parva) to match the then and now, the old and new with the simple aim of seeing what survived. This process caused us to think about the original research into the depiction of areas, contrasting how the area was described in the 1960s book with what we could observe in the 2000s. It is a technique used in the Jephcott work also. In an attempt to find the hidden traces of her life, to explore the 'trace of what once was back then, although this is but faintly seen' (Stanley, 2016), we followed a newspaper cutting of a house sale sent to us by a friend of Jephcott's, in an attempt to trace her earlier life in Alcester. Again, walking the field, it becomes easy to connect the past with the present, the then and now or the 'now/past' (Moore et al., 2016). Walking the roads and streets of Alcester the traces of the Jephcott family are all around: the memorial at the church to her brother Arthur, killed in action 4 August 1916 at Pozières while fighting for Australian forces; the road named after the family; Alcester grammar school to which she donated funds; and the Angel House, Pearl Jephcott's family home during the earlier years of her life.

The photograph taken while walking the field is more than a memento: it is a prompt for reflection. Here we can link Akeret (1973) to the approach of Smart (2007) in *Personal Life* who, when considering family photographs, suggests:

> [Try] to imagine their lives and to read into the photograph whether they were happy or not, whether their lives were very hard or reasonably comfortable, whether they were respected members of their community or not. (Smart, 2007: 1–2)

We can ask of Figure 10.5 (the Angel House) questions to help us imagine the life that was lived there. Visualise her father (a local auctioneer), her mother and her siblings before they emigrated to Australia and Argentina. We can reflect on what life was like in this small village between her birth and her going to Aberystwyth University in 1919. To answer Smart (2007), the Jephcotts were obviously comfortable, middle class, liberal and well-respected within their community.

Figure 10.5 Pearl Jephcott's family home, 'the Angel House', Alcester, UK in 2015. Photograph by John Goodwin

Other images found in informal archives have more direct and obvious analytical potential. Figure 10.6 emerged with the rediscovery of the Scotson files relating to the *Established and the Outsiders*. Although the social networks are described in the book there is no visual representation of these networks. However, Scotson's early hand-drawn social network clearly highlights the interrelationships between the main respondent 'Phyllis' and her network of friends – the strengths of relationships signified by the size of the circle and thickness of the interconnecting lines. Scotson's unused hand-drawn image provokes us to think about the networks that existed then and the networks that might exist now. Do these relationships still exist?

In summary, the third lesson is to not simply view images, drawings and other visual material as merely illustration but instead as prompts for further analysis, stimulating the imagination to make connections, fill in detail or suggest further lines of enquiry.

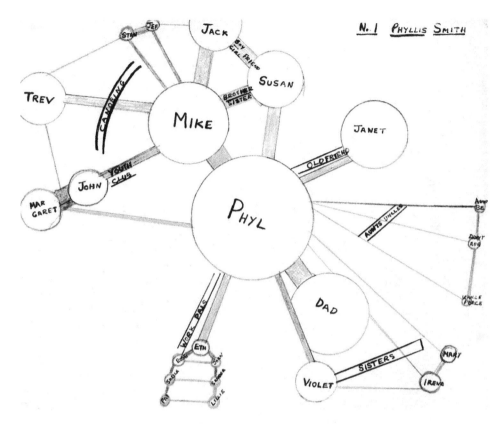

Figure 10.6 Scotson's network-analysis diagram c. 1958. See Goodwin et al., forthcoming

10.4.4 Lesson Four: Don't Forget about Ephemera

> ... the *Dead Sea* scrolls, *Cromwell's* death-mask, the gatepost of the *Vindolanda* Romano-British fort, *Emily Wilding Davison's* return rail-ticket to Epsom, the *Memphis* balcony where *Martin Luther King* was shot, the mountain of papers left by *Mohandas Gandhi* ... What gives these scrolls, masks, gateposts, tickets, balconies, political papers, forts and cities their still-resonant meanings are their specificities – their 'who, what, when, where and how' qualities. (Stanley, 2016: 1)

Like Stanley (2016) we have suggested above that our operationalisation of the idea of what 'data' is suitable for qualitative analysis is very broad and includes 'ephemera': those materials that are meant to be short-lived (not retained, preserved or valued) – the objects that most people discard in their daily routines and which are perceived to have very little long-term significance. Examples include: the receipt for many coloured paints amongst Elias's papers in the archive at Marbach; the word pairs or postcards in Mills's papers alongside seemingly random newspaper clippings; and the mixture of 'personal' and 'professional' materials with no distinction or demarcation between the two in Jephcott's notebooks. Epitomising the 'craft' advocated by Mills, Jephcott's Australia notebook, collated during her trip to Australia in 1971 aged 71, reveals an exceptional sociologist who methodically and richly documents her visit via notes, original artwork, clippings and postcards. These are augmented ephemera offering insights into Pearl's sociology that could not have been ascertained from any formally archived materials.

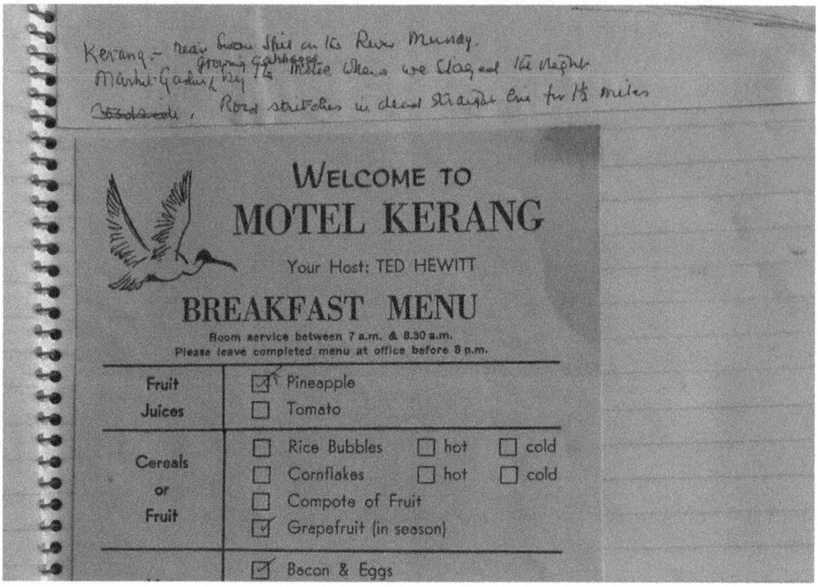

Figure 10.7 Ephemera example from Pearl Jephcott's Australia notebooks, April to October 1971. Courtesy of the Estate of Pearl Jephcott. Photograph by John Goodwin

Here, as shown in Figure 10.7, Jephcott has pasted into her files the room service breakfast menu for the Motel Kerang (Goodwin and O'Connor, 2017). Certainly ephemera, certainly something not meant to be kept, but a quirky document that reveals so much. It can be read literally in terms of what Peal ate for breakfast on that specific day. But it is also a marker as to where Jephcott visited during her Australia trip, and piecing together different bits of ephemera we can gain a real sense of the scale of her travels; it offers some suggestion to the funding she had (motels rather than hotels) and so forth.

A common piece of ephemera found through the formal and informal archives of Mills and Jephcott are newspaper cuttings. As suggested above some of the cuttings have an obvious and direct relevance to the content of the files. Other cuttings do not but were retained for some reason. They held some significance at some point in time. In line with the theme of his MA dissertation, Scotson

Figure 10.8 'The Regal Cinema' from *The Established and the Outsiders*, including research ephemera example from the Scotson Archive. Courtesy of the Estate of John Scotson. Photograph by John Goodwin, 2018 (see: https://le.ac.uk/research/images-of-research/john-goodwin)

clipped newspaper cuttings on juvenile delinquency in the Winston Parva area. One such clipping offered a detailed report on a fight that took place outside the Regal Cinema, the individuals and gangs involved, and the views of the local criminal justice system. This piece of ephemera is a tangible connection between the research concerns of the past and the location now. It promotes a discussion of change and transformation and stimulates imagination and creativity. The 'then' newspaper cutting is presented in front of the now 'Regal/Ritz cinema' in Figure 10.8. The juxtaposition between the cinema as a hive of youth activity (both pro- and anti-social behaviour, courtship and so forth) in the 1950s and 1960s, and the remnants of a 1980s bingo hall – compared to the seemingly run-down 'Retro Suite' of today – says something about urban decline.

The fourth lesson is to not ignore the seemingly ephemeral.

10.5 Conclusion

In this chapter we have tried to show how data can reveal itself to the researcher in many guises. Indeed, it is the data that was not collected as part of the formal process that often provides the most valuable insight. For example, the fieldnotes we are urged to keep as a record of sociological encounters during active data collection exercises, such as interviewing and observation, are a rich and almost-always untapped source of data. It is perhaps because as researchers we lack guidance on how to use such notes that the data are rarely used in the final analysis. The notes scribbled hastily in the margins of a survey during a doorstop encounter may be simply intended as an aide-memoire for the researcher during the analysis stage. Yet such notes can reveal as much if not more than the formal data. We have provided examples above that illustrate just how meaningful such marginalia can be – particularly to those, like us, who are revisiting past studies through a contemporary lens.

As described in this chapter, we have found that detailed interviewer notes, collected in the 1960s and intended originally only as a means of sharing additional information with the wider project team, have provided more contextual data than we could have gleaned from the interview questions themselves. Information on contemporary fashions, on housing quality, on crime, family formation, romantic relationships, youth culture, consumption ... the list is endless yet without looking to the paradata and marginalia we would not have benefited from such an abundance of period-specific contextual knowledge. Likewise the sketches and diary entries we have been lucky enough to access in relation to the works of Pearl Jephcott tell us so much more than the sanitised, edited, published versions of her work, and they bring elements of the research to life decades later through a simple drawing of a 1960s coffee shop or a child's account of a daily routine.

10.6 Pedagogical Resources

There are so many resources that can help researchers access unusual data – it is more a matter of reorientating to think about what constitutes useful data for social science research and what materials (whatever they may be) offer in terms of their analytical potential. A good place to start, especially if interested in long-term social processes, is in the archives. The Archives and Records Association of UK and Ireland have practical advice to offer in this regard via their websites (www.archives.org.uk/ and www.exploreyourarchive.org/). There are other archives that we have used that we would also highly recommend including the UK National Archives (www.nationalarchives.gov.uk/), the University of Glasgow Archives (www.gla.ac.uk/myglasgow/archives/collections/university/) and the Dolph Briscoe Center for American History at the University of Texas, Austin (www.cah.utexas.edu), which collects, preserves, and makes available documentary and material-culture evidence encompassing key themes in Texas and US history.

Also very useful are the following websites featuring the work of Liz Stanley: https://sites.google.com/site/thebookarchiveproject/ and www.whiteswritingwhiteness.ed.ac.uk/.

10.7 References

Akeret, R.U. (1973) *Photoanalysis: How to Interpret the Hidden Psychological Meaning of Personal and Public Photographs*. New York: P.H. Wyden.

Aronowitz, S. (2012) *Taking It Big: C. Wright Mills and the Making of Political Intellectuals*. New York: Columbia University Press.

Edwards, R., Goodwin, J., O'Connor, H. and Phoenix, A. (2017) *Working with Paradata, Marginalia and Fieldnotes: The Centrality of By-Products of Social Research*. Cheltenham: Edward Elgar.

Elias, N. and Scotson, J. (1965) *The Established and the Outsiders*. London: Frank Cass.

Goodwin, J. (2016) 'The cotton bobbin: Symbolic of a lost heritage?', *Social Worlds in 100 Objects*. Available at: www2.le.ac.uk/projects/social-worlds/all-articles/management/cotton-bobbin (accessed 30 May 2019).

Goodwin, J. (2018) 'Searching for pearls: "Doing" biographical research on Pearl Jephcott', *Contemporary Social Science*. Available at: https://doi.org/10.1080/21582041.2018.1470329 (accessed 30 May 2019).

Goodwin, J. and Hughes, J. (2011) 'Ilya Neustadt, Norbert Elias, and the development of sociology in Britain: Formal and informal sources of historical data', *British Journal of Sociology*, 26(4): 677–95.

Goodwin, J. and O'Connor, H. (2003) 'The Young Worker Project Renewed', in Dunning, E. and Mennell, S. (eds), *Norbert Elias*, London: Sage. pp. 39–43.

Goodwin, J. and O'Connor, H. (2006) 'Contextualising the research process: Using interviewer notes in the secondary analysis of qualitative data', *The Qualitative Report*, 11(2). Available at: www.nova.edu/ssss/QR/QR11-2/goodwin.pdf (accessed 30 May 2019).

Goodwin, J. and O'Connor, H. (2015a) 'Pearl Jephcott: The legacy of a forgotten sociological research pioneer', *Sociology*, 49(1): 139–55.

Goodwin, J. and O'Connor, H. (2015b) 'A Restudy of Young Workers from the 1960s: Researching Intersections of Work and Lifecourse in One Locality over 50 years', in Chapter 3 in Worth, N. and Hardhill, I. (eds), (2015) *Researching the Lifecourse: Critical Reflections from the Social Sciences*. London: Policy Press. pp. 63–80.

Goodwin, J. and O'Connor, H. (2017) *Welcome to Motel Kerang: Pearl Jephcott's Australia Notebook and the 'Craft of Sociology'*. Available at: www.whiteswritingwhiteness.ed.ac.uk/publications/archive-conferences/tracing-the-trace/goodwin-oconnor-abstract/ (accessed 30 May 2019).

Goodwin, J., Hughes, J. and O'Connor, H. (2016) 'Return to Winston Parva: Starting to reconstruct *The Established and the Outsiders* "from the margins"', *Historical Social Research*, 41(3): 18–30.

Goodwin, J., O'Connor, H., Hughes, J. and Dunning M. (forthcoming) *The Methodological Foundations of the Established and the Outsiders*, Media Communication and Sociology Occasional Papers.

Goudsblom, J. (1977) *Sociology in the Balance: A Critical Review*. New York: Columbia University Press,

Hughes, J. and Goodwin, J. (2014) *Documentary and Archival Research*, Sage Benchmarks in Research Methods (4 volumes). London: Sage.

Hughes, K., Goodwin, J. and Hughes, J. (2016) 'Human documents and artefacts as figurations/Documenti e reperti umani come figurazioni', *Cambio*, 6(11): 123.

Jephcott, P. (1962) *Married Women Working*. London: Routledge and Kegan Paul.

Kaufman, P. (1997) 'Michael Jordan meets C. Wright Mills: Illustrating the sociological imagination with objects from everyday life', *Teaching Sociology*, 25(4): 309–14.

Livingston, R.T. (1949) *Letter to C. Wright Mills, Department of Industrial Engineering*, 3 November, File 4B339, Dolphe Brisco Center For American Studies, University of Texas, Austin.

Miliband, R. (1962) 'C. Wright Mills', *New Left Review*, 1(15).

Mills, C.W. (1959) *The Sociological Imagination*. New York: Oxford University Press.

Mills K. and Mills, P. (eds) (2001) *C. Wright Mills: Letters and Autobiographical Writings*. California: University of California Press.

Moore, N., Salter, A., Stanley, L. and Tamboukou, M. (2016) *The Archive Project: Archival Research in the Social Sciences*. London: Routledge.

O'Connor, H. and Goodwin, J. (2012) 'Revisiting Norbert Elias's sociology of community: Learning from the Leicester restudies', *The Sociological Review*, 60(3): 476–97.

O'Connor, H. and Goodwin, J. (2017) 'Fieldnotes, marginalia and paradata in youth employment restudies 1960–1985', in R. Edwards, J. Goodwin, H. O'Connor and A. Phoenix (eds), *Working with Paradata, Marginalia and Fieldnotes: The Centrality of By-Products of Social Research*. Cheltenham: Edward Elgar.

Savage, M. (2005) 'Working-class identities in the 1960s: Revisiting the Affluent Worker Study', *Sociology*, 39(5): 929–46. Available at: https://doi.org/10.1177/0038038505058373 (accessed 30 May 2019).

Scott, J. and Nilsen, A. (2013) *C. Wright Mills and the Sociological Imagination: Contemporary Perspectives*. Cheltenham: Edward Elgar.

Smart, C. (2007) *Personal Life*. Bristol: Polity.

Stanley, L. (2016) *The Archive Project: 'The Trace'*. Available at: https://sites.google.com/site/thebookarchiveproject/the-trace (accessed 30 May 2019).

ELEVEN

USING QUANTITATIVE DATA IN QUALITATIVE SECONDARY ANALYSIS

Jane Gray and Ruth Geraghty

CHAPTER CONTENTS

11.1 Introduction

This chapter discusses the opportunities presented by bringing quantitative data into dialogue with qualitative data in qualitative secondary analysis. Drawing on examples from linked studies, we describe three ways in which such dialogue can take place: (i) in the original design of the study that generated the data; (ii) in the use of quantitative data to 'situate' qualitative data within research designs for secondary analysis; and (iii) in the development of theory. We show how quantitative data can assist us to: (i) place evidence from qualitative cases in the context of aggregate patterns, allowing us to understand how participants in the qualitative study were 'situated with respect to population heterogeneity' (Irwin, 2013); (ii) identify cases within a large qualitative database for in-depth analysis or for systematic comparison; and (iii) assemble qualitative cases for comparison. We argue that bringing qualitative secondary analysis into dialogue with representative quantitative data casts a spotlight on the extent to which our interpretation of macrosocial trends often implicitly draws on 'black box' inferences about the meanings and goals underpinning social action. By raising questions about these inferences, this dialogue can be generative for the development of theory and to identify new questions for qualitative secondary analysis. Finally, we discuss some problems that can arise in using quantitative methods in qualitative secondary analysis.

11.2 Designing Mixed Quantitative and Qualitative Longitudinal Studies

In this first section of the chapter, we begin by describing the three linked studies and two qualitative datasets that we refer to throughout. We describe how the qualitative datasets were based on interviews with people who had participated in quantitative panel studies, and discuss some implications of the similarities and differences between the two databases in terms of their research design, focusing on sampling strategy, method of interviewing and temporal orientation.

From 2005–2012, Jane Gray was a co-principal or principal investigator on three linked qualitative longitudinal studies: *Life Histories and Social Change* (hereafter LHSC, 2005–2008), *Poverty and the Life Cycle in 20th Century Ireland: A Childhood Centred Analysis* (2008–2009), and *Family Rhythms: Using Archived Qualitative Data to Examine the Changing Texture of Family Life in Ireland* (2011–2012).[1] Ruth

---

[1]The LHSC and *Family Rhythms* projects were funded by the Irish Research Council. *Poverty and the Life Cycle* was funded by the Combat Poverty Agency. The co-principal investigators on LHSC were Jane Gray, Seán Ó Riain and Aileen O'Carroll (all at Maynooth University).

Geraghty was a research assistant on the *Family Rhythms* project, and later worked on developing the LHSC data as a demonstrator project for the Digital Repository of Ireland (discussed further below).

LHSC was an infrastructural project that collected biographical interviews, life calendar and retrospective social network data from more than 100 Irish people born within different historical time periods across the twentieth century. *Poverty and the Life Cycle* used the LHSC data to examine change and variation over time in experiences of childhood poverty and the transition to young adulthood. Finally, *Family Rhythms* brought LHSC together with qualitative data collected as part of the *National Longitudinal Study on Children – Growing Up in Ireland* (hereafter, GUI-Qual). At the commencement of *Family Rhythms*, both datasets had been deposited (in part or in whole) in the Irish Qualitative Data Archive (Gray et al., 2015; Williams et al., 2017).[2] The *Family Rhythms* study had two aims: (1) to develop a fresh understanding of family change in modern Ireland, incorporating cutting-edge theoretical perspectives and drawing on archived qualitative data; (2) to disseminate learning from the experience of re-using qualitative data and to promote further sharing and re-use. As its principal output, the study led to the publication of an innovative textbook (Gray et al., 2016).

The Irish Qualitative Data Archive (IQDA) was established at Maynooth University in 2008 as a central access point for qualitative social science data generated in or about Ireland. It received initial funding under the Irish Government's Programme for Research in Third Level Institutions, Cycle 4 (PRTLI4). A national report led by the Higher Education Authority had identified the absence of data archives as a critical weakness in the research infrastructure for humanities and social science research (see HEA/Forfás, 2007). The Irish Social Science Data Archive, which acquires, preserves and disseminates *quantitative* data, also received support under PRTLI4. Subsequently, IQDA became a founding member of the Digital Repository of Ireland (DRI), which was established under PRTLI5 in 2015, and is currently funded by the Department of Education and Skills.

DRI is a 'trusted national infrastructure for the preservation, curation and dissemination of Ireland's humanities, social sciences, and cultural heritage data.' It received the 'Core Trust Seal' certification in 2018. This helps to ensure the reliability and durability of data repositories, so that researchers can be certain that their data 'remains useful and meaningful into the future'.[3] DRI develops policy

---

[2] These datasets are now available in the Digital Repository of Ireland (DRI). Work on ingesting LHSC data to the DRI is ongoing. At the time of writing, 85 of 98 interview transcripts available for archiving have been fully ingested into DRI.

[3] www.coretrustseal.org/why-certification.

for digital archiving and is a significant contributor to European policy on Open Science. It is a partner in international data archiving initiatives, including the European Digital Research Infrastructure for the Arts and Humanities (DARIAH), and is an active member of the international Research Data Alliance. Today, data deposited in IQDA are securely preserved and disseminated through the DRI. For qualitative social science researchers, this means that when they deposit their data, they can be confident that it will be safely stored and made available under licence to other approved researchers. DRI maintains internationally recognised metadata standards to support data management and enhance search and discovery. This means that qualitative social science researchers can find and access data relevant to their research question(s) through the DRI interface.

The qualitative datasets that fed into *Family Rhythms* (LHSC and GUI-Qual) have a shared feature which created interesting opportunities for the analysis of long-term patterns of family change. Both are linked to quantitative panel studies which are now available through the Irish Social Science Data Archive. Participants who opted in to LHSC had previously taken part in the Irish module of the European Community Household Panel (*Living in Ireland*), from 1994 to 2001 (ISSDA SN 0031-00). Participants in the qualitative module of *Growing Up in Ireland* were a subset of respondents to an ongoing panel study of two cohorts of Irish children and their families: a 'child cohort' aged nine years around the onset of the study in 2006 (ISSDA SN 0020-00), and an 'infant cohort' aged nine months (ISSDA SN 0019-00). Alongside the quantitative survey, qualitative data were collected with both cohorts during the first wave of data collection. The *Family Rhythms* study focused on the qualitative study with the child cohort, that is, with children born in 1997 or 1998, and their families.[4] Each of the archived datasets includes contextual information that helps the researcher to situate the qualitative data within the original quantitative studies (see Table 11.1).

Also, as discussed in one of the examples below, the original investigators on the LHSC study were able to link participants to their individual-level data within the original panel study.[5] Figure 11.1 summarises the relationships between the qualitative and quantitative datasets and studies discussed in this chapter.

---

[4]This is now referred to as the '98 cohort' in official *Growing Up in Ireland* documentation. See: www.growingup.ie/.

[5]For reasons of confidentiality, privacy and data protection, this is not possible with the archived data that are now available to other researchers through the Irish Social Science Data Archive. Similarly, it is not possible to link the archived qualitative GUI data to their records in the quantitative longitudinal study.

Table 11.1 Contextual data on the *Family Rhythms* datasets available in the Digital Repository of Ireland

	Archive ID	Pseudonym	Year of birth	Sex	Location	Socio-economic status	Family characteristics
LHSC	Yes	Yes	Yes - as generational cohort	Yes	Yes - NUTS III region	Yes - ISCO occupational category	No
GUI-Qual Parents	Yes	Yes	No	Implied by parental status	Yes - rural/urban and NUTS III region	Yes - household income high, medium or low	Yes - number of parents resident and family size
GUI-Qual Children	Yes	Yes	No but defined range (1997-98)	Yes	Yes - rural/urban and NUTS III region	Yes - household income high, medium or low	Yes - number of parents resident and family size

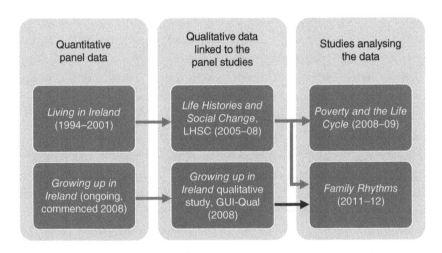

Figure 11.1 The data and the studies

While both qualitative datasets are linked to quantitative panels, there are also notable differences between them, first with respect to how participants were *selected* for inclusion in the qualitative studies; second in the method of interview; and third, in their *temporal* orientation. These differences posed interesting challenges and opportunities for situating the qualitative data, and in the case of *Family Rhythms*, bringing the datasets together in our secondary analysis. We discuss them in turn below.

11.3 Sampling and Recruiting Participants

Researchers in LHSC used quantitative data from the *Living in Ireland* panel study to select participants according to theoretical and substantive criteria. Drawing on existing scholarship, they first sought to identify birth cohorts of Irish people whose lives traversed periods of significant social change, and which were likely to have included innovators – that is, people who developed new social practices compared to those of earlier cohorts. They identified three broad *generational cohorts* of interest: people born before 1935; those born 1945–54; and those born 1965–74. Once the cohorts of interest had been identified, all participants within these age bands who had participated in the original quantitative study were invited to opt in to LHSC. This was carried out with the assistance of the Economic, Social and Research Institute (ESRI), which led the *Living in Ireland* survey. The ESRI wrote to relevant participants in the panel study, asking if they wished to participate in LHSC. They then forwarded the contact details of those who agreed to participate. The LHSC team then used the principle of maximising diversity by gender, social class and place of residence, to select participants from amongst those who opted in.

In contrast to LHSC, the inclusion of a qualitative study was part of the original project design in *Growing Up in Ireland*. Therefore, a question asking participants if they would like to participate in the qualitative study was included in the first wave of quantitative interviews. Almost two-thirds of the 8,500 families in the child cohort agreed to be included in the frame for selection. One hundred and fifty-eight families were invited to participate in the qualitative study, of which 120 were ultimately included. The *Growing Up in Ireland* team adopted a purposive, stratified approach to selecting participants for the qualitative study, based on the characteristics of the main, quantitative sample. They stratified the qualitative sample according to socio-economic status (high, medium, and low-income), urban/rural location, and family type (one or two resident parents) (Harris et al., 2011: 8).

The selection strategies adopted in the two studies, therefore, were forms of 'sampling for range', which is intended to ensure that there are a given number of participants within pre-determined categories (Small, 2009: 13). It is important to note that, in qualitative research, it is not meaningful to try to select cases on the basis of their 'representativeness'. This is because case selection for qualitative analysis is based on the logic of comparison, rather than that of inferential sampling (Small, 2009: 25–6). Many scholars would agree with Small (2009) that a strategy of sequential sampling, in which the researcher progressively refines his or her selection criteria according to what is learned with each new case, often represents a better approach to qualitative case selection than sampling for range. But this raises a wider question about the usefulness of linking qualitative cases to quantitative datasets in the manner described above.

We suggest that there is merit in doing so, especially when datasets are constructed for the purpose of qualitative *secondary* analysis, in which future researchers will approach the data with new and different theoretical and substantive questions. In these circumstances, a case selection strategy that allows researchers to match qualitative participants to representative categories within the quantitative sample can be a strength rather than a weakness. For example, in a study of young people's expectations for the future, Irwin (2009: 346) demonstrated how matching qualitative cases to cells in a table derived from analysis of a linked quantitative dataset facilitated comparison: 'Locating qualitative data in this way encourages consideration of diversity, and a form of comparative analysis that invites us to pay as much attention to atypical, as to typical, experiences both across, and within, social class groupings' (see also Irwin, Chapter 2 of this volume). So long as secondary researchers remain cognisant that the qualitative cases are not statistically representative of the wider categories within which they are located, situating them in this way can provide a useful starting point for comparison and process tracing. Later, we describe how a similar approach was used in the *Poverty and the Life Cycle* study.

11.4 Mixed Method Study Design

The LHSC study collected retrospective life narratives using a weakly structured, in-depth approach to interviewing. The interviewers were provided with a shared 'topic guide' and indicative 'question bank' (adapted from Thompson, 2000), but were instructed to encourage the participants to tell their life stories in their own words. Structured life history calendars and simple, retrospective social network schedules were also collected at the time of interview. [6] No explicit attempt was made to link the data collected in the life history interviews to questions on the original panel survey. By contrast, GUI-Qual took the form of semi-structured interviews, both with the children and with their parents, that were explicitly intended to 'map onto the domains of the main quantitative study' (Harris et al., 2011: 13).

The different sample selection and interview designs adopted within the two studies suggest differences in how the original researchers envisaged that the data would be used by secondary analysts. Small (2011) distinguished between mixed-method research designs that are intended to *confirm* (or 'triangulate') findings from one kind of data with those from another, and those in which the findings from both kinds of data are intended to *complement* one another by building on the strengths and weaknesses of each to develop a fuller understanding of social

---

[6]The data from these instruments are not currently available for re-use by other researchers.

phenomena (see also Brannen, 2005). The LHSC team aimed to generate qualitative data that would complement existing research, mainly quantitative, on social change in Ireland. By linking the cases to an existing panel study they aimed principally to *locate* them within a representative sample, so that future researchers could place them in the context of other information about Ireland's changing social structure.

By contrast, the *Growing Up in Ireland* team envisaged the development of 'detailed case studies of children and their families with particular socio-demographic profiles … enriching the quantitative findings relevant to such groups' (Harris et al., 2011: 8). The original study design envisaged that key issues identified within the cases could be tracked over time in future waves of *both* the quantitative and the qualitative study. The researchers planned to pursue a 'sequential, iterative' mixed method approach in which 'the results of the wave one qualitative studies will be fed into the next quantitative data-collection waves' (Harris and Greene, 2011: 21). Thus GUI-Qual was designed with both complementary and confirmatory mixed method research in mind.[7]

11.5 Temporal Orientations

Although they are each linked to a quantitative panel study, LHSC and GUI-Qual have different temporal orientations. LHSC was designed to collect *retrospective life narratives* from a concluded panel study. By contrast, the GUI qualitative interviews were embedded within a *continuing* panel, such that they have a *prospective* temporal orientation.

Neale (2018) has written eloquently of how: 'The temporal gaze is continually shifting as people look back and forth in the ever moving present, overwriting their biographies, reinterpreting wider social and structural forces, and confounding any sense of chronology and the orderly sequencing of events.' When qualitative interviews are linked to panel surveys, these fluid temporalities spill over the fixed chronologies and sequences built into the structure of quantitative longitudinal data. Thus in the LHSC study, participants' narratives ranged backwards in time to memories, experiences and stories that long pre-dated the time when they first participated in the quantitative panel. But they also included reflections on their present lives and narratives of anticipation about the future. Similarly, in GUI-Qual, the past leaked into interviews that were firmly oriented towards the present and future, for example, when parents reflected on how their own upbringing impacted on, or

---

[7]Unfortunately, no further waves of qualitative research were carried out in the *Growing Up in Ireland* study.

contrasted with, their current practices. Furthermore, in LHSC, participants' narratives varied in their biographical and temporal scope. In both studies, the rhythms of biographical, family and historical time overlapped in different ways across cases. Thus how temporalities intersected within participants' lives, and within the transcripts of their interviews, posed challenges for how we organised and assembled the data for *Family Rhythms*. We describe how we tried to address some of those challenges below.

11.6 Selecting and Assembling Qualitative Cases from Mixed Longitudinal Data

The previous sections described how a mixed approach was built into the construction of the qualitative longitudinal datasets discussed in this chapter, focusing on some of the implications of how qualitative cases were selected from within the quantitative panel studies, and of differences in the method of interviewing and related temporal scope. In this section, we discuss how these aspects provided important contexts for how we *selected* and *assembled* cases for qualitative secondary analysis.

There is a growing body of scholarship on the value of nested mixed method research designs in which linked qualitative cases are used either to confirm quantitative findings, or to complement them, for example through tracing the mechanisms leading to outcomes of interest (Small, 2011). Below, we describe how Gray (2010) adopted a version of this strategy in the *Poverty and the Life Cycle* study. In our second case, the *Family Rhythms* study, we were faced with a different challenge: how to bring together qualitative cases derived from different mixed studies in a pooled analysis. Davidson et al. (2018) have described this process as 'assemblage' to convey how it entails organising cases in new ways, including distributing them into categories that were not necessarily envisaged in the original study design. We describe how we assembled cases for *Family Rhythms* in order to develop an analysis of family change over time.

11.7 Selecting Qualitative Cases for Analysis

The *Poverty and the Life Cycle* study was informed by debates about individualisation and the de-standardisation of the life course in the context of contemporary policy interest in a 'developmental welfare state' that would flexibly respond to the different risks that people faced at different life stages. Building on earlier quantitative findings from the linked *Living in Ireland* panel study, *Poverty and the Life Cycle* aimed to develop a qualitative longitudinal analysis of the processes – or mechanisms – through which experiences of poverty in childhood gave rise to increased risk of poverty in adult-hood in different historical contexts. It therefore had two objectives: (1) to examine the changing experience of childhood poverty in different historical periods; (2) to explore the pathways through which the experience of poverty in childhood may have impacted on adult risk of poverty in different birth cohorts.

To meet these objectives, Gray (2010) used information about the individual participants in LHSC in the quantitative data to select cases for qualitative analysis across two phases. First, she selected all 47 LHSC participants who, in response to a standard question in the quantitative study, reported that their families had experienced 'great' or 'some' difficulty making ends meet in childhood. She then carried out a thematic analysis of their biographical interviews in order to understand what lay 'behind' the quantitative data on childhood hardship, and to explore continuity and change in different historical periods.

In the second phase of the study, Gray attempted a comparative biographical analysis of the pathways through which childhood poverty led to poverty in adulthood. This required a more onerous and stringent selection of cases using quantitative data on both origins and destinations. In order to move beyond some of the limitations associated with the subjective response on making ends meet (discussed in more detail later in the chapter), she added the level of education attained by a participant's father as a second criterion. She also limited the pool of potential cases to participants who, based on information provided to the quantitative study, had experienced income poverty as adults. Because just one person in the youngest birth cohort (born 1965–74) met all the criteria, she had to include people who met either of the two indicators of childhood poverty. By coincidence, all except one of the LHSC participants who met these criteria were women, simplifying the next stage of the analysis. Gray selected three cases in each cohort from this pool (nine in total) and carried out a person-centred (Singer et al., 1998; Elliott, 2005) comparative biographical analysis, similar to the approach described by Crompton (2001), that brought together information from the full range of data available on the participants.

The case selection strategy in *Poverty and the Life Cycle* was possible because the author had access to individual-level data within the original panel study. Other researchers could use the available contextual data (see Table 11.1) to adopt a similar approach to qualitative case selection and analysis, because the data are embedded within the quantitative studies. Thus, for example, a researcher interested in comparing the experiences of children living in households within different income categories could match the GUI-Qual cases to categories and findings from the quantitative study. However, the potential for selecting cases in this way is clearly limited by the contextual information that has been provided for the archived qualitative data. The level of detail provided in this contextual information, in turn, may be constrained by the requirement to maintain participant anonymity, by ensuring that data from the quantitative study cannot be linked directly to the qualitative data for individual study participants.

11.8 Assembling Qualitative Cases

In the *Family Rhythms* study, we aimed to document and explain changes in the textures of family life – the practices, meanings and displays through which Irish people 'did family' (Neale and Flowerdew, 2003) – across the twentieth century, first by tracing changes in how people remembered and described their family lives across the retrospective narratives in LHSC, and second, by comparing and contrasting those retrospective accounts with the qualitative data on contemporary families in GUI. In other publications (Gray et al., 2013; Geraghty and Gray, 2017), we have described our approach as 'working backwards and forwards' across different temporal horizons to bring the two datasets into dialogue from the perspective of different stages of the life course – childhood, early adulthood, the middle years and grandparenthood. Here we discuss how we addressed some of the challenges of organising and assembling the qualitative cases within historical and biographical time.

When working across the LHSC interviews we were constantly faced with the challenge of locating different narrative segments within their historical context. This was necessary because of our overall aim of understanding family change within a life-course perspective over an extended period of historical time. In other words, we sought to examine how the rhythms of biographical time within individual life stories intersected with those of long-term patterns of social change, including the trends identified in quantitative data. The oldest LHSC participant was born in 1912 and the youngest in 1974. Bringing LHSC and GUI-Qual together, therefore, involved working across a large pooled dataset that encompassed narratives of family life from a wide range of *generational standpoints*, within and across cases and datasets.

The *generational cohort* design built into LHSC provided the scaffolding with which we organised our cases. In our research for the textbook on family change (Gray et al., 2016) we relied principally on a thematic analysis of the qualitative interviews, organised by cohort and generational standpoint, that we carried out using the MAXQDA software package. To help locate narrative content from the life stories in chronological time, we developed visual representations of each cohort by life stage and decade (see Figure 11.2 for a version). These acted as 'aide-memoires' to help locate narrative segments within the historical time period to which they referred.

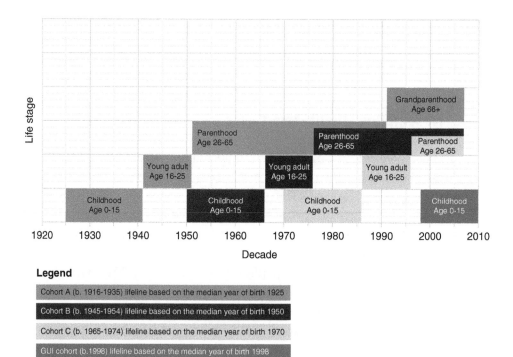

Figure 11.2   Life stage by decade for each cohort in *Family Rhythms*

Miller (1999: 37–40) demonstrated the usefulness of graphic representations for illustrating and differentiating time-related effects within and between lives. While they are immensely helpful, such schematic representations can also obscure other dimensions of the intersection of 'lives and historical times' (Elder, 1994). First, the normative scheduling of life transitions and social meanings of different life stages themselves change over time. Thus the social timing and significance of 'early adulthood' in Ireland were quite different in the 1940s and 1950s than in the 1980s and 1990s (a topic to which we return below). Second, demographic changes have had consequences for the distribution of family life stages in historical time, which in our study added to the challenge of understanding family change from different generational standpoints. For example, declining family size across the twentieth century meant that the number of years in which people were parenting young children was potentially greater for participants in the earlier than the later cohorts, with the consequence that the life stage of 'parenthood' in these cohorts extended over longer periods of historical time and, in consequence, across significant changes in normative and socio-economic contexts. Change in the average ages at which family life transitions occurred – such as starting a family or becoming a grandparent – also have consequences for how those life stages map onto historical time. For the qualitative researcher there is the third challenge of considerable variation on all these dimensions *amongst* cases and *within* cohorts. Addressing these challenges required continuous vigilance in situating narrative material from the biographical interviews within their appropriate historical and generational contexts, and our visual representations could work only as an indicative guide. In principle, linked quantitative data should assist with this work. We found the life history calendar data collected as part of the original LHSC study particularly helpful for this purpose although, inevitably, detailed information about timing was not available for all the events of interest in each case. Nevertheless, our experience strongly supports arguments in favour of mixed data collection in biographical, life-course research (see e.g., Nico, 2016).

11.9 Bringing Qualitative and Quantitative Data into Dialogue

The previous two sections centred on the implications of mixed quantitative and qualitative research designs for qualitative secondary analysis. In this section we discuss a more general way in which findings from qualitative and quantitative data can be brought into dialogue to yield surprising insights that challenge existing assumptions and raise new substantive and theoretical questions. We argue that this can happen for two reasons: first, because inductive analysis of qualitative data located in historical context can 'throw up' findings that go against the grain of established quantitative narratives; and second (and relatedly), because the social meanings underpinning changing trends often remain a 'black box' in quantitative data.

Traditionally, researchers distinguished between deductive and inductive approaches to observing and explaining social phenomena. The logic of deduction centred on using empirical evidence to test hypotheses derived from a general theoretical argument. By contrast, the logic of induction centred on the formulation of new theoretical arguments based on empirical observation. Conventionally, quantitative research was associated with deduction, and qualitative research with induction. However, most contemporary scholars recognise that all research involves both induction and deduction, and that: 'Any difference between quantitative and qualitative approaches in this respect is a matter of degree' (Cooper et al., 2012: 6).

Our first example begins with long-standing debates about historical variation and change in patterns of multi-generational household composition in Ireland. Scholars have expended considerable effort trying to calculate the prevalence of a 'stem-family' pattern using historical census data (for a recent comprehensive and definitive analysis, see Shimizu, 2016). Originating with the work of Frédéric Le Play, historians of the family identified the 'stem family' as a distinctive type of household living arrangement that occurred in some peasant societies. Under this system, the household head selected one son to inherit the family property. The heir would marry and continue the family line, but all other offspring would be obliged to leave the parental household or remain unmarried. Assuming the custom was for the household head to transmit ownership of the property before his death, we might expect to find *comparatively* high numbers of multi-generational households – i.e. where both an older couple (or widowed partner) co-resided with a younger couple and their children – in areas where stem-family practices prevailed (see Ruggles, 2010 for a recent overview of the international evidence from census data).

As we read through the interview transcripts of participants in the earliest LHSC cohort, we did find narratives of multi-generational co-residence consistent with stem-family practices. However, we also noted the frequency with which, in their childhood memories, participants described practices of exchange between households within extended family circles. These included circulations of children who spent time living in the homes of related adults (and sometimes even friends) for a range of reasons, including reducing the burden on mothers of large families, providing help to older or unmarried adults and gaining access to schooling (for a full account see Gray, 2014).

This led us to query whether or not scholars had been asking the 'wrong' question – or at least an incomplete question – in their focus on household composition. It also led us to look anew at patterns of circulation within extended family circles in later cohorts. Multi-generational households have become very uncommon in Ireland. In 2011, households with two or more families comprised just one percent of the total (Eurostat Census Hub). Fewer than two percent of infants shared a household with both a grandparent and their mother in 2008 (Williams et al., 2010: 26). Nevertheless, there is both qualitative and quantitative evidence of a continuing pattern of exchanges across generations and between households in extended families. In addition to being cared for by grandparents, children in GUI-Qual described warm relationships with their grandparents and spending time within extended family circles. This is consistent with other research suggesting that (similarly to the United Kingdom, see Emmel and Hughes, 2014) extended family relationships remain important for Irish families (see e.g., Ní Laoire, 2014). Consistent with new directions in family sociology (see e.g., Widmer, 2016 [2010]; Morgan, 2011), these findings indicate that our theoretical and empirical focus should shift to changes in structures, practices and meanings that transcend the boundaries of households.

However, developing a full understanding of the extent and significance of continuity and change in the structure of multi-generational ties will require attention, not just to the structure of family configurations, but also to the content of those relationships, including their meanings for people within different generational statuses and power relationships. Answering questions about how these have changed over time requires both quantitative and qualitative evidence. We have made an early attempt to address such questions with respect to changing relationships between grandparents and young grandchildren (Gray et al., 2013; Geraghty et al. 2014). There is considerable potential for further investigation of this kind bringing the evidence from qualitative longitudinal data into dialogue with data on quantitative trends. For example, while scholars anticipated that demographic ageing would lead to an increased significance of intergenerational ties within families (Bengtson, 2001), recent quantitative research has emphasised how variations in demographic trends and in the timing of life-course transitions – such as becoming a grandparent – may lead to substantial differences in the structure and form of intergenerational families across space and social groups (see e.g., Tarrant, 2010; Puur et al., 2011). This creates interesting opportunities for secondary analysis of qualitative data to enhance our understanding of change and variation in the meanings and textures of intergenerational family life, in dialogue with these new questions about the structure of intergenerational family change.

Our second example centres on changes in the timing and sequencing of events in early adulthood. There is now a significant body of scholarly research on the extension of early adulthood in western societies and how this pattern is associated with changes in the timing and sequencing of the transitions associated with family formation (Billari and Liefbroer, 2010). In particular, scholars have noted how these transitions have been postponed and 'unbundled' compared to the middle of the twentieth century, when young adults tended to marry, set up their own household and start a family in a tightly ordered sequence. Scholars have suggested that young people now spend a considerable period of time between adolescence and the attainment of 'full adulthood', largely because they must invest in more training and skills in order to succeed in the labour force (Furstenberg et al., 2004).

However, if we examine change over a more extended period of time using existing quantitative census data on the timing of early adult life transitions, we see that in some respects this pattern of extension follows a previous shift towards an earlier and more 'bundled' transition to adulthood. Ireland was characterised by a pattern of late marriage until the 1960s and 1970s when 'youthful and widespread marriage became the norm' (Lunn et al., 2009: 13). Whereas, early in the century, most young people had left school and were either in work (or assisting at home) after age 15, from the 1960s onwards there was an increasing trend for young people to remain in education. Figure 11.3 uses available census data to illustrate the changes for women.

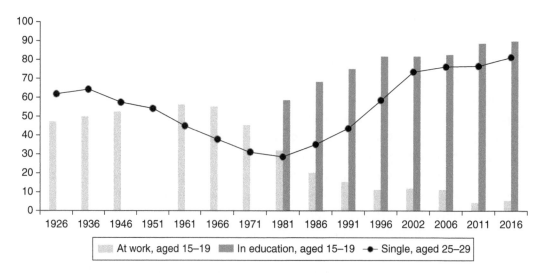

Figure 11.3 Percentage of Irish females in work or education (aged 15-19), and single (aged 25-29), 1926-2016

Source: Central Statistics Office Statbank, Census Time Series, Tables CNA21, CNA25 and CNML1

Note: Comparable data for 'In education aged 15-19' not available for census years before 1981

This suggests that early adulthood was 'extended' in a different way during the first half of the century. Young adults had to wait a considerable period of time between leaving education and attaining 'full adulthood' in what Furstenberg et al. (2004) describe as a state of 'semi-autonomy.' The contemporary experience of early adulthood is clearly different. For example, Lunn et al. (2009) show that, as people began to postpone marriage in the latter decades of the twentieth century, an increasing proportion of them were living in cohabiting relationships. Furthermore, contemporary young adults are not constrained by the strictures on sexual activity that their counterparts lived with during the first half of the last century.

Nevertheless, thinking about early adulthood in this longer historical time frame opens up interesting questions about continuities and changes in inter-generational relationships. It highlights the extent to which the second LHSC cohort (born 1945–54) were at the centre of a macro-social turning point in Irish family practices during the twentieth century. Longitudinal qualitative data offers the potential for in-depth examination of the experiences, motivations and meanings behind this shift. Furthermore, in the life stories of the earlier cohort (born before 1935), we found narratives of resentment and contestation on the part of young adults that open up interesting questions about the origins of social innovation and change (see Gray et al., 2016: 95–126). Interpreting these narratives requires us to take account of the fact that, having lived through significant social change, older people reflect on their lives through a greater variety of interpretive contexts (Brannen, 2004: 424). To take account of this, it is necessary to add contextual information from quantitative longitudinal data, but also from other sources, including contemporary ethnographies and literary accounts.

11.10 Conclusion

In this chapter we have discussed a variety of ways in which linkages to quantitative data can affect and assist qualitative secondary analysis by *situating* cases within population categories, by enabling the *selection* and *assemblage* of qualitative cases for analysis, and by *generating* new empirical and theoretical questions. In this final section we raise a 'cautionary' tale.

In a classic article on combining biographical data with representative quantitative analyses in the study of social mobility, Thompson (2004) discussed some of the challenges associated with working across qualitative and quantitative datasets, including how linked qualitative research frequently exposes 'mis-classification' of cases within quantitative data. This can be due to different kinds of error. The participant's response may have been incorrectly coded. Alternatively, the question may not have been well-designed to capture the 'true' underlying value within a given case. For the purposes of quantitative analysis, these errors may not matter very much if they are not widespread or systematically distributed within the dataset. However, in a mixed study design where the researcher is attempting to situate qualitative cases within categories derived from quantitative data, such 'mis-classification' can prove problematic.

For example, the linked variable on 'difficulty making ends meet' in childhood from the *Living in Ireland* panel study had proven valuable in an earlier quantitative study (Nolan et al., 2006), but when Gray (2010) sought to use this variable to identify cases for the qualitative *Poverty and the Life Cycle* study, she found that, amongst the LHSC set of cases, it included people from very diverse social-class backgrounds within the same categories. This can be thought of as a problem of 'mis-classification' in the quantitative data, but it is more broadly a problem associated with bringing together data collected for the purpose of 'variable-oriented' analysis with data collected for the purpose of 'case-oriented' analysis (see Ragin, 2014 [1987]). Treated as whole cases, each individual life unites a complex combination of factors that are organised and analysed as separate variables in a survey. This is both a strength of nesting qualitative cases within quantitative categories for 'process tracing', and a weakness. In practical terms, it means that researchers must be prepared to be flexible in their approach to selecting and analysing linked cases. However, even in comparatively large qualitative samples, this can quickly lead to a problematic reduction in the number of cases available for analysis. Furthermore, the problem can be more easily identified and addressed when the researcher has access to individual-level data on the cases in question within the quantitative study, but this will more commonly not be the case. Despite these challenges, we agree with Thompson's (2004: 241) conclusion that 'neither quantitative nor qualitative research can reach its full potential without drawing on each other's strengths', and that '[t]his is true both in terms of designing research questions, and of interpreting evidence.'

In this chapter, we have discussed how we brought qualitative and quantitative data into dialogue within a series of linked studies, to develop a fuller understanding of social change in twentieth century Ireland, focusing particularly on changes in the transition to adulthood and in intergenerational family relationships. We discussed the implications of this dialogue for qualitative secondary analysis across three phases of the research cycle: where a mixed approach was built into the original design for qualitative data collection (in LHSC and GUI-Qual); in the selection and assemblage of cases for secondary analysis (in *Poverty and the Life Cycle* and *Family Rhythms*); and in bringing existing quantitative and qualitative data together to develop new understandings of long-term patterns of family change (*Family Rhythms*).

Depending on data availability, and the questions to be answered, we provided examples of how researchers engaging in qualitative secondary analysis can make connections to quantitative data in three ways: (1) through a person-centred approach when it is possible to link qualitative cases to individual-level data in linked quantitative datasets; (2) by situating qualitative cases within socio-demographic categories, either directly linked to, or more commonly derived from, associated quantitative datasets; and (3) by bringing qualitative findings into dialogue with quantitative data from a variety of sources, such as census and survey data. Adopting such 'mixed' approaches to qualitative secondary analysis can be of considerable value for situating cases and developing theory.

11.11 Pedagogical Resources

Irish Qualitative Data Archive in the Digital Repository of Ireland – https://repository. dri.ie/catalog?f%5Binstitute_sim%5D%5B%5D=irish+qualitative+data+archive&mode=collections&search_field=all_fields&view=grid

Growing Up in Ireland: National Longitudinal Study of Children – www.growingup.ie/

Irish Social Science Data Archive – http://www.ucd.ie/issda/

11.12 References

Bengtson, V.L. (2001) 'Beyond the nuclear family: The increasing importance of multigenerational bonds: The Burgess Award Lecture'. *Journal of Marriage and Family*, 63(1): 1–16.

Billari, F.C. and Liefbroer, A.C. (2010) 'Towards a new pattern of transition to adulthood?', *Advances in Life Course Research*, 15(2–3): 59–75.

Brannen, J. (2004) 'Childhoods across the generations: Stories from women in four-generation English families', *Childhood*, 11(4): 409–28.

Brannen, J. (2005) 'Mixing methods: The entry of qualitative and quantitative approaches into the research process', *International Journal of Social Research Methodology*, 8(3): 173–84.

Cooper, B., Glaesser, J., Gomm, R. and Hammersley, M. (2012) *Challenging the Qualitative–Quantitative Divide: Explorations in Case-focused Causal Analysis*. London: Bloomsbury Publishing.

Crompton, R. (2001) 'Gender, comparative research and biographical matching'. *European Societies*, 3(2): 167–90.

Davidson, E., Edwards, R., Jamieson, L. and Weller, S. (2018) 'Big data, qualitative style: A breadth-and-depth method for working with large amounts of secondary qualitative data', *Quality and Quantity*, 53(1): 363–76. Available at: https://link.springer.com/article/10.1007/s11135-018-0757-y (accessed 30 May 2019).

Elder, G.H., Jr (1994) 'Time, human agency, and social change: Perspectives on the life course', *Social Psychology Quarterly*, 57(1): 4–15.

Elliott, J. (2005) *Using Narrative in Social Research: Qualitative and Quantitative Approaches*. London: Sage Publications.

Emmel, N. and Hughes, K. (2014) 'Vulnerability, intergenerational exchange and the conscience of generations', in J. Holland and R. Edwards (eds), *Understanding Families Over Time*. London: Palgrave Macmillan. pp. 161–75.

Furstenberg, F.F., Jr, Kennedy, S., McLoyd, V.C., Rumbaut, R.G. and Settersten, R.A., Jr (2004) 'Growing up is harder to do', *Contexts*, 3(3): 33–41.

Geraghty, R. and Gray, J. (2017) 'Family rhythms: Re-visioning family change in Ireland using qualitative archived data from Growing Up in Ireland and Life Histories and Social Change'. *Irish Journal of Sociology*, 25(2): 207–13.

Geraghty, R., Gray, J. and Ralph, D. (2014) '"One of the best members of the family": Continuity and change in young children's relationships with their grandparents', in L. Connolly (ed.), *The 'Irish' Family*. London: Routledge. pp. 124–39.

Gray, J. (2010) *Poverty and the Life Cycle in 20th Century Ireland: Changing Experiences of Childhood, Education and the Transition to Adulthood*, Combat Poverty Agency Working Paper Series 10/4. Available at: http://mural.maynoothuniversity.ie/2002/ (accessed 30 May 2019).

Gray, J. (2014) 'The circulation of children in rural Ireland during the first half of the twentieth century', *Continuity and Change*, 29(3): 399–421.

Gray, J., Geraghty, R. and Ralph, D. (2013) 'Young grandchildren and their grandparents: A secondary analysis of continuity and change across four birth cohorts', *Families, Relationships and Societies*, 2(2): 289.

Gray, J., O'Carroll, A., Ó Riain, S. and Geraghty, R. (2015) *Life Histories and Social Change Collection*, Digital Repository of Ireland [distributor], Irish Qualitative Data Archive [depositing institution]. Available at: https://doi.org/10.7486/DRI.9593xp97w (accessed 30 May 2019).

Gray, J., Geraghty, R. and Ralph, D. (2016) *Family Rhythms: The Changing Textures of Family Life in Ireland*. Manchester: Manchester University Press.

Harris, E. and Greene, S. (2011) *Qualitative Research Methodology: A Review of the Current Literature and its Application to the Qualitative Component of Growing Up in Ireland*. Dublin: Department of Children and Youth Affairs.

Harris, E., Sheila, G. and Merriman, B. (2011) *Growing Up in Ireland – National Longitudinal Study of Children: Technical Report on the 9-Year Qualitative Study*. Dublin: Department of Children and Youth Affairs.

HEA (Higher Education Authority) and Forfás (2017) *Research Infrastructure in Ireland: Building for Tomorrow*. Available at: http://hea.ie/assets/uploads/2017/06/Research-Infrastructure-in-Ireland-Building-for-Tomorrow.pdf (accessed 8 April 2019).

Irwin, S. (2009) 'Family contexts, norms and young people's orientations: Researching diversity', *Journal of Youth Studies*, 12(4): 337–54.

Irwin, S. (2013) 'Qualitative secondary data analysis: Ethics, epistemology and context', *Progress in Development Studies*, 13(4): 295–306.

Lunn, P., Fahey, T. and Hannan, C. (2009) *Family Figures: Family Dynamics and Family Types in Ireland, 1986–2006*. Dublin: Economic and Social Research Institute.

Miller, R.L. (1999) *Researching Life Stories and Family Histories*. London: Sage.

Morgan, D. (2011) *Rethinking Family Practices*. Basingstoke: Springer.

Neale, B. (2018) *What is Qualitative Longitudinal Research?* London: Bloomsbury Publishing.

Neale, B. and Flowerdew, J. (2003) 'Time, texture and childhood: The contours of longitudinal qualitative research', *International Journal of Social Research Methodology*, 6(3): 189–99.

Nico, M.L. (2016) 'Bringing life "back into life course research": Using the life grid as a research instrument for qualitative data collection and analysis', *Quality & Quantity*, 50(5): 2107–20.

Ní Laoire, C. (2014) 'Children, cousins and clans: The role of extended family and kinship in the lives of children in returning Irish migrant families', in L. Connolly (ed.), *The 'Irish' Family*. London: Routledge. pp. 154–72.

Nolan, B., Layte, R., Whelan, C.T. and Maître, B. (2006) *Day In, Day Out: Understanding the Dynamics of Child Poverty*. Dublin: Institute of Public Administration and Combat Poverty Agency.

Puur, A., Sakkeus, L., Põldma, A. and Herm, A. (2011) 'Intergenerational family constellations in contemporary Europe: Evidence from the Generations and Gender Survey', *Demographic Research*, 25: 135–72.

Ragin, C.C. (2014 [1987]) *The Comparative Method: Moving Beyond Qualitative and Quantitative Strategies*. Berkeley: University of California Press.

Ruggles, S. (2010) 'Stem families and joint families in comparative historical perspective', *Population and Development Review*, 36(3): 563–77.

Shimizu, Y. (2016) *Studies of Post-1841 Irish Family Structures*. Izumi, Osaka: Research Institute, St. Andrew's University.

Singer, B., Ryff, C.D., Carr, D. and Magee, W.J. (1998) 'Linking life histories and mental health: A person-centered strategy', *Sociological Methodology*, 28(1): 1–51.

Small, M.L. (2009) '"How many cases do I need?" On science and the logic of case selection in field-based research', *Ethnography*, 10(1): 5–38.

Small, M.L. (2011) 'How to conduct a mixed methods study: Recent trends in a rapidly growing literature', *Annual Review of Sociology*, 37: 57–86.

Tarrant, A. (2010) 'Constructing a social geography of grandparenthood: A new focus for intergenerationality', *Area*, 42(2): 190–97.

Thompson, P. (2000 [1978]) *The Voice of the Past: Oral History*, 3rd edn. Oxford: Oxford University Press.

Thompson, P. (2004) 'Researching family and social mobility with two eyes: Some experiences of the interaction between qualitative and quantitative data', *International Journal of Social Research Methodology*, 7(3): 235–57.

Widmer, E.D. (2016 [2010]) *Family Configurations: A Structural Approach to Family Diversity*. London: Routledge.

Williams, J., Greene, S., McNally, S., Murray, M. and Quail, A. (2010) *Growing Up in Ireland – National Longitudinal Study of Children: The Infants and their Families*. Dublin: Department of Health and Children.

Williams, J., Greene, S., Doyle, E., Harris, E., Layte, R., McCoy, S., McCrory, C., McDaid, R., McNally, S., Merriman, B., Murray, A., Nixon, E., O'Dowd, T., O'Moore, M., Quail, A., Smyth, E., Swords, L. and Thornton, M. (2017) *Growing Up in Ireland (GUI), 9-Year-Olds Cohort*, Digital Repository of Ireland [distributor], Irish Qualitative Data Archive [depositing institution]. Available at: https://doi.org/10.7486/DRI.6m31f4220 (accessed 30 May 2019).

INDEX